In Search of Pedagogy
Volume I

The selected works of Jerome S. Bruner

Jerome S. Bruner

Routledge
Taylor & Francis Group

LONDON AND NEW YORK

First published 2006
by Routledge
2 Park Square, Milton Park, Abingdon, Oxon, OX14 4RN

Simultaneously published in the USA and Canada
by Routledge
711 Third Avenue, New York, NY 10017

*Routledge is an imprint of the Taylor & Francis Group,
an informa business*

Transferred to Digital Printing 2008

© 2006 Jerome S. Bruner

Typeset in Sabon by
Newgen Imaging Systems (P) Ltd, Chennai, India

British Library Cataloguing in Publication Data
A catalogue record for this book is available
from the British Library

Library of Congress Cataloging in Publication Data
A catalog record for this book has been requested

ISBN13: 978-0-415-38668-5 (hbk)
ISBN13: 978-0-415-38670-8 (pbk)
ISBN13: 978-0-415-38682-1 (hbk set)
ISBN13: 978-0-415-38689-0 (pbk set)

In Search of Pedagogy Volume I

In the **World Library of Educationalists,** international experts themselves compile career-long collections of what they judge to be their finest pieces – extracts from books, key articles, salient research findings, major theoretical and practical contributions – so the world can read them in a single manageable volume. Readers will be able to follow themes and strands of the topic and see how their work contributes to the development of the field.

Jerome S. Bruner is one of the most distinguished and influential psychologists of his generation. His theories about cognitive development dominate psychology around the world today, but it is in the field of education where his influence has been especially felt. In this two volume collection, Bruner has selected and assembled his most important writing about education. Volume I spans the 20 years from 1957 to 1978. Volume II takes us from 1979 to 2006.

Each volume starts with a specially written introduction by Bruner, in which he gives us an overview of his career and contextualizes his selection of papers. The articles and chapters that follow reveal the thinking, the concepts, and the empirical research that have made Bruner one of the most respected and cited educational authorities of our time. Through chapters from his best-selling books, his autobiography, and original journal articles, the reader can follow Bruner's thinking on questions such as: How do human beings presume to educate their young, the only species on earth that does so? Do our ways of "educating" conform to what we have been learning about learning during these past centuries? How can we adapt what we know in general about the nature of learning processes to fit modern conditions such as poverty, race discrimination, and urban life?

Professor Bruner writes about these matters with the grace and passion for which he has become world famous. He discusses the scientific issues alongside the political and "administrative" ones, and draws on his research findings and his active participation in projects on improving schooling in America, the UK, and Europe. This two-volume set is the ultimate guide to Jerome Bruner's most important and influential work, and is ideal for students and academics who want to be able to follow the development of his thinking over his incredible 70-year career.

Jerome S. Bruner is a University Professor, principally teaching in the School of Law, New York University, USA.

Contributors to the series include: Richard Aldrich, Stephen J. Ball, James A. Banks, Jerome S. Bruner, John Elliott, Elliot W. Eisner, Howard Gardner, John K. Gilbert, Ivor F. Goodson, David Labaree, John White, E. C. Wragg.

World Library of Educationalists series

Other books in the series:

CONTENTS

ACKNOWLEDGMENTS

The following articles have been reproduced with the kind permission of the respective journals.

Bruner, J. S. "Learning and thinking." *Harvard Educational Review*, 1959, 29: 184–192.

Bruner, J. S. "The functions of teaching." *Rhode Island College Journal*, Rhode Island College, 1960, 1: 2ff.

Bruner, J. S. "The act of discovery." *Harvard Educational Review*, 1961, 31: 21–32.

Bruner, J. S. "The course of cognitive growth." *American Psychologist*, 1964, 19: 1–15.

Bruner, J. S. "Man: a course of study." *ESI Quarterly Report*, Educational Services Incorporated, Spring–Summer 1965, 3–13.

Bruner, J. S. "Child's play." *New Scientist*, London: IPC Magazines Ltd, 62, 694, 126–128.

Bruner, J. S. "Poverty and childhood." *Oxford Review of Education*, 1975, 1: 31–50. First published in J. S. Bruner, Relevance of Education, New York: W. W. Norton and Company Inc, 1971.

Bruner, J. S. "The role of tutoring in problem solving." D. Wood, J. S. Bruner, and G. Ross, *Journal of Child Psychology & Psychiatry and Allied Disciplines*, Pergamon Press, 1976, 17: 89–100.

The following chapters have been reproduced with the kind permission of the respective publishers.

Bruner, J. S. "Going beyond the information given." In Gruber H. *et al.* (eds), *Contemporary Approaches to Cognition: A Symposium held at the University of Colorado*, Cambridge: Harvard University Press, 1957.

Bruner, J. S. "The importance of structure." *The Process of Education*, Cambridge: Harvard University Press, 1960.

Bruner, J. S. "Readiness for learning." In *The Process of Education*, Cambridge: Harvard University Press, 1960.

Bruner, J. S. "The perfectibility of intellect." In P. H. Oeshser (ed.), *Knowledge among Men: Eleven Essays on Science, Culture and Society Commemorating the 200th Anniversary of the Birth of James Smithson*, New York: Simon & Schuster, 1966.

Bruner, J. S. "The will to learn." In *Toward a Theory of Instruction*, New York: W. W. Norton & Company Inc, 1966.

Bruner, J. S. "The growth of mind." In *The Relevance of Education*, New York: W. W. Norton & Company Inc, 1971.

Bruner, J. S. "Nature and uses of immaturity." In K. Connolly and J. S. Bruner (eds), *The Growth of Competence*, London: Academic Press, 1972.

Bruner, J. S. "Patterns of growth." (*Inaugural Lecture at Oxford University, May 25, 1973*), Oxford: Clarendon Press, 1974.

INTRODUCTION

The beginnings and the growth of one's interest in any form of inquiry are not easily reconstructed. How did I, initially an academic psychologist in a rather conservative academic setting at Harvard, develop such a long-lasting interest in education? And not until my early forties, at that, with a background principally in such hard-nosed psychological topics as perception! Education, in those days, was a "second-class" subject among "real" psychologists, a subject mostly confined to schools of education. To be sure, I had always had side-interests in what was then called "the psychological study of social issues" (as the politically oriented division of the American Psychological Association, of which I eventually became President, has long been called). But education in those days was not considered a "social issue."

But then, very abruptly in the mid-1950s, my interest in pedagogy and schooling grew by leaps and bounds. Was it because my two children were by then in the early stages of their student years? Well yes, that surely had a booster effect – though neither of my kids had any "learning problems" and both attended a notably humane primary school, Shady Hill, justly celebrated for its effective pedagogy. I was interested in the doings there, but that's not what precipitated my new concerns.

What led to my plunge, rather, was (how shall I call it?) a recognition of the relevance of education to the desperate ideological struggles of those times, the troubled early years of the Cold War. Let me explain.

My research in psychology was becoming increasingly preoccupied with the *activity* of cognition, with the highly selective and canny ways in which human beings achieve, categorize, remember, organize, and use their knowledge of the world. "Knowing," it soon became clear, was not just passively receiving and associating stimuli from "the world," and then responding in conformity with rewards or "reinforcements" from outside. I was one of a group of scholars who, quite unwittingly, were writing the first chapter of what later got to be called "the Cognitive Revolution." We were concerned (as Chapter 1 in this volume puts it) with how human being get "beyond the information given" from outside. Learning and thinking (to echo the title of Chapter 2) were by no means isolated from each other. Indeed, much of *learning* was guided by how you thought about what you were encountering – a point that was central to a book that I and two colleagues published in 1956. *A Study of Thinking.*

It so happened that those were the years in which the Russians launched Sputnik, the first manned space vehicle. America, self-assured as usual about its own technical superiority, was taken abruptly aback. Washington forthwith proclaimed the existence of a "Missile Gap," one that must have come inadvertently into being because the Soviets (for all their ideological shortcomings) were better at science *education* than "we" were. (Nobody, of course, could be better than us at *science*, given American technological vanity!). Soon our National Science Foundation was investing heavily in science curriculum projects to close the Missile Gap. Distinguished scientists threw themselves into creating new and striking school curricula in physics, mathematics, chemistry, and biology. Among them were several close friends of mine at the Massachusetts Institute of Technology who were not long in drawing me into their work at the Physical Science Study Committee, one of the pioneering curriculum groups.

Scientific brilliance concentrated as it was in those curriculum projects soon produced some stunning products, some real gems. The difficulty, predictably, was how to put those gems together in a manner suitable for teaching in classrooms taught by ordinary teachers to ordinary kids. Which led, of course, to some additional thinking about what we might mean by such banal terms as "classrooms," "ordinary teachers," or "curricula." And indeed, what *should* we take the aims of "pedagogy" to be?

More deeply, can education (even in the sciences) ever be conceived of as mainly in the service of bolstering "national defense" – or any other narrowly defined objective? In a democracy, surely, how we educate the young is an expression of a culture's goals in the large, its broader aspirations for the future, its sense of the limits of human possibility.

Issues of this sort (as well as shriller public demands that we "close" the Missile Gap) finally led our prestigious National Academy of Science to organize a special conference at Woods Hole on Cape Cod in the summer of 1959 to explore what those various curriculum projects were doing, how their work might be fitted into American educational practice, and what might indeed be envisaged for the future of American science education. Participants in those curriculum projects were invited as well as distinguished educators (including a few working teachers of known repute) plus, finally, recognized leaders in "the psychology of learning." The quotation marks around the last of these are well justified, for the psychology of learning was perhaps the most contentious and swords-drawn area in all of psychology. We resolved that dilemma by inviting the full spectrum of the best known learning researchers of the day, contending behaviorists like B.F.Skinner and Kenneth Spence, a strict Piagetian like Barbel Inhelder, information theorists like George Miller, and a classical psychometrician like Lee Cronbach, to help remind us of the eventual evaluation problems we would face. I had the daunting task of presiding!

It was a forming experience for most of us who participated. I wrote my "official report" for the National Academy of Science immediately afterward, and it was published at the gallop soon after by the Harvard University Press (*The Process of Education*, 1960). Chapters 4 and 5 of the present volume are taken from that book. Their main themes can be briefly summarized as follows:

1 Bodies of knowledge, like the sciences, cohere by dint of ideational structures that serve to organize and give meaning to their empirical details.
2 Understanding any particular body of knowledge requires grasping the underlying intellectual structure that renders its empirical details comprehensible.
3 Such structures vary from the highly intuitive and informal to the deductive-mathematical – from sensing intuitively that the hypotenuse of a right triangle, for example, "has to be" longer than either of the other two sides, to grasping the logical necessity of the Pythagorean Theorem.
4 In the course of coming to understand any particular body of knowledge, we tend naturally to begin with an initial intuitive grasp and progress with its help to a more formalized and verifiable form of understanding.

5   Indeed, the course of human mental growth itself typically progresses from an earlier intuitive stage to a later, more formalized and explicit form of verifiable reasoning. An early grasp of any body of knowledge, consequently, is typically intuitive and such a grasp facilitates later, more logical understanding. Intuition is but a step along the way to a fuller more rationally explicit grasp.

6   It follows then that any body of knowledge, whatever the subject, can be taught to anybody at any age in some initially intuitive form that does it justice. Indeed, in "teaching" we are well advised to cultivate an initial intuitive understanding before moving on to a more formal or mathematical insight. By the same logic, curricula and pedagogy in the sciences should be designed to aid initial intuitive understanding enroute to stricter mastery.

The participants at Woods Hole offered example after example of how such principles work in effective, day-to-day pedagogy. Though I tried to make them clear in my chairman's report as well as in the book that followed, I realize that they are not as obvious as they then seemed. I'm still sometimes asked, for example, "Are you claiming that the calculus can be taught to ten-year-olds?" Well, yes it can — in some form that is honest and intuitively self-evident as a step toward fuller understanding.

I confess I was surprised at the response to *The Process of Education*. For one thing, it sold like hotcakes — and continues to do so all these years later. And for another, it seemed to touch something deep in the imagination of teachers — some sort of recognition about their own best teaching practices. Teaching veterans still tell me about their excitement upon first reading the book years back.

I had written the book to address what I had thought were "American educational problems." But the book has had an astonishing translation career, having appeared by now in more than a couple of dozen languages. And given the "Missile Gap" crisis that precipitated the Woods Hole Conference, I was particularly amused that the very first translation to appear was in *Russian* — though without the usual request for permission, and without royalties or fees to either publisher or author.

Chapter 6 likens learning to an "act of discovery," as the outcome of a directed quest, and it can serve as an elaboration of points made in the two preceding chapters. And Chapter 7 explores in still further detail the "course of cognitive growth," particularly how human beings go from intuitive to more rational-symbolic forms of understanding — again emphasizing the precursory indispensability of the former to the latter.

Chapter 8 testifies to my own rapidly increasing involvement in the problems of school-teaching proper. How, for example, should one teach ten- or eleven-year-olds about the human or social sciences broadly conceived — my own specialties? A group of us in Cambridge (mostly close friends) decided we'd have a go at it. I shall always be grateful to academically "uptight" Harvard for giving me a year's leave of absence to help get this project started. And, of course, like the physicists, chemists, and biologists before us, we decided to create a school curriculum — this time on the nature and origins of the human condition, with particular reference to the emergence of human "culture." We named our project "Man: A Course of Study" (MACOS, as it came to be called) and with the aid of an initial grant from the Ford Foundation, we were soon installed and at work in a rickety old wooden building off Brattle Street in Cambridge, Massachusetts — an appropriately easy walking distance from the Harvard Yard!

We were anthropologists like Asen Belicki and Irvin DeVore, historians like Elting Morison, a linguist or two, a sprinkling of psychologists, even a then budding young ethologist. We even stole (on leave) some truly gifted teachers, like Peter Dow from Germantown Friends Academy, the famed Quaker school in Philadelphia.

What were our guiding questions to be? We decided (or rather, it was thrust upon us in our early discussions) that there were three that were essential:

1   What is distinctively human about human beings?
2   How did they get to be that way?
3   How might they become more so?

Our "consumers" were to be primary-school "sixth graders" in primary school, kids around ten and eleven, and their teachers.

MACOS is a long and troubling story. It's rationale and its procedures are detailed in Chapter 8. Its troubles, the political opposition it provoked among right-wing politicians in America, is well told by Peter Dow in his vivid little book, *Schoolhouse Politics* (Cambridge: Harvard University Press, 1991). I've also sketched it in my own autobiography, *In Search of Mind*. All I need say here is that we learned that views of the human condition – and aspirations regarding it – involve deeply political issues as well as educational ones. The briefest account is that, unexpectedly, we found ourselves handily defeated in distributing MACOS to American schools by fierce opposition sparked by the then Governor of California, Ronald Reagan, who actively opposed its adoption in his home State.

Comparing the human condition in different cultures is, alas, too easily interpreted as finding fault with our own. Never mind how the Netsilik Eskimo culture copes selflessly with old age or with scarce Arctic resources, nor how the !Kung Bushmen in Africa manage to live at a leisurely pace though they are mere hunter-gatherers. If such accounts risk alerting children to our own shortcomings, keep them out of our schools. Ironically, the Canadian Film Board, who helped us film our Netsilik Eskimo footage, brilliantly as always, issued a striking video disk in 2005 celebrating MACOS and revisiting the Netsilik in the far-north Pelly Bay district of Canada! But MACOS, still feared as a political hot potato, is not to be found in American public schools – only in highly select urban private schools or in such far-off lands as Australia's New South Wales.

In the years after MACOS, my own academic research took me increasingly toward studies of early cognitive activities in infancy and early childhood, with particular reference to the precursors and preconditions for the development of spoken language. It was a newly revived field of inquiry, and a flood of new and striking research was appearing around the world. What soon became evident was that the so-called "higher mental processes" began much earlier than had been previously recognized. But what was also becoming increasingly plain was that deprivation of opportunities to exercise early-appearing mental processes in social settings could put a child seriously at risk, interfering with later mental development. It was in these years that we had set up our "baby lab" at the Center for Cognitive Studies at Harvard, and we were hard at work – "we" referring not just to myself but to visiting scholars as varied as the linguist Roman Jakobson, the philosopher Nelson Goodman, and such laboratory magicians as Hanus Papousek.

During those years, in the mid-1960s, I was once or twice a month in Washington serving on President Johnson's Advisory Panel on Education. It was in the so-called civil-rights period in which we Americans were "discovering" the blight of inequality, injustice, and poverty in our midst. Indeed, it was becoming increasingly plain by then that grinding poverty could produce serious damage to early mental development through its disruption of family life and child care. Several colleagues and I (notably Nicholas Hobbs and Urie Bronfenbrenner) began arguing at our Panel meetings in Washington that Federal support was urgently needed to provide preschools that could counteract the serious impact of poverty on the family care of young children. We argued strongly that the children of poverty needed preschools that might give them, as it were, a "head start" before they started school and risked entering a career of failure. Daniel Patrick Moynahan, the beloved "Pat," (then at the Department of Labor, and later Senator from my native New York) was an enormous assist in all this. He helped turn our lower-case proposal for a federally funded "head start" into today's official Head Start program in America. I tell some of that story in Chapter 15, "Poverty and Childhood" – my first publication upon arriving in Oxford in the early 1970s.

Perhaps the most searching general discussion of the theoretical and practical issues involved in assuring adequate early childhood care is to be found in Chapter 12, "The Nature and Uses of Immaturity." It was an Invited Address to the 20th International Congress of Psychology in Tokyo in 1972 and deals particularly with the "burdens" of growing up in a culturally shaped, man-made environment in contrast to a natural habitat.

In any case, I was off to Oxford in 1972. "Why are you leaving Harvard for Oxford," I was often asked in those days. I think I was in search of some sort of "new start," somehow disenchanted with the American scene. The student "uprisings" in the later 1960s, while they had raised new possibilities, ended with little more than an anticlimactic return to ordinariness. I was, how shall I say, bored. So when I received an invitation to come be the Watts Professor of Psychology at Oxford, a newly founded Chair, I accepted (somewhat, indeed, to my own surprise!). Indeed, to keep the sense of venture bubbling, I even sailed to England in my beloved, somewhat aging yawl, *Wester Till*!

Once established at Oxford, and in collaboration with my colleague Harry Judge, I set about establishing a Preschool Research Group with the hope of advising the then Minister of Education, Margaret Thatcher, on how to improve preschool provisions for British children. Professor Judge was co-chairman with me and, together, we brought out a series of books on early educational provision. Echoes of that work can be found in Chapter 16, the final chapter in Volume I. I shall have more to say about our adventures in Volume II.

I must mention one other theme that keeps appearing in the papers included in this volume. It concerns the role and function of play and the ludic in mental development and mental functioning generally – a theme that has always fascinated me. It comes front and center (if too briefly) in Chapter 13. I have long been convinced that play and "playfulness" free us from the narrowing immediacy of pressing demands, enabling us better to explore the combinatorial possibilities that are opened to us by our cognitive powers. Play is indeed serious business, as one of my Oxford students once summed it up in a tutorial paper!

I've little further to say about the chapters in Volume I. I've included some seemingly rather straightforward research papers, sensing that they relate to educational issues as well. Chapter 16, for example, is about "tutoring" – though hardly in the university sense of that term. It has to do with how adults "scaffold" the problem-solving efforts of children: indeed, how human beings help each other master problems that one of them understands better than another. It's a "laboratory study" and, like all such, quite "artificial." Scaffolding, of course, is rather an odd term for how the more knowledge-able (teachers, parents, older siblings) support the problem-solving efforts of the less knowledgeable. But it well describes how a teacher or parent provides a containing structure to help organize the efforts of a pupil or a child until they can manage on their own. That chapter, "The role of tutoring in problem solving" was co-authored by my then colleague and former Harvard student, Dr. Kathy Sylva, who has since gone on to practice what we then preached, and well beyond it, on a worldwide scale.

This Introduction, I hope, will provide some organizing context for the disparate papers collected in the pages following. Volume II, covering the years 1978–2006, continues the story.

CHAPTER 1

GOING BEYOND THE INFORMATION GIVEN

H. Gruber *et al.* (eds), *Contemporary Approaches to Cognition:*
A Symposium held at the University of Colorado (1957),
Cambridge: Harvard University Press

More than thirty years ago, Charles Spearman (1923) undertook the ambitious task of characterizing the basic cognitive processes whose operations might account for the existence of intelligence. He emerged with a triad of non-genetic principles, as he called them, the first of these being simply an affirmation that organisms are capable of apprehending the world they live in. The second and third principles provide us with our starting point. One of these, called, as you know, "the education of relations," holds that there is an immediate evocation of a sense of relation given the mental presentation of two or more things. "White" and "black" evoke "opposite" or "different." The third principle, the "education of correlates," states that in the presence of a thing and a relation one immediately educes another thing. "White" and "opposite of" evokes "black." I think that Spearman was trying to say that the most characteristic thing about mental life, over and beyond the fact that one apprehends the events of the world around one, is that one constantly goes beyond the information given. With this observation I find myself in full agreement, and it is here that my difficulties start. For, as Professor Bartlett (1951, p. 1) put it in a recent paper, "...whenever anybody interprets evidence from any source, and his interpretation contains characteristics that cannot be referred wholly to direct sensory observation or perception, this person thinks. The bother is that nobody has ever been able to find any case of the human use of evidence which does not include characters that run beyond what is directly observed by the senses. So, according to this, people think whenever they do anything at all with evidence. If we adopt that view we very soon find ourselves looking out upon a boundless and turbulent ocean of problems." Bother though it be, there is little else than to plunge right in.

Some instances of going beyond the information given

It may help to begin with some rather commonplace examples of the different ways in which people go beyond information that is given to them. The first of these represents the simplest form of utilizing inference. It consists of learning the defining properties of a class of functionally equivalent objects and using the presence of these defining properties as a basis of inferring that a new object encountered is or is not an exemplar of the class. The first form of "going beyond," then, is to go beyond sense data to the class identity of the object being perceived. This is the more remarkable an achievement when the new object encountered differs from in more respects than it resembles other exemplars of the class that have been previously encountered. A speck on the horizon surmounted by a plume of smoke is identified as a ship, so too a towering transatlantic liner at its dock, so too a few schematic lines in a drawing. Given the presence of a few defining properties or cues, we go beyond them to the inference of identity. Having done so, we infer that the instance so categorized or identified has the other properties characteristic of membership in a category. Given the presence of certain cues of shape, size, and texture, we infer that the thing before us is an apple: *ergo*, it can be eaten, cut with a knife, it relates by certain principles of classification to other kinds of fruits, and so on. The act of rendering some given event equivalent with a class of other things, placing it in an identity class, provides then one of the most primitive forms of going beyond information given.

William James (1890) wrote picturesquely of this process, remarking that cognitive life begins when one is able to exclaim, "Hollo! Thingumbob again." The adaptive significance of this capacity for equivalence grouping is, of course, enormous. If we were to respond to each event as unique and to learn anew what to do about it or even what to call it, we would soon be swamped by the complexity of our environment. By last count, there were some 7.5 million discriminable differences in the color solid alone. Yet for most purposes we get by treating them as if there were only a dozen or two classes of colors. No two individuals are alike, yet we get by with perhaps a dozen or so "types" into which we class others. Equivalence categories or concepts are the most basic currency one can utilize in going beyond the sensory given. They are the first steps toward rendering the environment generic.

Consider a second form of going beyond the information given, one that involves learning the redundancy of the environment. I present the word, P*YC*OL*GY, and with no difficulty at all you recognize that the word is PSY-CHOLOGY. Or the finding of Miller, Heise, and Lichten (1951) that words masked by noise are more easily recognized when they are in a meaningful or high-probability context than when they are presented in isolation. Indeed, the missing word in the sentence, "Dwight _____ is currently President of the United States" can be completely masked by noise and yet "recognized" correctly by any-body who knows the subject matter. Or we find that subjects in some experiments currently in progress check off about an average of thirty trait words from the Gough list as being characteristic of a person who is only described as being either "intelligent," or "independent," or "considerate." Any one of these key traits has at least thirty possible avenues for going beyond it, based on learned probabilities of what things are likely to go with what in another person. Once one learns the probability texture of the environment, one can go beyond the given by predicting its likely concomitants.

We move one step beyond such probabilistic ways of going beyond the information given and come now to certain formal bases for doing so. Two propositions are presented:

$$A > B$$
$$B > C$$

and with very little difficulty most people can readily go beyond to the inference that

$$A > C$$

Or I present a series of numbers, with one missing one to be supplied:

2, 4, 8, *, 32, 64

and as soon as you are able to see that the numbers are powers of two, or that they represent successive doublings, you will be able to provide the missing number 16. Or in an experiment by Bruner, Matter, and O'Dowd, rats are taught to find their way through a four-unit T-maze by threading the path LRLR. Given the proper conditions (and to these we will return later), an animal readily transfers to the mirror-image pattern of RLRL – provided he has learned the path as an instance of single alternation and not as a set of specific turns.

What it is that one learns when one learns to do the sort of thing just described, whether it be learning to do syllogisms or learning the principle of single alternation, is not easily described. It amounts to the learning of certain formal schemata that may be fitted to or may be used to organize arrays of diverse information. We shall use the expression *coding* to describe what an organism does to information under such circumstances, leaving its closer examination until later. Thus, we can conceive of an organism capable of rendering things into equivalence classes, capable of learning the probabilistic relationships between events belonging to various classes, and capable of manipulating these classes by the utilization of certain formal coding systems.

We often combine formal codes and probability codes in making inferences beyond the data. Studies such as those by Wilkins (1928) provide instructive examples. One finds, for example, that a typical deduction made from the proposition "If all A are B" is that "All B are A," and to the proposition "If some A are not B" a typical conclusion is that "Some B are not A." Yet none of the subjects ever agrees with the proposition that "If all men are mammals, then all mammals are men," or with the proposal that "If some men are not criminals, then some criminals are not men." In sum, it may often be the case that "common sense" – the result of inductive learning of what is what and what goes with what in the environment – may often serve to correct less well learned formal methods of going beyond information given. In short, one may often have alternative modes of going beyond, sometimes in conflict with each other, sometimes operating to the same effect.

One final case before we turn to the difficult business of trying to specify what is involved in utilizing information in this soaring manner. This time we take a scientist, and we shall take him unprepared with a theory, which, as we know, is a rare state for both the scientist and the layman alike. He has, let us say, been working on the effects of sound sleep, and in pursuit of his inquiries has hit on the bright idea of giving his subjects a complete rest for five or six days – "just to see what happens." To add to their rest, he places them on a soft bed, covers their eyes with translucent ground-glass goggles, lulls their ears with a soft but persistent homogeneous masking noise, and in general makes life as homogeneously restful as possible for them. At the end of this time, he tests them and finds, lo and behold, that they are incapable of doing simple arithmetic problems, that they cannot concentrate, that their perceptual constancies are impaired, and so on down the list of findings that have recently been reported from McGill by Bexton, Heron, Scott (1954), and their collaborators. (Please note that the McGill investigators started with a hypothesis about sensory deprivation; our example is a fiction, but it will serve us and may even relate to our Canadian colleagues before they are through.) Once one has got some data of this order, one is in a funk unless one can go beyond them. To do so requires a theory. A theory, of course, is something we invent. If it is a good theory – a good formal or probabilistic coding system – it should permit us to go beyond the present data both retrospectively and prospectively. We go backward – turn around on our own schemata – and order data that before seemed unrelated to each other. Old loose ends now become part of a new pattern. We go forward in the sense of having new hypotheses and predictions about other things that should be but that have not been tested. When we have finished the reorganizing by means of the new theoretical coding system, everything then seems obvious, if the thing fits. We mention theory construction as a final example of coding processes largely because it highlights several points that are too easily overlooked in the simpler examples given earlier. Coding may involve inventive behavior and we must be concerned with what is involved in the construction of coding systems. And coding systems may be effective or ineffective in permitting one to go beyond information. Later we shall inquire into the conditions that make for construction of new coding systems and what may lead to the construction of adequate ones.

On coding systems

A coding system may be defined as a set of contingently related, nonspecific categories. It is the person's manner of grouping and relating information about his world, and it is constantly subject to change and reorganization. Bartlett's memory *schemata* are close to what is intended here, and the early work of Piaget (1930) on the child's conception of nature represents a naturalistic account of coding systems in the child.

Let it be clear that a coding system as I describe it here is a hypothetical construct. It is inferred from the nature of antecedent and consequent events. For example, in the rat experiment cited earlier, I teach an organism to wend a course that goes LRLR through a maze. *I wish to discover how the event is coded.* I transfer the animal to a maze that goes RLRL. He transfers with marked savings. I infer now that he has coded the situation as single alternation. But I must continue to test for the genericalness of the coding system used. Is it alternation in general or alternation only in spatial terms? To test this I set up a situation in the maze where the correct path is defined by taking alternate colors, now a black, now a white member of black-white pairs, without regard to their position. If there is saving here too, I assume that the original learning was coded not as positional alternation but as alternation in general. Of course, I use the appropriate control groups along the way. Note that the technique I am using is identical with the technique we use to discover whether children are learning proper codes in school. We provide training in addition, then we move on to numbers that the child has not yet added, then we move to abstract symbols like $a + a + a$ and see whether $3a$ emerges as the answer. Then we test further to see whether the child has grasped the idea of repeated addition, which we fool him by calling multiplication. We devise techniques of instruction along the way to aid the child in building a generic code to use for all sorts of quantities. If we fail to do this, we say that the child has learned in rote fashion or that, in Wertheimer's (1945) moralistic way of putting it, we have given the child "mechanical" rather than "insightful" ways of solving the problem. The distinction is not between mechanical and insightful, really, but whether or not the child has grasped and can use the generic code we have set out to teach him.

You will sense immediately that what I have been describing are examples of "transfer of training," so-called. But nothing is being transferred, really. The organism is learning codes that have narrower or wider applicability.

Let me give you some examples of how one uses the transfer paradigm to investigate what kind of coding systems are being learned. William Hull, a teacher in a Cambridge school, raised the question whether the learning of spelling involved simply the learning by rote of specific words or whether instead it did not also involve learning the *general coding system* for English words from which the child might then be able to reconstruct the letters of a word. He took children of the fifth grade and separated them into those who had done well and those who had done poorly on a standard spelling achievement test, taking as subjects those who fell in the highest and lowest quartile of the class. He then presented these children brief exposures of pseudowords, which they were to write down immediately after the card bearing each word was removed. Some of the words were first-order approximations to English, essentially random strings of letters that had the same frequency distribution of letters as does English. Some were third- and fourth-order approximations to English constructed by Miller, Bruner, and Postman (1954) in connection with another experiment, words like MOSSIANT, VERNALIT, POKERSON, ONETICUL, APHYSTER, which reflected the probability structure of English very closely and which, but for the grace of God, might have been in the dictionary. Take the case for five-letter and six-letter pseudowords. For the first-order or random words, there was little difference between good and poor spellers. But for nonsense approximations to English, there was a great difference between the two, the good spellers showing a much superior performance.

The difference between the two groups is in *what* they had been learning while learning to spell English words. One group had been learning words more by rote, the others had been learning a general coding system based on the transitional probabilities that characterize letter sequences in English. Along the same lines, Mr Robert Harcourt of Cambridge University and I used the occasion of an international seminar at Salzburg to test Italian, German, Swedish, French, Dutch, and English speakers on their ability to reproduce random strings of letters presented briefly (that is, zero-order approximations to any language), and third-order approximations to each of these languages. As you would expect, there was no difference in ability to handle random strings, but a real difference in ability, favoring one's mother tongue, in reproducing nonsense in one's own language. You will sense immediately to what language stock each of the following nonsense words belongs: MJÖLKKOR, KLOOK, GERLANCH, OTIVANCHE, TRIANODE, FATTOLONI, and so on. When one learns a language one learns a coding system that goes beyond words. If Benjamin Lee Whorf is right, the coding system goes well beyond even such matters as we have described.

Let us sum up the matter to this point. We propose that when one goes beyond the information given, one does so by virtue of being able to place the present given in a more generic coding system and that one essentially "reads off" from the coding system additional information either on the basis of learned contingent probabilities or learned principles of relating material. Much of what has been called transfer of training can be fruitfully considered a case of applying learned coding systems to new events. Positive transfer represents a case where an appropriate coding system is applied to a new array of events, negative transfer being a case either of misapplication of a coding system to new events or of the absence of a coding system that may be applied. It follows from this that it is of the utmost importance in studying learning to understand systematically *what it is* that an organism has learned. This is the cognitive problem in learning.

There is perhaps one additional thing that is learned by an organism when he acquires information generically and this must be mentioned in passing although it is not directly germane to our line of inquiry. Once a situation has been mastered, it would seem that the organism alters the way in which new situations are approached in search of information. A maze-wise rat, for example, even when put into a new learning situation, seems not to nose about quite so randomly. In an experiment by Goodnow and Pettigrew (1955), for example, once their subjects have learned one pattern of pay-off on a "two-armed bandit," they approach the task of finding other patterns by responding more systematically to the alternatives in the situation. Even when they are trying to discover a pattern in what is essentially a random series of pay-offs, their sequential choice behavior shows less haphazardness. It is interesting that this acquired regularity of response makes it possible for them to locate new regularities in pay-off pattern when these are introduced after a long exposure to random positional pay-offs. Even though the behavior is designed to discover whether the old pattern will recur again, its regularity makes it possible to discover new patterns.

Three general problems now emerge. The first problem concerns the conditions under which efficient and generalizable coding systems will be acquired. What will lead a rat to learn the sequence LRLR in such a generic way that it will be transferable to the sequence of turns RLRL? What will lead a child to learn the sequence 2, 4, 8, 16, 32 ... in such a way that it transfers to the sequence 3, 9, 27, 81 ...? This we shall call *the conditions of code acquisition.*

The second we may label the *problem of creativity.* It has two aspects. The first has to do with the *inventive* activity involved in constructing highly generic and widely appropriate coding systems, armed with which a person will subsequently, in a highly predictive way, be able to deal with and go beyond much of the information he encounters in his environment. The other aspect of the problem of creativity is the development of a readiness to *utilize* appropriately already acquired coding systems. James long ago called this "the electric sense of analogy" and it consists in being able to recognize something before one fits it into or finds it to be a case of some more generic class of things that one has dealt with before – being able to see, for example, that laws that were originally related to statistical physics also fit the case of the analysis of transmitted information, the leap that carries us from Boltzmann's turn-of-the-century conception of entropy to modern theories of communication as initiated by Claude Shannon (1948). The equation of entropy with information was a creative analogical leap indeed, even if it did not require any new invention. Very well, the problem of creativity involves then the invention of efficient and applicable coding systems to apply to the information given and also the proper sense of knowing when it is appropriate to apply them.

The third and final problem to be considered is the *problem of instruction,* and it is a practical one. It concerns the best coding system in terms of which to present various subject matters so as to guarantee maximum ability to generalize. For example, the statement $S = 1/2 \, gt^2$ is an efficient and highly generalizable coding system for learning about falling bodies, and by using the code one can go beyond any partial data given one about falling bodies. But how does one teach somebody "about a country" in general so that given some new specific knowledge about the country he can effectively "go beyond it" by appropriate inferences based on an effective coding system?

We consider each of these problems in turn.

Conditions affecting the acquisition of coding systems

Essentially, we are asking under what conditions will an organism learn something or, as we put it, code something in a generic manner so as to maximize the transferability of the learning to new situations?

Let me propose four general sets of conditions that may be relevant here. The first of these is *set* or *attitude*. The second is *need state*. The third is *degree of mastery* of the original learning from which a more generic coding system must be derived. The fourth is *diversity of training*.

The role of set

It is a perennial source of embarrassment to psychologists interested in the learning process that "set to learn" is such a massive source of variance in most experiments on human learning. We make the distinction between incidental learning and intentional learning. What is the difference between the two?

Take typical experiments in the field of concept attainment as a case in point. In most such experiments since Hull's classic study (1920), the subject is given the task of *memorizing* what nonsense syllables go with what figures or pictures or words. One subset of pictures in the array presented – ones that all contain unbeknownst to the subject a certain common defining property – will have the label CIV and another subset, let us say, will have the label DAX. The task as presented is one in which the subject is to learn which label goes with which pictures. Insofar as the task is understood as one involving the memorization of labels, the subject is engaged in what can only be called incidental concept attainment. An interesting experiment by Reed (1946) shows that when subjects operate under such a set, they attain concepts more slowly and remember them less well than under instructional conditions where the subject is told frankly what is the real objective of the experiment – that is, to find what makes certain designs CIV's and other DAX's. In an extensive series of experiments by Bruner, Goodnow, and Austin (1955), moreover, it is evident that the search for the defining attributes of a class of objects – the search for a generic code in terms of which a class of objects may be rendered equivalent – leads to certain forms of behavior strategies or learning sets that are absent when the task is seen as one of rote memorization. The subject learns ways of testing instances to gather an optimum amount of information leading him to final discovery of the defining attributes of CIV's and DAX's. Once success has been achieved in this way, new instances can be recognized with no further learning and the memory of the instances already encountered need no longer depend upon sheer retention. For now, knowing the code, the subject can reconstruct the fact that all positive instances encountered were all marked by certain critical attributes.

In short, an induced set can guide the person to proceed non-generically and by rote or to proceed as if what was to be learned was a principle or a generic method of coding events. Instructions serve, if you will, as a switching mechanism or set producer that brings different forms of coding into play and tunes the organism to the kind and level of generic activity that seem appropriate to the situation.

Obviously, the principal giver of instruction is our own past history. For by virtue of living in a certain kind of professional or social setting, our approach to new experience becomes constrained – we develop, if you will, a professional deformation with respect to ways of coding events. The mathematician tends with time to code more and more events in terms of certain formal codes that are the stock in trade of his profession. The historian has his particular deformations, and so too the psychologist. With experience, Harlow's (1949) monkeys gradually develop a deformation too and attempt to solve all discrimination problems as exemplars of the oddity principle.

It is perhaps Kurt Goldstein (1939) who has insisted most strongly that one may in general characterize the typical sets a person brings to problems along the dimensions of abstractness and concreteness. The person who is high in concreteness deals with information or events in terms of their own specific identity and does not tend to genericize what is learned. The abstract attitude is one in which the individual can not only tear himself away from the given, but actually may not deal with the given save as an exemplar of more generic categories. How people "get to be" one way and the other or how they maintain an ability to operate at both levels is something we do not understand with any clarity, although some tentative proposals will be put forth in the following section.

To sum up: the manner and the degree with which newly learned knowledge is coded generically can be influenced in a transient way by situational instruction and in a more permanent way by the regimen of one's past experience. One's "attitude" toward learning, whether a transient or an enduring thing, will then determine the degree to which one is equipped with coding systems that can be brought to bear on new situations and permit one to go beyond them.

Need state

I should like to dust off the Yerkes-Dodson Law at this point and propose that the generality of the coding system in terms of which newly acquired information is organized depends upon the presence of an optimum motivational state. Very high and very low drive lead, I think, to an increase in concreteness of cognitive activity. There is a middle state of drive level that produces the strongest tendency toward generic learning.

Let me illustrate this by going back to the experiment of Bruner, Matter, and O'Dowd previously referred to. Consider two of their groups. Each group was given enough training to reach a criterion in learning the turn pattern LRLR and then given eighty additional trials of overlearning. The only difference between the groups was that one group did its learning under thirty-six hours of food deprivation, the other under twelve hours of deprivation. When the two groups were then transferred to the reversal pattern, RLRL, the moderately motivated group showed positive transfer, learning the new single alternation pattern significantly faster than they had learned the original pattern. The very hungry group showed marked negative transfer.

The behavior of the two groups at the time of transfer is revealing. When transferred, the moderately motivated groups showed much more disturbance in behavior. When these highly trained animals found the old reliable door at the first turn blocked, they drew back from the choice-point and sometimes took as long as twenty minutes before they could make up their minds about what to do next. They defecated, seemed upset, and spent a great deal of time looking back and forth at the two doors. Several of the animals, at the end of this period of delay, then charged through the now correct first door and continued to charge right through the now correct single alternation pattern and made no errors from then on. Others made somewhat more errors, but on the whole, their learning was rapid.

The other group, the highly skilled and highly motivated rats of the thirty-six-hour deprived group, showed quite different behavior. Finding the first door locked, they barged right over and took the alternative door, and then attempted unsuccessfully at each successive alley to make their old turn. Some of these animals persisted in this for many trials and then shifted to other forms of systematic response – such as one-sided position habits – that were not single alternation. In sum, it seemed as if they had to unlearn the old pattern of LRLR responses and then relearn a new one.

There is one particular feature of the behavior of the animals in the two groups that wants special attention. It is the amount of "looking around" or VTE-ing or scanning that went on in the two groups. As Tolman (1938) has observed, highly motivated organisms show less VTE behavior, less looking back and forth at choice points. So, too, our thirty-six-hour hungry animals during original learning in contrast with the twelve-hour ones. The difference in VTE was particularly marked during the early transfer trials as well, and it was exhibited by the less hungry rats predominantly in the first unit of the maze, at the choice-point that was the only real alternative, for once the first turn was correctly mastered, the rest of the pattern followed.

It would seem, then, that under conditions of high drive, if a path to the goal has been learned, it is learned, so to speak, as "*this* path to *this* goal" and is not coded or acquired as an example of a more generic pattern, "this *kind* of path to this *kind* of goal." In consequence, when a new situation arises, the driven creature does not have a generic coding system that permits him to go beyond it "insightfully." It is as if one of the students of geometry in Wertheimer's study (1945) had learned to do the operations necessary for solving the area of *this* parallelogram but had not generalized the knowledge into a coding system for handling parallelograms of slightly different size, shape, or position.

Impelling drive states seem also to affect the extent to which a person is able to apply already very firmly acquired coding systems to new material encountered, permitting him to go appropriately beyond the information given. An illustrative study is provided by the experiment of Postman and Bruner (1948) on perception under stress. Two groups of subjects were used. They began by having to recognize brief, three-word sentences presented tachistoscopically under usual laboratory conditions. Then the stress group was given an impossible perceptual recognition task to perform (reporting on the details on a complex picture presented at an exposure level too brief in duration for adequate performance). During these stress trials they were rather mercilessly badgered by the experimenter for performing so poorly and were urged to try harder. The other group was given a simple task of judging the illumination level at which the same picture was presented at the same exposure levels. And they were not badgered. Then additional sentences were given subjects in both groups. The stress group showed no further improvement in their sentence- and word-recognition thresholds, the nonstress group continued to improve. What was striking about the performance of the two groups in the latter half of the experiment was that the stress subjects either overshot the information given and made wild inferences about the nature of the briefly presented words, or they undershot and seemed unable to make words out of the briefly presented data at all. In terms of the Jamesian electric sense of analogy, it was as if the stress introduced either too many ohms of resistance into the circuit or removed too many of them. The stress subjects, let it be noted, did not behave consistently in the overshoot or the undershoot fashion, but seemed to go back and forth between the two.

Let me note finally in connection with code acquisition and/or the transfer of acquired codes to new situations that there is one interesting feature of the Harlow (1949) experiments on the acquisition of learning sets that is not often enough remarked. Recall that in the typical experiment of this kind, an animal is trained to choose the odd member of a set of stimuli, and that after training on a variety of such problems he is able to do so regardless of what characteristics the stimuli have: the odd one of several shapes, of several colors, of several junk stimuli, and so on. These experiments are carried out with animals who are only very lightly motivated. They are well fed before they are run, the reward used consists of a half or even a quarter of a peanut, and it would almost be fair to say that the most impelling drive operative is the manipulative-curiosity drive that Harlow has rightly made so much of in his recent writing. The use of such a mild motivational regimen is well advised. The fact of the matter is that one does not get such elegant principle learning in more highly motivated animals. A very hungry monkey may not develop such learning sets at all. Again, more generic coding seems to be inhibited by a condition in which the information to be acquired has too great instrumental relevance to a need state then in being.

Let me conclude this section on the role of need states in acquiring and utilizing coding systems with an important caveat, one that has been insisted upon particularly by George Klein (1951). One cannot specify the cognitive or behavioral resultants of need states without specifying the manner in which the organism has learned to deal with his need states. The resultant of "learning to deal with needs" is the establishment in behavior of what Klein calls general regulatory systems. In a sense, we have been implying such systems in the rat and monkey when we speak of the fact that a high need state has the effect of specializing the organism to deal with the here-and-now without regard to the more generic significance of what is being learned. It is conceivable that in some higher organisms this may not always be the case.

Degree of mastery and its relationship to generic coding

Let me begin again with that overworked species, the rat. Starling Reed (1953) reports that animals who have been over-trained on a black–white discrimination, with black the positive stimulus, are able to transfer more easily to a black–white discrimination with white positive than are animals trained simply to criterion and then reversed. In the Bruner, Matter, and O'Dowd study already referred to, three groups of twelve-hour and three groups of thirty-six-hour hungry animals were used. High- and low-motivation groups were paired in terms of amount of original training given. One pair of groups was given original training on an LRLR pattern until they just reached criterion; a second pair was given twenty additional trials of practice beyond criterion; and the third pair was given eighty additional overtraining trials. The biggest effect in the study was in the interaction of drive level and amount of overtraining. For the twelve-hour groups, the more their overtraining, the better they did on transfer to the reverse pattern. But only the highly overtrained group showed positive transfer. All the strongly motivated animals showed about the same amount of negative transfer. We may take as a tentative conclusion that overtraining and mastery aids generic coding provided motivation is not severe.

We are in the midst of a controversial area, for the wisdom of common sense and of the psychologist divides sharply on the matter of practice and drill. "Practice makes perfect" is a well-thumbed proverb and the darling of practically all S-R learning theory. To be sure, it is a moot point in these theories just *what* it is that practice makes one perfect at. Nobody denies that it makes one perfect at the thing being practiced, but there is still debate on whether it also improves one at things beyond what one has practiced. The position of most stimulus-response theorists has been that it does not make one perfect at anything save the thing itself and that transfer to other things depends upon whether the other things contain elements identical to those that existed in the first task. We shall leave aside the question of how fast and loose one can play with the word "identical" in the expression "identical elements," for it is obvious that exploring its usage will be a discouraging venture. Even in the original monograph of Thorndike (1903) it was claimed that one form of identical element shared by two problems was that they could be solved by the same principle!

In any case, to return to the main issue at hand, there is another school of thought that proposed insight and understanding as a more important factor than drill in improving both performance of a particular task and in guaranteeing wider generalization of the learning to other situations. The names of Wertheimer (1945), Katona (1940), Duncker (1945), and Köhler (1925) are associated with this position, and the modern proverb has been provided by International Business Machines: THINK. The progressive school and its apostles have perhaps been the chief carriers of the practical banner.

I think the issue is a pseudoissue. The nature and effect of drill and overtraining is a function of what has to be learned. Moreover, one cannot speak of drill without specifying the nature of the set and the drive conditions under which it takes place. We cannot talk about practice or training as if it were being administered to an indifferently constructed black box.

First about the nature of materials to be learned. Take Katona's example of the string of numbers:

58121519222629

If subjects are asked to remember it, the amount of practice required to become perfect depends upon their method of recoding the numbers. If they recognize that the numbers are grouped as follows

5–8–12–15–19–22–26–29

and that this series begins with 5 and is made up of successive additions of 3 and 4, then what they had better practice is "5 then add 3 and then 4 and keep repeating this alternation." Mastering this coding system requires less practice and it is different practice than trying to remember the series by rote. As George Miller (1951) puts it in his delightful discussion of recoding systems, "Suppose that we want to know how far a body falls through space when it has been falling freely for a given number of seconds. One way to tackle this problem is to make measurements, summarize the measurements in a table, and then memorize the table ... This is a very stupid way to proceed because we memorize each number as if it were unrelated to all the other numbers ... All the measurements can be recoded into a simple rule that says the distance fallen at the end of t seconds is $gt^2/2$. The value of g is about 32. All we need remember is $16t^2$. Now we store all the measurements away in memory by storing this simple formula" (p. 234). Again, we had better practice remembering the formula and the value of g, and never mind practicing on the table of measurements from which it was produced.

But yet this fails to meet the question squarely. For where we do not know the appropriate coding system in advance, what is the best practice procedure for discovering it? Our rats and those of Starling Reed obviously had to do a fair amount of drilling at their task before they learned it in a generic way. And it seems to be frequently the case that a certain amount of skill development is necessary at a simpler level of coding before more generic recoding of the learning can occur. The earliest studies of code learning, the classic study by Bryan and Harter (1897) of telegraphic code learning, can be reproduced in many later studies: one first learns to code the messages in terms of letters, then in terms of words, then in terms of sentences. Later methods of regrouping or recoding depend upon prior mastery of less generic methods of coding. One's limited immediate memory span requires one to deal first with the dits and dahs of single letters. Then gradually when the dit-dah arrangement of a letter takes on unitary properties, that is, can be categorized as a unit, it may be grouped with other unitary dit-dah arrangements into words. When words are codable as units, then one goes to sentences. So too with the rats: they must master the regularity of a set of turns before it becomes possible to reorganize or recode in terms of a single alternation principle.

In sum, then, the question of mastery comes down to this. Learning often cannot be translated into a generic form until there has been enough mastery of the specifics of the situation to permit the discovery of lower-order regularities which can then be recombined into higher-order, more generic coding systems. Once a system of recoding has been worked out whereby information is condensed into more generic codes, the problem of mastery becomes one of mastering the recoding system rather than mastering the original set of events. Moreover, the nature of practice cannot be simply specified in terms of repetition to and beyond mastery of a specific task. Rather, one must specify the conditions under which practice takes place, whether with the auxiliary intention to search out a generic coding system or whether simply with a rote learning intention. Finally, the need level at which the organism is practicing a task must also be specified. Practice at a high rate of drive may produce no generic learning. Low-drive practice may.

Diversity of training

I think that we know intuitively that if we wish to make a group of students understand the Pythagorean theorem in plane geometry, it helps to illustrate the intuitive proof of the theorem to use several right triangles of different dimensions, and indeed it might also help to demonstrate that the theorem does not apply to nonrectilinear triangles. It also seems intuitively right, does it not, that if monkeys are to be taught Harlow's oddity problem it helps or indeed may be essential to give them training choosing the odd member of several *different* arrays? So too when we play the original word game with children, we point to several exemplars of the word "dog" and several exemplars of "cat" in demonstrating the linguistic code utterance "cats and dogs are different." The quantitative informational importance of diversity of instances in concept attainment has been dealt with elsewhere and I would only like to consider some of the common-sense implications of the matter here.

The process of finding out what is generic about a given situation so that one can then deal with similar situations later – know their solution without having to go through the tedious business of learning all over again – consists essentially of being able to isolate the defining properties of the class of events to which the present situation belongs. In a concept-formation experiment, for example, if a subject is trying to discover what makes certain cards "positive" and certain ones "negative," his task is to discover which of the discriminable attributes or which combination of discriminable attributes are present in the positive instances and absent in the negative ones. I think one can think of the matter of diversity in terms of the interesting old proverb. "The fish will be the last to discover water," as indeed man was very late in discovering the atmosphere. Unless one is exposed to some changes, genericizing does not seem to be stimulated. Kurt Lewin had a subtle point when he urged that the best way to understand the nature of a social process was to try to change it, for only in the face of changes in events does one begin to have the information necessary to abstract generic properties.

This suggests a rather simple but rather startling conclusion. If we are to study the conditions under which generic learning occurs, the pattern of much of present learning research needs drastic change. The present approach is to study the speed of acquisition of new learning and, possibly, to study the conditions that produce extinction. When we have carried our experimental subjects through these steps, we either dismiss them or, if they are animal subjects, dispose of them. The exception, of course, is the clinician, but even his research on learning and cognition is of the cross-sectional type. We have been accustomed to speaking of maze-wise rats and test-wise human beings, but in the spirit of being annoyed by an inconvenience. The fact of the matter is, as Beach (1954) has recently pointed out, that early and diverse training of lower organisms seems to be one of the conditions for producing "intelligent" behavior in the more mature organism. If we really intend to study the conditions of generic learning by the use of the transfer-of-training paradigm I have proposed, then we shall have to keep our organisms far longer and teach them original tasks of greater diversity than we now do if we are to discover the conditions affecting generic learning.

The invention or creation of coding systems

The past half century has witnessed a profound revolution against the conception of science inherited from the Newtonian period. Newton saw the task of the scientist as a journey on the sea of discovery whose objective was to discover the islands of truth. The conception was essentially Baconian. Newton's *Principia* was not proposed as a theoretical system but as a description of discoveries about nature. His *Opticks* was in like vein a disquisition into the secrets of light. Indeed, Jonathan Edwards preached to his parishioners in Western Massachusetts on Newton's discovery of the spectral composition of white light as an instance of the fact that God had given man sufficient capacities to see through to some of the deepest secrets of God's design. To a considerable extent, the layman's view of science is still dominated by the spirit of discovery, by the spirit of naturalistic realism.

The temper of modern science is more nominalistic. The scientist constructs formal models or theories that have predictive value, that have a value in going beyond the information available. One works with sets of observations that one fits into a theory. If the theory cannot take one beyond one's observations, if it does not have the "surplus value" that is demanded of a theory, then the theory is trivial. The universe is a set of perspectives devised by scientists for understanding and rendering predictable the array of observations that are possible. Whoever has read Robert Oppenheimer's account of "Lord Rutherford's World" in his Rieth Lectures (Oppenheimer, 1954) or whoever has read Max Wertheimer's account (1945) of his conversations with Einstein on the formulation of the special and general theories of relativity cannot but be struck by the emphasis on the constructive, nominalistic, and essentially subjective conception of science-making that prevails in modern physical theory.

The activity of constructing formal models and theoretical constructs is a prototype of what we mean by the creation of generic coding systems that permits one to "go beyond" the data to new and possibly fruitful predictions.

Let us consider the creative acts by which a person constructs a "theory" for dealing with a problem. The given, let us say, is as it is in a Duncker-type problem. Here is x-ray apparatus capable of destroying a tumor in the center of a body. The difficulty is that the amount of radiation sufficient to destroy the tumor is also sufficient to destroy the healthy tissue through which it must pass in reaching the tumor. How solve the difficulty? Let us assume that the problem solver did not learn a routine technique in medical school for dealing with this problem.

We will assume (and it is not an outrageous assumption, as we shall see) that the person has had experiences that provide the elements out of which a solution may be fashioned. The child knows, for example, that if a plank is too weak to take two children across a gap simultaneously, the children can get across one at a time in successive order or get across the gap at the same time if they can find two planks to throw across it. This is highly relevant knowledge. But this is not a "theory" nor by remembering it does one either solve the problem or create a relevant coding system.

Suppose now that the person comes, through whatever processes are involved, to a solution of the problem: using two x-ray beams, each of less than lethal dose, to converge at some angle upon the tumor. This solution, insofar as it is specific to the single problem at hand, is still not a theory; indeed it is not altogether clear that anything new has been "produced" or "created." What we mean by a theory or model or generic coding system is a representation of the criterial characteristics of the situation just described, a contentless depiction of the ideal case, empty in the sense that geometry is empty of particulars. It is this emptying operation, I would propose, that constitutes the creative step in inventing or producing a coding system. It is also the step that is involved when one learns something generically. In this sense there is only a difference in degree between what we have spoken of as generic learning and what we here call the production of a generic coding system.

Pursue the matter a bit further. The problem solver says to himself, "This must be a general characteristic of loads, media, and destinations within the medium. Every medium has an array of paths to a destination within it and each path has a capacity. The number of paths required for the simultaneous transmission of a load to a destination is the size of the load divided by the capacity of any single path." Now we say the person has a theory: he has to some degree emptied the problem of specific content.

When we ask what leads to such an emptying operation (or abstraction, if one prefers the more conventional term), we are forced to answer by describing the conditions that inhibit it. What then inhibits "theory construction"? I would submit that the conditions inhibiting theory construction of this kind are the same ones that inhibit generic learning – the conditions of code acquisition described in the preceding section. For generic learning and the abstracting or "emptying" operation are, I think, the same thing.

But consider one other aspect of the creation or acquisition of generic coding systems. It consists of a form of combining activity that is made possible by the use of abstracted or "empty" codes. Take the formulation just given – the theory of loads, media, destinations, and path capacities. It now becomes possible to combine *this* formalized system with other formalized systems to generate new predictions. For example, suppose the problem solver goes on to combine his new formulation with the equally abstract formulations of analytic geometry. The number of paths converging through a medium to an enclosed destination is infinity. Therefore, the combined path capacity of an over-all medium is infinity, and therefore, in principle, an infinite load (radiation or whatnot) can be delivered to a destination. In principle, then, one may go beyond to the hypothesis that *no* load is too large to deliver simultaneously across a medium, given the solution of technical limitations.

It seems to me that the principal creative activity over and beyond the construction of abstracted coding systems is the combination of different systems into new and more general systems that permit additional prediction. It is perhaps because of this that, in Whitehead's picturesque phrase, progress in science seems to occur on the margins between fields. There is virtually no research available on this type of combinatorial creativity. How, for example, do physiological psychologists combine the coding systems of biology and psychology, or biophysicists their component disciplines to derive a new emergent? We might begin by looking.

The problem of instruction

What we have said thus far obviously has implications for educational practice, and it is with one of these that we wish to conclude. How shall we teach a subject matter? If the subject matter were geometry we readily answer that we teach the person those axioms and theorems – a formal coding system – that will maximize the ability of the individual to go beyond the information given in any problem he might encounter. A problem in geometry is simply an incomplete statement, one that has unknowns in it. We say, "Here is a three-sided figure: one side measures x, and the other y, the angle between them is z degrees and the problem is to find the length of the other side and the size of the other two angles as well as the area of the triangle." One must, in short, go beyond what is given. We know intuitively that if the person has learned the formal coding system, he will be able to perform such feats.

But how describe the history of a people or, say, Navaho culture? I would propose that much the same criterion should prevail here as we apply to geometry. The best description of a people's history is that set of propositions that permits a given individual to go beyond the information given to him. This, if you will, is *"the"* history of a people, the information that is necessary to make all other information as redundant or predictable as possible. So too in characterizing Navaho culture: that minimum set of propositions that will permit the largest reconstruction of unknowns by people to whom the propositions are revealed.

Let me in general propose this test as a measure of the adequacy of any set of instructional propositions – that once they are grasped, they permit the maximum reconstruction of material unknown to the reconstructor. My colleague Morton White (1950) argues persuasively for this position when he says (pp. 718–719),

> We ought to start by observing that a history contains true statements about the whole course of … [an] object's existence. True statements about the future of the object will be as much part of its history as true statements about its remote past. We must observe that some of these statements have causal implications whereas others do not … . The next thing to observe is that there are two kinds of historians, two kinds of students who *want* to approximate the whole truth about a given object. First there are those who conceive it as

their task to amass as many true singular statements as can be amassed at a given moment, and in this way approximate the ideal of the historian. Clearly this seems like the way to approach an infinite or very large number of statements – gather as many as you can. But then there are historians who are more discriminating, who recognize that some singular statements are historically more important than others, not because they fit in with some moral point of view, but because they are more useful for achieving the history of the object as here defined. The first group is near-sighted. It tries to amass everything in sight on the theory that this is a sure method of getting close to the whole truth. But it fails to realize that those who select facts which seem to have causal significance are more apt to come to know things about the future and past of the object.

White then goes on to compare the criterion of "causal fertility" in history with the criterion of "deductive fertility" in logic, noting that "both attempts at brevity…are motivated by a desire for intellectual economy." In the broadest sense, the economy is a predictive economy – to be able to go beyond givens to a prediction of unknowns.

I would submit, I think, that it is only by imparting "causally fertile" propositions or generic codes that general education in the broad range of human knowledge is made possible. General education does best to aim at being generic education, training men to be good guessers, stimulating the ability to go beyond the information given to probable reconstructions of other events.

Conclusion

This has been a programmatic essay on the conditions by which it becomes possible for people to go beyond the information given them, or as Bartlett (1957) has put it, to go beyond evidence, to fill in gaps, to extrapolate. We have posed the problem as one involving the learning of coding systems that have applicability beyond the situation in which they were learned. In essence, our proposal is that we emphasize those conditions that maximize the transferability of learning and in pursuit of that we have urged that psychologists examine more closely what is involved when we learn generically – the motivational conditions, the kinds of practice required, the nature of the set designed for gaining an optimally generic grasp of materials. Rate of acquisition and rate of extinction in learning have occupied us for a generation. Perhaps in the coming generation we can concern ourselves more directly with the utility of learning: whether, one thing having been learned, other things can be solved with no further learning required. When we have achieved this leap, we will have passed from the psychology of learning to the psychology of problem solving.

Bibliography

Bartlett, F. C. *Thinking: An Experimental and Social Study*. Cambridge: Cambridge University Press, 1957.

Beach, F. A. and J. Jaynes. The effects of early experience on the behavior of animals. *Psychol. Bull.*, 51: 239–263 (1954).

Bexton, W. H., W. Heron, and T. H. Scott. Effects of decreased variation in the sensory environment. *Canadian J. Psychol.*, 8: 70–76 (1954).

Bryan, W. L. and N. Harter. Studies on the telegraphic language. The acquisition of a hierarchy of habits. *Psychol. Rev.*, 6: 345–375 (1897).

Duncker, K. On problem solving. *Psychol. Monogr.*, 58: 1–112 (1945).

Goldstein, K. *The Organism*. New York: American Book Co. (1939).

Goodnow, J. J. and T. Pettigrew. Effect of prior patterns of experience upon strategies and learning sets. *J. Exp. Psychol.*, 49: 381–389 (1955).

Harlow, H. F. The formation of learning sets. *Psychol. Rev.*, 56: 51–65 (1949).

Hull, C. L. Quantitative aspects of the evolution of concepts. *Psychol. Monogr.*, 123 (1920).

Humphrey, G. *Thinking*. New York: Wiley (1941).

Jamés, W. *The Principles of Psychology*. New York: Holt (1890).

Katona, G. *Organizing and Memorizing*. New York: Columbia University Press (1940).

Klein, G. S. "The personal world through perception," in R. R. Blake and G. V. Ramsey (eds), *Perception: An Approach to Personality*. New York: Ronald (1951).

Köhler, W. *The Mentality of Apes*. New York: Harcourt Brace (1925).

Miller, G. A. *Language and Communication*. New York: McGraw-Hill (1951).

Miller, G. A., G. A. Heise, and W. Lichten. The intelligibility of speech as a function of the context of the test materials. *J. Exp. Psychol.*, 41: 329–335 (1951).

Miller, G. A., J. S. Bruner, and L. Postman. Familiarity of letter sequences and tachistoscopic identification. *J. Gen. Psychol.*, 50: 129–139 (1954).

Oppenheimer, J. R. *Science and the Common Understanding*. New York: Simon and Schuster (1954).

Piaget, J. *The Child's Conception of Physical Causality*. London: Kegan, Paul (1930).

Postman, L. and J. S. Bruner. Perception under stress. *Psychol. Rev.*, 55: 314–323 (1948).

Reed, H. B. Factors influencing the learning and retention of concepts. I. The influence of set. *J. Exp. Psychol.*, 36: 71–87 (1946).

Reed, S. The development of noncontinuity behavior through continuity learning. *J. Exp. Psychol.*, 46: 107–112 (1953).

Shannon, C. E. A mathematical theory of communication. *Bell Syst. Tech. J.*, 27: 379–423, 623–656 (1948). Also in C. E. Shannon and W. Weaver, *The Mathematical Theory of Communication*, Urbana: University of Illinois Press (1949).

Smith, S. cited by G. A. Miller, The Magic Number 7 ± 2. Address given at the 1955 meetings of the Eastern Psychological Association, Philadelphia (1955).

Spearman, C. *The Nature of Intelligence and the Principles of Cognition*. London: Macmillan (1923).

Thorndike, E. L. *Educational Psychology*. New York: Lencke and Buechner (1903).

Tolman, E. C. The determiners of behavior at a choice point. *Psychol. Rev.*, 45: 1–41 (1938).

Wertheimer, M. *Productive Thinking*. New York: Harper (1945).

White, M. G. "Toward an analytic philosophy of history," in M. Farber (ed.), *Philosophical Thought in France and the United States*, Buffalo: University of Buffalo Press (1950).

Wilkins, M. C. The effect of changed material on ability to do formal syllogistic reasoning. *Arch. Psychol.*, 102 (1928).

CHAPTER 2

LEARNING AND THINKING

Harvard Educational Review (1959) 29, 184–192

I

I have been engaged, these last few years, in research on what makes it possible for organisms – human and subhuman alike – to take advantage of past learning in attempting to deal with and master new problems before them now. It is a problem with a deceptively simple ring to it. In pursuit of it, my colleagues and I have found ourselves observing children in schoolrooms, watching them learning. It has been a revealing experience.

We have come to recognize in this work that one of the principal objectives of learning is to save us from subsequent learning. This seems a paradox, but it is not. Another way of putting the matter is to say that when we learn something, the objective is to learn it in such a way that we get a maximum of travel out of what we have learned. A homely example is provided by the relationship in arithmetic between addition and multiplication. If the principle of addition has been grasped in its deeper sense, in its generic sense, then it is unnecessary to learn multiplication. For, in principle, multiplication is only repeated addition. It is not, as we would say in our curricula, another "unit."

Learning something in a generic way is like leaping over a barrier. On the other side of the barrier is thinking. When the generic has been grasped, it is then that we are able to recognize the new problems we encounter as exemplars of old principles we have mastered. Once over the barrier, we are able to benefit from what William James long ago called "the electric sense of analogy."

There are two interesting features in generic learning – in the kind of learning that permits us to cross the barrier into thinking. One of them is *organization*; the other is *manipulation*. If we are to use our past learning, we must organize it in such a way that it is no longer bound to the specific situation in which the learning occurred. Let me give an example from the history of science. It would have been possible for Galileo to have published a handbook of the distances traversed per unit time by falling bodies. School boys for centuries thereafter could easily have been tortured by the task of having to remember the Galilean tables. Such tables, cumbersome though they might have been, would have contained all the necessary information for dealing with free-falling bodies. Instead, Galileo had the inspiration to reorganize this welter of information into a highly simplified form. You recall the compact expression $S = 1/2 \ gt^2$: it not only summarizes all possible handbooks but organizes their knowledge in a way that makes manipulation possible. Not only do we know the distances fallen, but we can use the knowledge for bodies that fall anywhere, in any gravitational field – not just our own.

One of the most notable things about the human mind is its limited capacity for dealing at any one moment with diverse arrays of information. It has been known for a long time that we can deal only with about seven independent items of information at once; beyond that point we exceed our "channel capacity," to use our current jargon. We simply cannot manipulate large masses of information. Because of these limits, we must condense and recode. The seven things we deal with must be worth their weight. A simple formula that can regenerate the distance fallen by any free body, past or future, is under these conditions highly nutritious for its weight. Good organization achieves the kind of economical representation of facts that makes it possible to use the facts in the future. Sheer brute learning, noble though it may be, is not enough. Facts simply learned without a generic organization are the naked and useless untruth. The proper reward of learning is not that it pleases the teacher or the parents, nor is it that we become "quiz kids." The proper reward is that we can now use what we have learned, can cross the barrier from learning into thinking. Are we mindful of these matters in our conduct of teaching?

What has been said thus far must seem singularly lacking in relevance to magic, to art, and to poetry. It appears to relate principally to the learning of mathematics, science, and the social studies. But there is an analogous point to be made about the learning of the arts and literature. If one has read literature and beheld works of art in such a way as to be able to think with their aid, then one has also grasped a deeper, simplifying principle. The underlying principle that gives one the power to use literature and the arts in one's thinking is not of the order of a generic condensation of knowledge. Rather it is metaphoric in nature, and perhaps the best way of describing this class of principles is to call them guiding myths.

Let me take an example from mythology. Recall when you read for the first time the story of Perseus slaying the hateful Medusa. You recall that to look directly upon the Medusa was to be turned to stone. The secret of Perseus was to direct the killing thrust of his sword by the reflection of Medusa on his polished shield. It is an exciting story, full of the ingenuity that Hercules had taught us to expect. Beneath the story, beneath all great stories, there is a deeper metaphoric meaning. I did not understand this meaning for many years, indeed, not until my son asked me what the myth of Perseus "meant." It occurred to me that the polished shield might symbolize all of the devices by which we are able to take action against evil without becoming contaminated by it. The law suggested itself as one such device, enabling us to act against those who trespassed against morality without ourselves having to trespass in our action. I do not wish to hold a brief for my interpretation of the Perseus myth. But I would like to make one point about it.

Man must cope with a relatively limited number of plights – birth, growth, loneliness, the passions, death, and not very many more. They are plights that are neither solved nor by-passed by being "adjusted." An adjusted man must face his passions just as surely as he faces death. I would urge that a grasp of the basic plights through the basic myths of art and literature provides the organizing principle by which knowledge of the human condition is rendered into a form that makes thinking possible, by which we go beyond learning to the use of knowledge. I am not suggesting that the Greek myths are better than other forms of literature. I urge simply that there be exposure to, and interpretation of, literature that deals deeply with the human condition. I have learned as much from Charley Brown of *Peanuts* as I have learned from Perseus. The pablum school readers, stripped of rich imagery in the interest of "readability," stripped of passion in the erroneous belief that the deeper human condition will not interest the child – these are no more the vehicles for getting over the barrier to thinking than are the methods of teaching mathematics by a rote parrotting at the blackboard.

II

I should like to consider now some conditions in our schools today that promote and inhibit progress across the barrier from learning to thinking. I should point out in advance that I am not very cheerful on this subject.

The passivity of knowledge-getting

I have been struck during the past year or so, sitting in classrooms as an observer, by the passivity of the process we call education. The emphasis is upon gaining and storing information, gaining it and storing it in the form in which it is presented. We carry the remainder in long division so, peaches are grown in Georgia, transportation is vital to cities, New York is our largest port, and so on. Can the facts or the methods presented be mimicked? If so, the unit is at an end. There is little effort indeed which goes into the process of putting the information together, finding out what is generic about it. Long division is a skill, like threading a needle. The excitement of it as a method of partitioning things that relates it to such matters as subtraction is rarely stressed. One of the great inventions of man – elementary number theory – is presented as a cookbook. I have yet to see a teacher present one way of doing division and then put it squarely to the class to suggest six other ways of doing it – for there are at least six other ways of doing it than any one that might be taught in a school. So too with algebra. Algebra is not a set of rules for manipulating numbers and letters except in a trivial sense. It is a way of thinking, a way of coping with the drama of the unknown. Lincoln Steffens, in his *Autobiography*, complains upon his graduation from the University of California that his teachers had taught him only of the known, how to commit it to mind, and had done little to instruct him in the art of approaching the unknown, the art of posing questions. How does one ask questions about the unknown? Well, algebra is one technique, the technique for arranging the known in such a way that one is enabled to discern the value of an unknown quantity. It is an enriching strategy, algebra, but only if it is grasped as an extended instance of common sense.

Once I did see a teacher specifically encourage a class to organize and use minimal information to draw a maximum number of inferences. The teacher modeled his technique, I suppose, on the tried method of the storyteller. He presented the beginnings of the Whiskey Rebellion and said to his pupils, much in the manner of Ellery Queen speaking to his readers, "You now have enough to reconstruct the rest of the story. Let's see if we can do it." He was urging them to cross the barrier from learning into thinking. It is unhappily true that this is a rare exception in our schools.

So knowledge-getting becomes passive. Thinking is the reward for learning, and we may be systematically depriving our students of this reward as far as school learning is concerned.

One experiment which I can report provides encouragement. It was devised and carried out by the research group with which I am associated at Harvard in collaboration with teachers in the fifth grade of a good public school. It is on the unpromising topic of the geography of the North Central States and is currently in progress so that I cannot give all of the results. We hit upon the happy idea of presenting this chunk of geography not as a set of knowns, but as a set of unknowns. One class was presented blank maps, containing only tracings of the rivers and lakes of the area as well as the natural resources. They were asked as a first exercise to indicate where the principal cities would be located, where the railroads, and where the main highways. Books and maps were not permitted and "looking up the facts" was cast in a sinful light. Upon completing this exercise, a class discussion was begun in which the children attempted to justify why the major city would be here, a large city there, a railroad on this line, etc.

The discussion was a hot one. After an hour, and much pleading, permission was given to consult the rolled up wall map. I will never forget one young student, as he pointed his finger at the foot of Lake Michigan, shouting, "Yipee, *Chicago* is at the end of the pointing-down lake." And another replying, "Well, OK: but Chicago's no good for the rivers and it should be here where there is a big city (St. Louis)." These children were thinking, and learning was an instrument for checking and improving the process. To at least a half dozen children in the class it is not a matter of indifference that no big city is to be found at the junction of Lake Huron, Lake Michigan, and Lake Ontario. They were slightly shaken up transportation theorists when the facts were in.

The children in another class taught conventionally, got their facts all right, sitting down, benchbound. And that was that. We will see in six months which group remembers more. But whichever does, one thing I will predict. One group learned geography as a set of rational acts of induction – that cities spring up where there is water, where there are natural resources, where there are things to be processed and shipped. The other group learned passively that there were arbitrary cities at arbitrary places by arbitrary bodies of water and arbitrary sources of supply. One learned geography as a form of activity. The other stored some names and positions as a passive form of registration.

The episodic curriculum

In a social studies class of an elementary school in a well-to-do suburb of one of our great eastern cities, I saw groups of twelve-year-old children doing a "project" on the southeastern states. Each team was gathering facts that might eventually end up on a map or a chart or some other graphic device. The fact-gathering was atomized and episodic. Here were the industrial products of North Carolina. There was the list of the five principal cities of Georgia. I asked the children of one team what life would be like and what people would worry about in a place where the principal products were peanuts, cotton, and peaches. The question was greeted as "unfair." They were gathering facts.

It is not just the schools. The informational environment of America seems increasingly to be going through such an atomization. Entertainment is in fifteen minute episodes on TV, to be taken while sitting down. The school curriculum is built of episodic units, each a task to itself: "We have now finished addition. Let us now move to multiplication." Even in our humor the "gag" threatens to replace the shrewd observer of the human comedy. I have seen an elementary school play fashioned entirely on a parody of radio commercials. It was a brave effort to tie the 10-second atoms together.

I do not wish to make it seem as if our present state of education is a decline from some previous Golden Age. For I do not think there has ever been a Golden Age in American public education. The difference now is that we can afford dross less well than ever before. The volume of positive knowledge increases at a rapid rate. Atomizing it into facts-to-be-filed is not likely to produce the kind of broad grasp that will be needed in the world of the next quarter century. And it is certainly no training for the higher education that more and more of our children will be getting.

I have not meant the above as a plea for the "central subject" or the "project" method of teaching. It is, rather, a plea for the recognition of the continuity of knowledge. One hears professional educators speak of "coverage," that certain topics must be covered. There are indeed many things that must be covered, but they are not unconnected things. The object of learning is to gain facts in a context of connectivity that permits the facts to be used generatively. The larger the number of isolated facts, the more staggering the number of connections between them – unless one can reduce them to some deeper order. Not all of them can. Yet it is an ideal worth striving for, be it in the fifth grade or in graduate school. As Robert Oppenheimer put it in a recent address before the American Academy, "Everything cannot be connected with everything in the world we live in. Everything can be connected with anything."

The embarrassment of passion

I should like to consider now the guiding myth. Let me begin with a summary of the young Christopher Columbus as he is presented in a popular social studies textbook. Young Chris is walking along the water front in his home town and gets to wondering where all those ships go. Eventually he comes back to his brother's cobbler shop and exclaims, "Gee, Bart, I wonder where all those ships go, whether maybe if they just kept going they wouldn't come back because the world is round." Bart replies with pleasant brotherly encouragement. Chris is a well-adjusted kid. Bart is a nice big brother. And where is the passion that drove this obsessed man across uncharted oceans? What impelled this Columbus with such force that he finally enlisted the aid of Ferdinand and Isabella over the protest of their advisors? Everything is there in the story except the essential truth – the fanatical urge to explore in an age of exploration, the sense of an expanding world. Columbus did not have a schoolboy's whim, nor was he the well-adjusted grownup of this account. He was a man driven to explore, to control. The justification for the pablum that makes up such textbooks is that such accounts as these touch more directly on the life of the child.

What is this "life of the child" as seen by text writers and publishers? It is an image created out of an ideal of adjustment. The ideal of adjustment has little place for the driven man, the mythic hero, the idiosyncratic style. Its ideal is mediocentrism, reasonableness above all, being nice. Such an ideal does not touch closely the deeper life of the child. It does not appeal to the dark but energizing forces that lie close beneath the surface. The Old Testament, the Greek Myths, the Norse legends – these are the embarrassing chronicles of men of passion. They were devised to catch and preserve the power and tragedy of the human condition – and its ambiguity, too. In their place, we have substituted the noncontroversial and the banal.

Here a special word is needed about the concept of "expressing yourself," which is our conception of how one may engage the deeper impulses of the child, I have seen a book review class in a public school in which the children had the choice of reporting on any book they wished to choose, in or out of the school library, and where the discussion by the other children had to do entirely with the manner in which the reciting child presented his material. Nothing was said about the book in the discussion. The emphasis was on nice presentation, and whether the book sounded interesting. I have no quarrel with rewarding self-expression. I wonder simply whether it is not perhaps desirable, too, to make known the canons of excellence. The children in this class were learning to be seductive in their recounting; they were not concerned with an honest accounting of the human condition. The books they had read were cute, there was no excitement in them, none to be extracted. Increasingly the children in American elementary schools grow out of touch with the guiding myths. Self-expression is not a substitute. Adjustment is a worthy ideal, if not an ennobling one. But when we strive to attain it by shutting our eyes to the turmoils of human life, we will not get adjustment, but a niggling fear of the unusual and the excellent.

The quality of teachers

I do not wish to mince words. The educational and cultural level of the majority of American teachers is not impressive. On the whole they do not have a good grasp of the subject matter that they are teaching; courses on method will not replace the absent subject matter. In time and with teaching experience this deficiency is often remedied. But in so many cases there is no time: the turnover in the teaching profession as we all know is enormous; the median number of years of teaching before departure for marriage or motherhood is around three.

This leaves us with a small core of experienced teachers. Do we use them to teach the new teachers on the job? No. The organization of the school with respect to utilization of talent is something short of imaginative. It consists of a principal on top and a group of discrete teachers beneath her, and that is all. In large metropolitan high schools this is sometimes supplemented by having departments at the head of which is an experienced teacher. The communication that goes on between teachers is usually at a highly informal level and can scarcely be called comprehensive. It is usually about problem-children, not about social studies or mathematics or how to bring literature alive.

I would urge, and I believe that educators have taken steps in this direction, that we use our more experienced teachers for on-the-job training of less experienced, new teachers. I would also urge that there be established some means whereby the substantive topics taught in our elementary and high schools be included in some kind of special extension program provided by our eighteen hundred colleges and universities in the United States for the benefit of teachers. I am not speaking only of teachers colleges, but rather of all institutions of higher learning. Institutions of higher learning have a responsibility to the lower schools, and it can be exercised by arranging for continuous contact between those, for example, who teach history at the college level and those who are teaching history or social studies at the lower levels. And so, too, with literature or mathematics, or languages. To assume that somehow a teacher can be "prepared" simply by going through teacher training and then by taking courses on methods in summer school is, I think, fallacious. Often it is the case that the teacher, like her students, has not learned the material well enough to cross the barrier from learning to thinking.

III

It is quite plain, I think, that the task of improving the American Schools is not simply one of technique – however comforting it would be to some professional educators to think so. What is at issue, rather, is a deeper problem, one that is more philosophical than psychological or technological in scope. Let me put it in all innocence. What do we conceive to be the end product of our educational effort? I cannot help but feel that this rather overly simplified question has become obscured in cant. There is such an official din in support of the view that we are "training well-rounded human beings to be responsible citizens" that one hesitates to raise the question whether such an objective is a meaningful guide to what one does in classroom teaching. Surely the objective is worthy, and it has influenced the techniques of education in America, not always happily. For much of what we have called the embarrassment of passion can, I think, be traced to this objective, and so too the blandness of the social studies curriculum. The ideal, sadly, has also led to the standardization of mediocrity by a failure of the schools to challenge the full capacity of the talented student.

Since the war, there has been a perceptible shift in the problems being faced by schools and parents alike. It is the New Competition. Will Johnny and Sally be able to get into the college of their first choice or, indeed, into any college at all? The origins of the concern are obvious enough – the "baby bulge" has made itself felt. The results are not all bad, I would urge, or need not be. There are, to be sure, severe problems of overcrowding that exacerbate the difficulties already inherent in public education. And it is true that parental pressures for grades and production are increasing the proportion of children with "learning blocks" being referred to child guidance clinics.

But the pressures and the competition are also rekindling our awareness of excellence and how it may be nurtured. The shake-up of our smugness by the evident technical thrust of the Soviet Union has added to this awareness. Let me urge that it is this new awareness that requires shaping of expression in the form of a new set of ideals. Grades, admission to college, followed by admission to graduate school – these are surely not the ideals but, rather, the external signs.

Perhaps the fitting ideal is precisely as we have described it earlier in these pages, the active pragmatic ideal of leaping the barrier from learning into thinking. It matters not *what* we have learned. What we can *do* with what we have learned: this is the issue. The pragmatic argument has long been elaborated on extrinsic grounds, that the higher one has gone in the educational system the greater the economic gain. Indeed, at least one eminent economist has proposed that parents finance college education for their children by long-term loans to be repaid by the children on the almost certain knowledge that higher earning results from such education. All of this is the case, and it is indeed admirable that educational progress and economic success are so intimately linked in our society. I would only suggest that the pragmatic ideal be applied also to the intrinsic aspects of education. Let us not judge our students simply on *what* they know. That is the philosophy of the quiz program. Rather, let them be judged on what they can generate from what they know – how well they can leap the barrier from learning to thinking.

Note

This was a paper presented to the Massachusetts Council on Teacher Education on February 13, 1958.

CHAPTER 3

THE FUNCTIONS OF TEACHING

An address delivered at Rhode Island College of Education,
April 13, 1959

I should like to beg of you that you grant me the privilege of innocence. It is not my intention of passing in review the various theories that now exist concerning the proper function of teaching, then to weigh and evaluate these in the interest of a synthesis. I do not have the requisite learning for such a venture. Nor is it what really I want to do. My intent, rather, is to examine the nature of the processes involved in communicating knowledge and, in a certain measure, to examine the structure of knowledge as we have come to understand it in the past decade, and in the light of these two considerations, to examine what the unique position of teaching and teachers might be. My warrant for asking this privilege of innocence is not very strong, for though I have taught for fifteen years and been taught still longer, that gives me no more warrant to speak than I would have if the subject were the nature of prose, and I have been speaking prose longer than I have either taught or been taught. The remainder of my warrant rests upon the fact that I have busied myself for more than a decade with the nature of the knowing process – cognition as it is called in the catalogues. But what my efforts have yielded is the firm conviction that while we know a certain amount about learning and about thinking, we know precious little about teaching and its functions. So I shall use this opportunity to examine the shape of the gaps. I hope I fare as well as Lord Russell who long ago gave a lecture at Harvard on the philosophical implications of quantum theory and relativity when these implications were even less well understood than they are today. When his exposition was completed, Alfred North Whitehead, who was chairing the meeting, congratulated Lord Russell by saluting him for not having obscured the great darkness of the subject.

Sparing the learner the more dangerous consequences of learning

Let me begin by proposing that the first function of the teacher and teaching is to spare the learner the more dangerous consequences of learning. That is to say, the existence of the teacher makes possible the commission of error without irreversible harm occurring. Let me put it in terms of food gathering behavior and the learning involved therein. A hungry young organism is out gathering food and he sees something that might be either a mushroom or a toadstool. The most direct way of finding out which it is would be to pick the object from its stalk and eat it. If it is a mushroom, the child will live to pick another day. If it is not, he has removed himself irreversibly from the arena of learning. The teacher enters by playing the role of vicar for consequences, and his existence makes feasible the committing of error. In short, the teacher states in one way or another that eating this particular thing will kill you or not kill you as the case may be. It follows from this, does it not, that one of the first functions of teaching is to make possible the presence of error, and, as we shall see shortly, to make error possible in an instructive way. The consequences of error, then, should always be less grave when there is teaching present than when learning is direct and unmediated by a teacher. This is an obvious point, but it is not a trivial one and it may easily be forgotten.

Instructive error

I used the expression "instructive error," and we must now look at what such an error amounts to. To be instructive, an error must have the effect of reducing the range of alternative errorful acts that the learner will perform in comparable situations later. To use the language of commonsense rather than information theory, this means that the learner must have some sense of what it was about his act that was in error so that he may be spared committing one like it again. What is most interesting about errors is that they have a logical structure, some of them quite interesting and others quite trivial. The trivial errors are errors such as those we make in spelling – failures to observe convention. Teaching spelling as a set of rote conventions turns out, in consequence, to be rather a dull enterprise. So, too, learning spelling. Yet on closer inspection it turns out that spelling is something more than a set of simple rote conventions – something more than that the vocalic/sla/ can be written as SLEIGH or SLAY, with a somewhat different arbitrary meaning in each case. In fact, the sequential letter structure of all Western languages is a beautiful pattern of transitional probabilities that make possible the construction of nonsense words with a high degree of approximation to the language – so high in fact that the words are not in the dictionary only by chance. VERNALIT, MOSSIANT, POKERSON, APHYSTER, RICANING, ANTHROPAND – all of these are words we have constructed by the use of formal robots programmed to obey the transitional rules of English orthography. We know from the work of William Hull that one can effect real improvements in the spelling of real words by teaching children to practice recognizing brief exposures of such nonsense words as these and writing down the letters that they see – indeed, doing this without ever encountering the same pseudo-word twice. In short, we can even convert the errors of convention into something more interestingly generic – where an error can be interpreted as something not that violates an arbitrary convention concerning the spelling of a word, but something that violates a general rule about how things are put together.

But this is a bit of a diversion. The real point about instructive error and the logical structure that underlies it is that when there is a teacher present, it should be possible to utilize the error to increase its instructiveness, to make the error understandable. In most cases this consists of making clear the distinction between signal and noise, or essence and accident as it used to be called in the classical philosophy. In the case of the mushroom-toadstool example, it consists of calling attention to the fact that the toadstool in contrast to a mushroom has certain distinctive features of size and shape and color and habitat. In the case of our spelling example, it consists of pointing out that a given way of spelling does or does not violate a rule of transitional probability in English – does or does not regardless of whether the particular spelling used constitutes a word correctly or incorrectly. In short, if we can say that teaching makes possible the commission of error, it also serves the function of an analyzer, as the physicist would say – it analyzes the essential from the non-essential, and thereby elucidates error.

Machines programmed for artificial intelligence

Before we turn to a third function of teaching, let me comment briefly on one universal feature of all minds and of all instruments that simulate mind – machines programmed for artificial intelligence. It is a feature worthy of being mentioned over and over again. They all are characterized by a limited span of attention or immediate memory as it is sometimes called. That is to say, we can hold in mind simultaneously only a certain number of independent items, hold them in mind and manipulate or transform them. The estimate for human beings is that about seven unrelated items can be held in mind, and that much beyond this there is interference between the items and a notable drop in their manipulability. This limited span is not something to lament, and it is not something on whose expansion you can reasonably hope to work. Brute memory training is a rather unrewarding form of exercise for it yields only the realization that not much can be done about it – not much in the sense of expanding the simple span. The only reasonable thing that you can do is to see that, as my colleague George Miller puts it, the seven slots are filled with gold rather than dross. Let me explain this by an example.

Turning dross into gold consists of recoding materials into a form such that one can not only hold more in mind, but hold it in mind in a way such that one can regenerate information. Let me duly inform you, for example, that a certain free falling body dropped a distance of 144 units in 3 seconds, 256 units in 4 seconds, had reached a distance of 1600 units at 10 seconds, and at 13 seconds was observed at a distance of 2704 units from its point of origin. This is pretty dull stuff, and fortunately we know that you will have forgotten it in a few minutes. In the form presented it just about chokes up your channel capacity, as span is sometimes called by communications engineers. If you teach well, you will have had your students scurrying for a recoding by now, one that will permit easy holding in mind and ready manipulation – in this case the manipulation that results in adequate interpolation and extrapolation: "Where was the object at 5 seconds, where was it at a minute?" Or, "Is this happening on earth or on the moon?" Some of you have already recognized that the numbers are readily recodable in terms of the formula for falling bodies in the earth's gravitational field with a constant of gravitation of about 32, the formula being as ancient as Galileo. You can hold it in mind and leave enough room to hold in mind simultaneously a correction formula to take account of atmospheric densities. The two formulae taken in conjunction will permit you to regenerate any and all information you need about distances fallen on any planet in any atmospheric field, and if you do a little more recoding, you may rediscover some more laws of nature.

Teaching can never be just the presentation of material

My digression, intricate in detail though it was, has an overwhelmingly important point to be drawn from it about the nature of teaching. It is that teaching can never be just the presentation of material, material about some subject. It cannot be that unless you have no respect for nor knowledge about the nature of the human span. For it is the proper function of the teacher to present information in such a way and in terms of such a structure that the learner can get maximum regenerative travel from the material to which he has been exposed. This immediately brings up the rewardingly complicated issue of how one presents different kinds of material in order to honor properly this particular function of teaching. What materials should be presented to the learner at different stages, and in what order and pattern? We have experts who are charged with the task of devising subject-matter curricula, and I do not mean to belittle the importance of what they do. Usually they are highly knowledgeable about children and what they can absorb, and likely as not they have had such direct experience in dealing with children in the process of learning particular subjects. Almost never, however, are they the great creative minds in the substantive fields for which they are designing a curriculum. And here I wish to make a debatable point. It is that the structure of a field and therefore the order of approach to it is best understood by the person who has the deepest understanding of the field – he is the one who best knows what things are worth struggling to understand and when. If we are to do an adequate job of presenting models or structures in terms of which facts and data can be recoded for better retention and subsequent use, the great men in the substantive fields will have to work with the expert on the process of child learning to devise curricula that are comprehensible and worth comprehending. It is far from clear, for example, that the particulars of primary arithmetic are worth teaching first in view of the fact that they are such a special case of more general mathematics which, once grasped, provides a simple basis for deriving ordinary arithmetic. The difficulty with ordinary arithmetic is that it is so special – however useful it may be in toting up the cost of milk and barley – that it is hard to generalize.

To me, one of the happy signs of our times is that precisely what I am urging is now taking place – alas, only in the sciences, however. The Physical Sciences Study Committee at MIT, under the direction of such distinguished physicists as Jerrold Zacharias and Francis Friedman are devising courses in high school physics; comparable projects are in progress at Yale and Illinois in mathematics; at Colorado in biology; and the National Academy of Sciences is now instituting a special study group to investigate the way to regularize on a long-term basis such enterprises across the whole spectrum of the sciences and other branches of learning. It is still too early to say much about the project save that the guiding principle will be to bring together the efforts of three kinds of people: men of the deepest learning in the substantive fields to be taught; students of the principles and techniques of the communication of knowledge such as psychologists, information theorists, specialists in the theory of display, etc.; and finally, experts in the learning capacities of children with experience in the reality of teaching in school settings.

Additional functions of teaching

Let me turn now to some additional functions of teaching. I should like to consider next something that is as paradoxical as it is simple. It has to do with the protected nature of the learning situation where school teaching occurs. When we learn in the process of doing, *in situ*, there is little separation between the act of learning and doing something with what we have learned. Teaching has the effect of separating the two, learning and doing. This is partly a function of the fact that the teacher is present properly to cushion the consequences of learning which removes learning from its usual context. It is partly due, too, to the fact that the teacher, in order to set forth the structure of a subject matter, must remove the learning from the context of action so that various alternative ways of looking at material may be considered. It is a necessary *antimony*, this distinction between reflection and action. Yet it has a danger. The danger is that that learning may become passive and benchbound, that the learner (as I have put it elsewhere) does not make the leap over the boundary between learning and thinking. By thinking I mean the operation of utilizing information to go beyond that which has been given to that which might be likely. Any operation that involves going beyond the information given is what constitutes the link between the isolated learning of the teaching situation to the requirement of action based upon what has been learned. It is such internalized action – these operations of going beyond – that constitutes the condition for getting travel out of what has been learned. Let me spell out this matter a little.

Reversibility

Mental growth from childhood to adolescence and then to adulthood consists, according to Piaget and others, of internalizing action, rendering it into symbolic form, and then endowing it with what has been called reversibility. The last point is of huge importance, reversibility. Overt action once learned tends not to have this property. Having learned to write words from left to right, for example, we are not thereby enabled to trace out the same words from right to left. Cognitive or mental operations, on the other hand, are notably reversible. In simplest form, we imagine that we have eaten something, and we can then immediately imagine the reverse of not having eaten it, considering the two simultaneously if necessary. In more formal terms, reversibility in the case of mathematical operations consists of being able to add two quantities together and then to reverse them back to their original form by subtraction. It is the internal means whereby we are enabled to scan alternatives, to work without being irreversibly committed to action.

Now the only way in which I know of to assure that operations are performed on what has been learned – that thinking occurs – is to shift emphasis from time to time from the intake side to the output side, to *make* learners do something with what they have learned. Indeed, the learning process geared together with good teaching can combine the two. The simplest version of this is to make the student predict or extrapolate to new facts before they are told to him so that the new information has the effect of confirming or infirming the cognitive operations in terms of which he is using his already mastered knowledge. The story is told of the great English historian Trevelyan that on the occasions when he had gone home to his study without the source materials that he needed for the next sections of his work, he would often reconstruct by prediction what must have happened. Needless to say, he would be quite uncannily correct on all matters save the inessentials – names, dates, and places. I do not mean to say that names, dates, and places are unimportant. Rather, what is centrally important is what happens. So perhaps students ought to have the kinds of historical textbooks in which the next chapter can be sealed up and the student tested on his ability to foretell what would be in it before reading it. I could not be more serious. Is it not the function of historical intuition that it presumes to aid one in a sense of what our own times mean? Would it not be a modest start in the development of such intuition to ask a student who has just completed a "unit" on the age of discovery to try some predictions about the age of colonization?

Once I did see a teacher specifically encourage a class to organize and use minimal information to draw a maximum number of inferences and it impressed me deeply. The teacher modeled his technique, I suppose, on the tried method of the storyteller. He presented the beginnings of the Whiskey Rebellion and said to his pupils, much in the manner of Ellery Queen speaking to his readers, "You now have enough to reconstruct the rest of the story. Let's see if we can do it." He was urging them to cross the barrier from learning into thinking. It is unhappily true that this is a rare exception in our schools.

Research experiment at Harvard

I do have one experiment to report that provides encouragement, one that was devised and carried out by the research group with which I am associated at Harvard in collaboration with teachers in the fifth grade of a good public school. It is on the unpromising topic of the geography of the North Central States and is currently in progress so that I cannot give all of the results. We hit upon the happy idea of presenting this chunk of geography not as a set of knowns, but as a set of unknowns. One class was presented blank maps, containing only tracings of the rivers and lakes of the area as well as simple notation of the natural resources. The students were asked as a first exercise to indicate where the principal cities would be located, where the railroads, and where the main highways. Books and maps were not permitted and "looking up the facts" was cast in a sinful light. Upon completing this exercise, a class discussion was begun in which the children attempted to justify why the major city would be here, a large city there, a railroad on this line, etc.

The discussion was a hot one. After an hour, and much pleading, permission was given to consult the rolled-up wall map. I will never forget one young student, as he pointed his finger at the foot of Lake Michigan, shouting "Yipee, *Chicago* is at the end of the pointing-down lake." And another replying, "Well, OK: but Chicago's no good for the rivers and it should be here where there *is* a big city (St. Louis)." These children were thinking, and learning was an instrument for checking and improving the process. To at least half a dozen children in the class it is not a matter of indifference that no big city is to be found at the junction of Lake Huron, Lake Michigan, and Lake Ontario. They were slightly shaken up transportation theorists when the facts were in.

The children in the conventional class got their facts all right, sitting down, benchbound. And that was that. We will see in six months which group remembers more. But whichever does, one thing I will predict. One group learned geography as a set of rational acts of induction – that cities spring up where there is water, where there are natural resources, where there are things to be processed and shipped. The other group learned passively that there were arbitrary cities at arbitrary places by arbitrary bodies of water and arbitrary sources of supply. One learned geography as a form of activity. The other stored some names and positions as a passive form of registration.

If I have made it appear up to this point that teaching has to do principally with the task of rendering the world less dangerously consequential, more economical to handle cognitively, and more predictable, I have left out one important feature of the teaching task. It has to do with the degree to which the adult teacher is in a more advantageous position than the child to recognize and communicate a sense of the alternative plights into which man can fall. In a somewhat more formal context a moment ago, I remarked in passing that the teacher, by delaying the necessity for external action and emphasizing reversible internal operations, gave the child a sense of alternatives. With respect to the life of a society, there are similarly alternative models upon which one can pattern oneself. These are frequently called the myths of a society, and myth in this sense does not mean untruth. Penelope as a faithful wife is not an untruth by virtue of being a fiction, nor is Emma Bovary in the plight of *la femme incomprise* faced with the grievous problems of love and adultery. Hercules is not just a story, but a symbolizing of aspirations for omni-competence and infinite wiles. If one grasps the symbolism of Perseus slaying the hateful Medusa, guiding the telling thrust by her reflection in his polished shield rather than by looking upon her directly and being turned to stone, then one has grasped the metaphoric meaning of the law and wherein one becomes the victim of evil attacked directly – the protection of the mediating shield.

The enduring body of a culture's literature is a storehouse of myths that symbolize and condense the myriad forms of the rather limited range of plights that characterize the life of a people. The great student of myth and legend, Joseph Campbell, remarks that there has been a breakdown in what he calls the "mytho-logically instructed community," the community that shares a set of instructive myths about life and its alternative ways. In contrast to the classic times of Greece, we are indeed without a unified corpus of myth. In its place have arisen the forms of modern literature, notably the novel, and in the literature of the last century and a half one finds traced not so much externalized myth as what might better be called a record of voyages into the interior. It is by knowledge of those voyages that one comes to a sense of the alternative forms of coping or fleeing, one gains a knowledge of life beyond what one might immediately encompass in direct experience however long one lives.

And how does this relate to the function of teaching? I should like to propose that the teacher of literature has a function akin to the teacher of empirical subjects such as science and history. Where the latter attempts somehow to provide a model, indeed alternative models of the *external* world one encounters, it seems to me that it is the function of the teacher of literature to use the corpus of novels and drama to elucidate the *internal* world and its alternative expressions. And indeed, much of what I said earlier about learning and thinking might well hold here. What better exercise for the development of a tragic sense – without which there can be no sense of compassion – than to have to make an attempt at writing the last act of *Hamlet* having read the others that preceded it. Or if not writing the last act anew, at least considering the various ways in which it might come out and why.

Criteria for judging the adequacy of a theory of teaching

Consider now a more general matter that may have the effect of binding together what I have said thus far about the functions of teaching. It would appear, upon reading the literature on the subject in a sketchy way, that there is a certain lack of adequate theory in the field of teaching. Rest easy, I do not propose to set forth a theory of teaching at short notice! Rather, I would like to consider what might be taken to be adequate criteria for judging whether a theory of teaching is adequate, whether it condenses and provides a means for generating new ideas. And let me say that when I use the word theory, I have in mind a very useful thing.

I should begin by commenting that theory is often misunderstood. It is in effect a heuristic or guide that gets you from where you happen to find yourself to where it is that you want to be – particularly so when we are dealing as now with a theory of practice, and all theory is that, once one tries to operate with it. It should be self-evident, should it not, that a theory-in use has an objective: you wish to build a faster sloop or predict eclipses of the moon or to educate a child in some particular way. Characteristically, a theory-in-use is derived from a more general model or theory about the nature of things that has prediction as its aim. The construction of sloops is a good case in point, for it is guided by theoretical understanding of principles of aerodynamics, hydrodynamics, and the doctrine of the parallelogram of forces. In order to use such knowledge, you have to have in mind what it is that you want to accomplish – whether you want a rough weather boat, one that can operate in shoal water, whether the objective is a spacious hold, and so on. So it goes with the theory of education. Before you can use theoretical formulations concerning the learning process, the nature of child development, and the structure of knowledge in substantive fields you must be clear what you want to use the knowledge for. I have very strongly the impression that one of the grave sources of confusion in the field of education is that educational theorists have difficulty using available knowledge not so much because the knowledge is shaky, but because they do not know what they want to use it for. In short, we are not clear in our image of what constitutes an educated person – the place that we want to get with a learner starting from here. Nor do I think that our confusion is all an affliction. At least it guarantees a certain pluralism in our approach to young people and saves us from the temptation to squeeze everybody into the same mold.

Minimum objectives in fashioning a theory of teaching

But there is a limit to proclaiming the virtues of our confusions. I would like to bring my remarks to a close by suggesting some of the minimum objectives that seem to me to be worthwhile in fashioning a theory of teaching.

The first of them should be that the educated person should be one who has internalized a sense of the instructiveness of error. This means in effect that he knows how to try out his ideas with the aid of advice and that error does not stand for defeat. If teaching has succeeded, then fear of error should have been made to subside. In essence, this implies that the individual is better enabled to try out his ideas and to determine whether they are useful or not. It is a simple objective, but it is an exceedingly important one.

A second objective has to do with what some of my colleagues on the Cognition Project at Harvard refer to as "recoding push." Good teaching should have the effect of leading a person to condense and transform what he has encountered into a form that honors the deeper general structure of whatever he has experienced. He, the learner, must have learned ways of respecting his limited cognitive capacities by rendering the welter of material to which he is exposed into something more manageable and he must first recognize when things have become unmanageable. This holds as much for daily life where the "he said, she said, I said" approach to understanding what goes on between oneself and others often blocks deeper understanding, as it holds for any other aspect of life – such as reading the newspaper or attempting to understand technical problems in one's business or profession.

A third objective is that the learner end his formal exposure to teaching well equipped with a set of models or condensations of the nature of the world with which he must cope – the physical world, the biological, the social. Here I have in mind that the task of communicating substantive knowledge is as paramount in fact as we sometimes make out in giving it lip service. I do not think that we will make the desired progress along this front until we reexamine freshly and critically the structure of the knowledge that is to be communicated, and in this endeavor

I sense that a revolution is about to take place which will have the effect of bringing the man of learning back into working contact with the teacher.

Finally, it seems to me, the well educated learner should have acquired a sense of the varieties of the human condition – and now I am speaking less of social studies and more of human intuition. So long as the schools feel the need to avoid controversial materials in their teaching of literature – and make no mistake about it, the artistically gripping presentation of human lives is likely to be controversial in the school setting, even if it is becoming less so in that startling medium called television – so long as there is the need to avoid the controversial, we will be tempted to teach pablum rather than plight. I have seen a social studies book in which the passionately fixated Christopher Columbus was presented as a nice kid with a brother Bart amiably going about the task of convincing people that an ocean crossing would be interesting. Its readability figure was superbly low, but it was a lie against the passion to explore. The justification was that it related the experience of Columbus to the experience of the sixth grader. And we in an age in which artificial moons have become a part of common sense!

These are minimum objectives, and obviously there are many more – like making the student aware of the nature of the government under which he lives and what his prerogatives are thereunder. I do not mean to belittle these objectives. The ones I have suggested, if achieved, can only make the achievement of the others more worthwhile.

I have said nothing about the ideal of personal adjustment in education, for it is not within the purview of this essay. I do know that an overburden of personal problems, creating the ground for neurotic processes, can be the prime enemy of the type of vigorously open mind that I have been urging we take as an objective in our teaching efforts. But it is not my impression that good teaching of genuinely worthwhile subject matter has ever had the effect of creating neurosis. What I would suggest is that we pursue our teaching with the utmost vigor while at the same time combatting the kinds of forces in the home, the school, and the society at large that produce crippling effects on the learner. It will not avail us much, will it, if we produce the well adjusted child whose principal virtue is that he is not disturbed. The task is to produce students who, by virtue of the teaching they have received, are able to go beyond what they have been taught to the formulation of their own identity and individuality.

CHAPTER 4

THE IMPORTANCE OF STRUCTURE

The Process of Education (1960), Cambridge: Harvard University Press

The first object of any act of learning, over and beyond the pleasure it may give, is that it should serve us in the future. Learning should not only take us somewhere; it should allow us later to go further more easily. There are two ways in which learning serves the future. One is through its specific applicability to tasks that are highly similar to those we originally learned to perform. Psychologists refer to this phenomenon as specific transfer of training; perhaps it should be called the extension of habits or associations. Its utility appears to be limited in the main to what we usually speak of as skills. Having learned how to hammer nails, we are better able later to learn how to hammer tacks or chip wood. Learning in school undoubtedly creates skills of a kind that transfers to activities encountered later, either in school or after. A second way in which earlier learning renders later performance more efficient is through what is conveniently called nonspecific transfer or, more accurately, the transfer of principles and attitudes. In essence, it consists of learning initially not a skill but a general idea, which can then be used as a basis for recognizing subsequent problems as special cases of the idea originally mastered. This type of transfer is at the heart of the educational process – the continual broadening and deepening of knowledge in terms of basic and general ideas.

The continuity of learning that is produced by the second type of transfer, transfer of principles, is dependent upon mastery of the structure of the subject matter, as structure was described in the preceding chapter. That is to say, in order for a person to be able to recognize the applicability or inapplicability of an idea to a new situation and to broaden his learning thereby, he must have clearly in mind the general nature of the phenomenon with which he is dealing. The more fundamental or basic the idea he has learned, almost by definition, the greater will be its breadth of applicability to new problems. Indeed, this is almost a tautology, for what is meant by "fundamental" in this sense is precisely that an idea has wide as well as powerful applicability. It is simple enough to proclaim, of course, that school curricula and methods of teaching should be geared to the teaching of fundamental ideas in whatever subject is being taught. But as soon as one makes such a statement a host of problems arise, many of which can be solved only with the aid of considerably more research. We turn to some of these now.

The first and most obvious problem is how to construct curricula that can be taught by ordinary teachers to ordinary students and that at the same time reflect clearly the basic or underlying principles of various fields of inquiry. The problem is twofold: first, how to have the basic subjects rewritten and their teaching materials revamped in such a way that the pervading and powerful ideas and attitudes relating to them are given a central role; second, how to match the levels of these materials to the capacities of students of different abilities at different grades in school.

The experience of the past several years has taught at least one important lesson about the design of a curriculum that is true to the underlying structure of its subject matter. It is that the best minds in any particular discipline must be put to work on the task. The decision as to what should be taught in American history to elementary school children or what should be taught in arithmetic is a decision that can best be reached with the aid of those with a high degree of vision and competence in each of these fields. To decide that the elementary ideas of algebra depend upon the fundamentals of the commutative, distributive, and associative laws, one must be a mathematician in a position to appreciate and understand the fundamentals of mathematics. Whether schoolchildren require an understanding of Frederick Jackson Turner's ideas about the role of the frontier in American history before they can sort out the facts and trends of American history – this again is a decision that requires the help of the scholar who has a deep understanding of the American past. Only by the use of our best minds in devising curricula will we bring the fruits of scholarship and wisdom to the student just beginning his studies.

The question will be raised, "How enlist the aid of our most able scholars and scientists in designing curricula for primary and secondary schools?" The answer has already been given, at least in part. The School Mathematics Study Group, the University of Illinois mathematics projects, the Physical Science Study Committee, and the Biological Sciences Curriculum Study have indeed been enlisting the aid of eminent men in their various fields, doing so by means of summer projects, supplemented in part by year-long leaves of absence for certain key people involved. They have been aided in these projects by outstanding elementary and secondary school teachers and, for special purposes, by professional writers, film makers, designers, and others required in such a complex enterprise.

There is at least one major matter that is left unsettled even by a large-scale revision of curricula in the direction indicated. Mastery of the fundamental ideas of a field involves not only the grasping of general principles, but also the development of an attitude toward learning and inquiry, toward guessing and hunches, toward the possibility of solving problems on one's own. Just as a physicist has certain attitudes about the ultimate orderliness of nature and a conviction that order can be discovered, so a young physics student needs some working version of these attitudes if he is to organize his learning in such a way as to make what he learns usable and meaningful in his thinking. To instill such attitudes by teaching requires something more than the mere presentation of fundamental ideas. Just what it takes to bring off such teaching is something on which a great deal of research is needed, but it would seem that an important ingredient is a sense of excitement about discovery – discovery of regularities of previously unrecognized relations and similarities between ideas, with a resulting sense of self-confidence in one's abilities. Various people who have worked on curricula in science and mathematics have urged that it is possible to present the fundamental structure of a discipline in such a way as to preserve some of the exciting sequences that lead a student to discover for himself.

It is particularly the Committee on School Mathematics and the Arithmetic Project of the University of Illinois that have emphasized the importance of discovery as an aid to teaching. They have been active in devising methods that permit a student to discover for himself the generalization that lies behind a particular mathematical operation, and they contrast this approach with the "method of assertion and proof" in which the generalization is first stated by the teacher and the class asked to proceed through the proof. It has also been pointed out by the Illinois group that the method of discovery would be too time-consuming for presenting all of what a student must cover in mathematics. The proper balance between the two is anything but plain, and research is in progress to elucidate the matter, though more is needed. Is the inductive approach a better technique for teaching principles? Does it have a desirable effect on attitudes?

That the method of discovery need not be limited to such highly formalized subjects as mathematics and physics is illustrated by some experimentation on social studies carried out by the Harvard Cognition Project. A sixth-grade class, having been through a conventional unit on the social and economic geography of the Southeastern states, was introduced to the North Central region by being asked to locate the major cities of the area on a map containing physical features and natural resources, but no place names. The resulting class discussion very rapidly produced a variety of plausible theories concerning the requirements of a city – a water transportation theory that placed Chicago at the junction of the three lakes, a mineral resources theory that placed it near the Mesabi range, a food-supply theory that put a great city on the rich soil of Iowa, and so on. The level of interest as well as the level of conceptual sophistication was far above that of control classes. Most striking, however, was the attitude of children to whom, for the first time, the location of a city appeared as a problem, and one to which an answer could be discovered by taking thought. Not only was there pleasure and excitement in the pursuit of a question, but in the end the discovery was worth making, at least for urban children for whom the phenomenon of the city was something that had before been taken for granted.

How do we tailor fundamental knowledge to the interests and capacities of children? This is a theme we shall return to later, and only a word need be said about it here. It requires a combination of deep understanding and patient honesty to present physical or any other phenomena in a way that is simultaneously exciting, correct, and rewardingly comprehensible. In examining certain teaching materials in physics, for example, we have found much patient honesty in presentation that has come to naught because the authors did not have a deep enough understanding of the subject they were presenting.

A good case in point is to be found in the usual attempt to explain the nature of tides. Ask the majority of high school students to explain tides and they will speak of the gravitational pull of the moon on the surface of the earth and how it pulls the water on the moon's side into a bulge. Ask them now why there is also a bulge of less magnitude on the side of the earth opposite to the moon, and they will almost always be without a satisfactory answer. Or ask them where the maximum bulge of the incoming tide is with respect to the relative position of the earth and moon, and the answer will usually be that it is at the point on the earth's surface nearest to the moon. If the student knows there is a lag in the tidal crest, he will usually not know why. The failure in both cases comes from an inadequate picture of how gravity acts upon a free-moving elastic body, and a failure to connect the idea of inertia with the idea of gravitational action. In short, the tides are explained without a share of the excitement that can come from understanding Newton's great discovery of universal gravitation and its mode of action. Correct and illuminating explanations are no more difficult and often easier to grasp than ones that are partly correct and therefore too complicated and too restricted. It is the consensus of virtually all the men and women who have been working on curriculum projects that making material interesting is in no way incompatible with presenting it soundly; indeed, a correct general explanation is often the most interesting of all. Inherent in the preceding discussions are at least four general claims that can be made for teaching the fundamental structure of a subject, claims in need of detailed study.

The first is that understanding fundamentals makes a subject more comprehensible. This is true not only in physics and mathematics, where we have principally illustrated the point, but equally in the social studies and literature. Once one has grasped the fundamental idea that a nation must trade in order to live, then such a presumably special phenomenon as the Triangular Trade of the American colonies becomes altogether simpler to understand as something more than commerce in molasses, sugar cane, rum, and slaves in an atmosphere of violation of British trade regulations. The high school student reading *Moby Dick* can only understand more deeply if he can be led to understand that Melville's novel is, among other things, a study of the theme of evil and the plight of those pursuing this "killing whale." And if the student is led further to understand that there are a relatively limited number of human plights about which novels are written, he understands literature the better for it.

The second point relates to human memory. Perhaps the most basic thing that can be said about human memory, after a century of intensive research, is that unless detail is placed into a structured pattern, it is rapidly forgotten. Detailed material is conserved in memory by the use of simplified ways of representing it. These simplified representations have what may be called a "regenerative" character. A good example of this regenerative property of long-term memory can be found in science. A scientist does not try to remember the distances traversed by falling bodies in different gravitational fields over different periods of time. What he carries in memory instead is a formula that permits him with varying degrees of accuracy to regenerate the details on which the more easily remembered formula is based. So he commits to memory the formula $s = 1/2 \, gt^2$ and not a handbook of distances, times, and gravitational constants. Similarly, one does not remember exactly what Marlowe, the commentator in *Lord Jim*, said about the chief protagonist's plight, but, rather, simply that he was the dispassionate onlooker, the man who tried to understand without judging what had led Lord Jim into the straits in which he found himself. We remember a formula, a vivid detail that carries the meaning of an event, an average that stands for a range of events, a caricature, or picture that preserves an essence – all of them techniques of condensation and representation. What learning general or fundamental principles does is to ensure that memory loss will not mean total loss, that what remains will permit us to reconstruct the details when needed. A good theory is the vehicle not only for understanding a phenomenon now but also for remembering it tomorrow.

Third, an understanding of fundamental principles and ideas, as noted earlier, appears to be the main road to adequate "transfer of training." To understand something as a specific instance of a more general case – which is what understanding a more fundamental principle or structure means – is to have learned not only a specific thing but also a model for understanding other things like it that one may encounter. If a student could grasp in its most human sense the weariness of Europe at the close of the Hundred Years' War and how it created the conditions for a workable but not ideologically absolute Treaty of Westphalia, he might be better able to think about the ideological struggle of East and West – though the parallel is anything but exact. A carefully wrought understanding should also permit him to recognize the limits of the generalization as well. The idea of "principles" and "concepts" as a basis for transfer is hardly new. It is much in need of more research of a specific kind that would provide detailed knowledge of how best to proceed in the teaching of different subjects in different grades.

The fourth claim for emphasis on structure and principles in teaching is that by constantly reexamining material taught in elementary and secondary schools for its fundamental character, one is able to narrow the gap between "advanced" knowledge and "elementary" knowledge. Part of the difficulty now found in the progression from primary school through high school to college is that material learned earlier is either out of date or misleading by virtue of its lagging too far behind developments in a field. This gap can be reduced by the kind of emphasis set forth in the preceding discussion.

Consider now some specific problems that received considerable discussion at Woods Hole. One of them has to do with the troubled topic of "general science." There are certain recurrent ideas that appear in virtually all branches of science. If in one subject one has learned them well and generally, that achievement should make the task of learning them again in a different form elsewhere in science much easier. Various teachers and scientists have raised the question whether these basic ideas should not be "isolated," so to speak, and taught more explicitly in a manner that frees them from specific areas of science. The type of idea can be easily illustrated: categorization and its uses, the unit of measure and its development, the indirectness of information in science and the need for operational definition of ideas, and so forth. With respect to the last, for example, we do not *see* pressure or the chemical bond directly but infer it indirectly from a set of measures. So too body temperature. So too sadness in another person. Can these and similar ideas be presented effectively and with a variety of concrete illustrations in the early grades in order to give the child a better basis for understanding their specific representation in various special disciplines later? Is it wise to teach such "general science" as an introduction to disciplinary sciences in the later grades? How should they be taught and what could we reasonably expect by way of easier learning later? Much research is needed on this promising topic – research not only on the usefulness of such an approach, but also on the kinds of general scientific ideas that might be taught.

Indeed, it may well be that there are certain general attitudes or approaches toward science or literature that can be taught in the earlier grades that would have considerable relevance for later learning. The attitude that things are connected and not isolated is a case in point. One can indeed imagine kindergarten games designed to make children more actively alert to how things affect or are connected with each other – a kind of introduction to the idea of multiple determination of events in the physical and the social world. Any working scientist is usually able to say something about the ways of thinking or attitudes that are a part of his craft. Historians have written rather extensively on this subject as far as their field is concerned. Literary men have even evolved a genre of writing about the forms of sensibility that make for literary taste and vigor. In mathematics, this subject has a formal name, "heuristic," to describe the approach one takes to solving problems. One may well argue, as it was argued at Woods Hole by men in widely differing disciplines, that it might be wise to assess what attitudes or heuristic devices are most pervasive and useful, and that an effort should be made to teach children a rudimentary version of them that might be further refined as they progress through school. Again, the reader will sense that the argument for such an approach is premised on the assumption that there is a continuity between what a scholar does on the forefront of his discipline and what a child does in approaching it for the first time. This is not to say that the task is a simple one, only that it is worthy of careful consideration and research.

Perhaps the chief arguments put forward in opposition to the idea of such efforts at teaching general principles and general attitudes are, first, that it is better to approach the general through the specific and, second, that working attitudes should be kept implicit rather than being made explicit. For example, one of the principal organizing concepts in biology is the persistent question, "What function does this thing serve?" – a question premised on the assumption that everything one finds in an organism serves some function or it probably would not have survived. Other general ideas are related to this question. The student who makes progress in biology learns to ask the question more and more subtly, to relate more and more things to it. At the next step he asks what function a particular structure or process serves in the light of what is required in the total functioning of an organism. Measuring and categorizing are carried out in the service of the general idea of function. Then beyond that he may organize his knowledge in terms of a still more comprehensive notion of function, turning to cellular structure or to phylogenetic comparison. It may well be that the style of thought of a particular discipline is necessary as a background for learning the working meaning of general concepts, in which case a general introduction to the meaning of "function" might be less effective than teaching it in the context of biology.

As for "attitude" teaching or even the teaching of heuristic in mathematics, the argument runs that if the learner becomes too aware of his own attitudes or approach, he may become mechanical or trick-oriented in his work. No evidence exists on the point, and research is needed before any effort is made to teach in this way. Work is now going on at Illinois on training children to be more effective in asking questions about physical phenomena, but much more information is needed before the issue is clear.

One hears often the distinction between "doing" and "understanding." It is a distinction applied to the case, for example, of a student who presumably understands a mathematical idea but does not know how to use it in computation. While the distinction is probably a false one – since how can one know what a student understands save by seeing what he does – it points to an interesting difference in emphasis in teaching and in learning. Thus one finds in some of the classic books on the psychology of problem solving (such as Max Wertheimer's *Productive Thinking*) a sharp line drawn between "rote drill" and "understanding." In point of fact, drill need not be rote and, alas, emphasis on understanding may lead the student to a certain verbal glibness. It has been the experience of members of the School Mathematics Study Group that computational practice may be a necessary step toward understanding conceptual ideas in mathematics. Similarly one may try to give the high school student a sense of styles by having him read contrasting authors, yet final insight into style may come only when the student himself tries his hand at writing in different styles. Indeed, it is the underlying premise of laboratory exercises that doing something helps one understand it. There is a certain wisdom in the quip made by a psychologist at Woods Hole: "How do I know what I think until I feel what I do?" In any case, the distinction is not a very helpful one. What is more to the point is to ask what methods of exercise in any given field are most likely to give the student a sense of intelligent mastery over the material. What are the most fruitful computational exercises that one can use in various branches of mathematics? Does the effort to write in the style of Henry James give one an especially good insight into that author's style? Perhaps a good start toward understanding such matters would be to study the methods used by successful teachers. It would be surprising if the information compiled failed to suggest a host of worthwhile laboratory studies on techniques of teaching – or, indeed, on techniques of imparting complex information generally.

A word is needed, finally, on examinations. It is obvious that an examination can be bad in the sense of emphasizing trivial aspects of a subject. Such examinations can encourage teaching in a disconnected fashion and learning by rote. What is often overlooked, however, is that examinations can also be allies in the battle to improve curricula and teaching. Whether an examination is of the "objective" type involving multiple choices or of the essay type, it can be devised so as to emphasize an understanding of the broad principles of a subject. Indeed, even when one examines on detailed knowledge, it can be done in such a way as to require an understanding by the student of the connectedness between specific facts. There is a concerted effort now under way among national testing organizations like the Educational Testing Service to construct examinations that will emphasize an understanding of fundamental principles. Such efforts can be of great help. Additional help might be given to local school systems by making available to them manuals that describe the variety of ways in which examinations can be constructed. The searching examination is not easy to make, and a thoughtful manual on the subject would be welcome.

To recapitulate, the main theme of this chapter has been that the curriculum of a subject should be determined by the most fundamental understanding that can be achieved of the underlying principles that give structure to that subject. Teaching specific topics or skills without making clear their context in the broader fundamental structure of a field of knowledge is uneconomical in several deep senses. In the first place, such teaching makes it exceedingly difficult for the student to generalize from what he has learned to what he will encounter later. In the second place, learning that has fallen short of a grasp of general principles has little reward in terms of intellectual excitement. The best way to create interest in a subject is to render it worth knowing, which means to make the knowledge gained usable in one's thinking beyond the situation in which the learning has occurred. Third, knowledge one has acquired without sufficient structure to tie it together is knowledge that is likely to be forgotten. An unconnected set of facts has a pitiably short half-life in memory. Organizing facts in terms of principles and ideas from which they may be inferred is the only known way of reducing the quick rate of loss of human memory.

Designing curricula in a way that reflects the basic structure of a field of knowledge requires the most fundamental understanding of that field. It is a task that cannot be carried out without the active participation of the ablest scholars and scientists. The experience of the past several years has shown that such scholars and scientists, working in conjunction with experienced teachers and students of child development, can prepare curricula of the sort we have been considering. Much more effort in the actual preparation of curriculum materials, in teacher training, and in supporting research will be necessary if improvements in our educational practices are to be of an order that will meet the challenges of the scientific and social revolution through which we are now living.

There are many problems of how to teach general principles in a way that will be both effective and interesting, and several of the key issues have been passed in review. What is abundantly clear is that much work remains to be done by way of examining currently effective practices, fashioning curricula that may be tried out on an experimental basis, and carrying out the kinds of research that can give support and guidance to the general effort at improving teaching.

How may the kind of curriculum we have been discussing be brought within the intellectual reach of children of different ages? To this problem the rest of the book is devoted.

CHAPTER 5

READINESS FOR LEARNING

The Process of Education (1960), Cambridge: Harvard University Press

We begin with the hypothesis that any subject can be taught effectively in some intellectually honest form to any child at any stage of development. It is a bold hypothesis and an essential one in thinking about the nature of a curriculum. No evidence exists to contradict it; considerable evidence is being amassed that supports it.

To make clear what is implied, let us examine three general ideas. The first has to do with the process of intellectual development in children, the second with the act of learning, and the third with the notion of the "spiral curriculum" introduced earlier.

Intellectual development

Research on the intellectual development of the child highlights the fact that at each stage of development the child has a characteristic way of viewing the world and explaining it to himself. The task of teaching a subject to a child at any particular age is one of representing the structure of that subject in terms of the child's way of viewing things. The task can be thought of as one of translation. The general hypothesis that has just been stated is premised on the considered judgment that any idea can be represented honestly and usefully in the thought forms of children of school age, and that these first representations can later be made more powerful and precise the more easily by virtue of this early learning. To illustrate and support this view, we present here a somewhat detailed picture of the course of intellectual development, along with some suggestions about teaching at different stages of it.

The work of Piaget and others suggests that, roughly speaking, one may distinguish three stages in the intellectual development of the child. The first stage need not concern us in detail, for it is characteristic principally of the pre-school child. In this stage, which ends (at least for Swiss school children) around the fifth or sixth year, the child's mental work consists principally in establishing relationships between experience and action; his concern is with manipulating the world through action. This stage corresponds roughly to the period from the first development of language to the point at which the child learns to manipulate symbols. In this so-called preoperational stage, the principal symbolic achievement is that the child learns how to represent the external world through symbols established by simple generalization; things are represented as equivalent in terms of sharing some common property. But the child's symbolic world does not make a clear separation between internal motives and feelings on the one hand and external reality on the other. The sun moves because God pushes it, and the stars, like himself, have to go to bed. The child is little able to separate his own goals from the means for achieving them, and when he has to make corrections in his activity after unsuccessful attempts at manipulating reality, he does so by what are called intuitive regulations rather than by symbolic operations, the former being of a crude trial-and-error nature rather than the result of taking thought.

What is principally lacking at this stage of development is what the Geneva school has called the concept of reversibility. When the shape of an object is changed, as when one changes the shape of a ball of plasticene, the preoperational child cannot grasp the idea that it can be brought back readily to its original state. Because of this fundamental lack the child cannot understand certain fundamental ideas that lie at the basis of mathematics and physics – the mathematical idea that one conserves quantity even when one partitions a set of things into subgroups, or the physical idea that one conserves mass and weight even though one transforms the shape of an object. It goes without saying that teachers are severely limited in transmitting concepts to a child at this stage, even in a highly intuitive manner.

The second stage of development – and now the child is in school – is called the stage of concrete operations. This stage is operational in contrast to the preceding stage, which is merely active. An operation is a type of action: it can be carried out rather directly by the manipulation of objects, or internally, as when one manipulates the symbols that represent things and relations in one's mind. Roughly, an operation is a means of getting data about the real world into the mind and there transforming them so that they can be organized and used selectively in the solution of problems. Assume a child is presented with a pinball machine which bounces a ball off a wall at an angle. Let us find out what he appreciates about the relation between the angle of incidence and the angle of reflection. The young child sees no problem: for him, the ball travels in an arc, touching the wall on the way. The somewhat older child, say age ten, sees the two angles as roughly related – as one changes so does the other. The still older child begins to grasp that there is a fixed relation between the two, and usually says it is a right angle. Finally, the thirteen- or fourteen-year-old, often by pointing the ejector directly at the wall and seeing the ball come back at the ejector, gets the idea that the two angles are equal. Each way of looking at the phenomenon represents the result of an operation in this sense, and the child's thinking is constrained by his way of pulling his observations together.

An operation differs from simple action or goal-directed behavior in that it is internalized and reversible. 'Internalized' means that the child does not have to go about his problem-solving any longer by overt trial and error, but can actually carry out trial and error in his head. Reversibility is present because operations are seen as characterized where appropriate by what is called "complete compensation;" that is to say, an operation can be compensated for by an inverse operation. If marbles, for example, are divided into subgroups, the child can grasp intuitively that the original collection of marbles can be restored by being added back together again. The child tips a balance scale too far with a weight and then searches systematically for a lighter weight or for something with which to get the scale rebalanced. He may carry reversibility too far by assuming that a piece of paper, once burned, can also be restored.

With the advent of concrete operations, the child develops an internalized structure with which to operate. In the example of the balance scale, the structure is a serial order of weights that the child has in his mind. Such internal structures are of the essence. They are the internalized symbolic systems by which the child represents the world, as in the example of the pinball machine and the angles of incidence and reflection. It is into the language of these internal structures that one must translate ideas if the child is to grasp them.

But concrete operations, though they are guided by the logic of classes and the logic of relations, are means for structuring only immediately present reality. The child is able to give structure to the things he encounters, but he is not yet readily able to deal with possibilities not directly before him or not already experienced. This is not to say that children operating concretely are not able to anticipate things that are not present. Rather, it is that they do not command the operations for conjuring up systematically the full range of alternative possibilities that could exist at any given time. They cannot go systematically beyond the information given them to a description of what else might occur. Somewhere between ten and fourteen years of age the child passes into a third stage, which is called the stage of "formal operations" by the Geneva school.

Now the child's intellectual activity seems to be based upon an ability to operate on hypothetical propositions rather than being constrained to what he has experienced or what is before him. The child can now think of possible variables and even deduce potential relationships that can later be verified by experiment or observation. Intellectual operations now appear to be predicated upon the same kinds of logical operations that are the stock in trade of the logician, the scientist, or the abstract thinker. It is at this point that the child is able to give formal or axiomatic expression to the concrete ideas that before guided his problem-solving but could not be described or formally understood.

Earlier, while the child is in the stage of concrete operations, he is capable of grasping intuitively and concretely a great many of the basic ideas of mathematics, the sciences, the humanities, and the social sciences. But he can do so only in terms of concrete operations. It can be demonstrated that fifth-grade children can play mathematical games with rules modeled on highly advanced mathematics; indeed, they can arrive at these rules inductively and learn how to work with them. They will flounder, however, if one attempts to force upon them a formal mathematical description of what they have been doing, though they are perfectly capable of guiding their behavior by these rules. At the Woods Hole Conference we were privileged to see a demonstration of teaching in which fifth-grade children very rapidly grasped central ideas from the theory of functions, although had the teacher attempted to explain to them what the theory of functions was, he would have drawn a blank. Later, at the appropriate stage of development and given a certain amount of practice in concrete operations, the time would be ripe for introducing them to the necessary formalism.

What is most important for teaching basic concepts is that the child be helped to pass progressively from concrete thinking to the utilization of more conceptually adequate modes of thought. But it is futile to attempt this by presenting formal explanations based on a logic that is distant from the child's manner of thinking and sterile in its implications for him. Much teaching in mathematics is of this sort. The child learns not to understand mathematical order but rather to apply certain devices or recipes without understanding their significance and connectedness. They are not translated into his way of thinking. Given this inappropriate start, he is easily led to believe that the important thing is for him to be "accurate" – though accuracy has less to do with mathematics than with computation. Perhaps the most striking example of this type of thing is to be found in the manner in which the high school student meets Euclidian geometry for the first time, as a set of axioms and theorems, without having had some experience with simple geometric configurations and the intuitive means whereby one deals with them. If the child were earlier given the concepts and strategies in the form of intuitive geometry at a level that he could easily follow, he might be far better able to grasp deeply the meaning of the theorems and axioms to which he is exposed later.

But the intellectual development of the child is no clockwork sequence of events; it also responds to influences from the environment, notably the school environment. Thus instruction in scientific ideas, even at the elementary level, need not follow slavishly the natural course of cognitive development in the child. It can also lead to intellectual development by providing challenging but usable opportunities for the child to forge ahead in his development. Experience has shown that it is worth the effort to provide the growing child with problems that tempt him into next stages of development. As David Page, one of the most experienced teachers of elementary mathematics, has commented:

> In teaching from kindergarten to graduate school, I have been amazed at the intellectual similarity of human beings at all ages, although children are perhaps more spontaneous, creative, and energetic than adults. As far as I am concerned young children learn almost anything faster than adults do if it can be given to them in terms they understand. Giving the material to them in terms they understand, interestingly enough, turns out to involve knowing the mathematics oneself, and the better one knows it, the better it can be taught. It is appropriate that we warn ourselves to be careful of assigning an absolute level of difficulty to any particular topic. When I tell mathematicians that fourth-grade students can go a long way into "set theory" a few of them reply: "Of course." Most of them are startled. The latter ones are completely wrong in assuming that "set theory" is intrinsically difficult. Of course it may be that nothing is intrinsically difficult. We just have to wait until the proper point of view and corresponding language for presenting it are revealed. Given particular subject matter or a particular concept, it is easy to ask trivial questions or to lead the child to ask trivial questions. It is also easy to ask impossibly difficult questions. The trick is to find the medium questions that can be answered and that take you somewhere. This is the big job of teachers and textbooks.

One leads the child by the well-wrought "medium questions" to move more rapidly through the stages of intellectual development, to a deeper understanding of mathematical, physical, and historical principles. We must know far more about the ways in which this can be done.

Professor Inhelder of Geneva was asked to suggest ways in which the child could be moved along faster through the various stages of intellectual development in mathematics and physics. What follows is part of a memorandum she prepared for the Conference.

"The most elementary forms of reasoning – whether logical, arithmetical, geometrical, or physical – rest on the principle of the invariance of quantities: that the whole remains, whatever may be the arrangement of its parts, the change of its form, or its displacement in space or time. The principle of invariance is not a priori datum of the mind, nor is it the product of purely empirical observation. The child discovers invariance in a manner comparable to scientific discoveries generally. Grasping the idea of invariance is beset with difficulties for the child, often unsuspected by teachers. To the young child, numerical wholes, spatial dimensions, and physical quantities do not seem to remain constant but to dilate or contract as they are operated upon. The total number of beads in a box remains the same whether subdivided into two, three, or ten piles. It is this that is so hard for the child to understand. The young child perceives changes as operating in one direction without being able to grasp the idea that certain fundamental features of things remain constant over change, or that if they change the change is reversible.

A few examples among many used in studying the child's concept of invariance will illustrate the kinds of materials one could use to help him to learn the concept more easily. The child transfers beads of a known quantity or liquids of a known volume from one receptacle to another, one receptacle being tall and narrow, the other flat and wide. The young child believes there is more in the tall receptacle than the flat one. Now the child can be confronted concretely with the nature of one-to-one correspondence between two versions of the same quantity. For there is an easy technique of checking: the beads can be counted or the liquid measured in some standard way. The same operations work for the conservation of spatial quantity if one uses a set of sticks for length or a set of tiles for surface, or by having the child transform the shape of volumes made up of the same number of blocks. In physics dissolving sugar or transforming the shapes of balls of plasticene while conserving volume provides comparable instruction. If teaching fails to bring the child properly from his perceptual, primitive notions to a proper intuition of the idea of invariance, the result is that he will count without having acquired the idea of the invariance of numerical quantities. Or he will use geometrical measures while remaining ignorant of the operation of transitivity – that if A includes B, and B includes C, then A also includes C. In physics he will apply calculations to imperfectly understood physical notions such as weight, volume, speed, and time. A teaching method that takes into account the natural thought processes will allow the child to discover such principles of invariance by giving him an opportunity to progress beyond his own primitive mode of thinking through confrontation by concrete data – as when he notes that liquid that looks greater in volume in a tall, thin receptacle is in fact the same as that quantity in a flat, low vessel. Concrete activity that becomes increasingly formal is what leads the child to the kind of mental mobility that approaches the naturally reversible operations of mathematics and logic. The child gradually comes to sense that any change may be mentally cancelled out by the reverse operation – addition by subtraction – or that a change may be counterbalanced by a reciprocal change.

A child often focuses on only one aspect of a phenomenon at a time, and this interferes with his understanding. We can set up little teaching experiments in such a way that he is forced to pay attention to other aspects. Thus, children up to about age seven estimate the speed of two automobiles by assuming that the one that gets there first is the faster, or that if one passes the other it is faster. To overcome such errors, one can, by using toy automobiles, show that two objects starting at different distances from a finish line cannot be judged by which one arrives first, or show that one car can pass another by circling it and still not finish first. These are simple exercises, but they speed the child toward attending to several features of a situation at once.

In view of all this it seems highly arbitrary and very likely incorrect to delay the teaching, for example, of Euclidian or metric geometry until the end of the primary grades, particularly when projective geometry has not been given earlier. So too with the teaching of physics, which has much in it that can be profitably taught at an inductive or intuitive level much earlier. Basic notions in these fields are perfectly accessible to children of seven to ten years of age, *provided that they are divorced from their mathematical expression and studied through materials that the child can handle himself.*

Another matter relates particularly to the ordering of a mathematics curriculum. Often the sequence of psychological development follows more closely the axiomatic order of a subject matter than it does the historical order of development of concepts within the field. One observes, for instance, that certain topological notions, such as connection, separation, being interior to, and so forth, precede the formation of Euclidian and projective notions in geometry, though the former ideas are newer in their formalism in the history of mathematics than the latter. If any special justification were needed for teaching the structure of a subject in its proper logical or axiomatic order rather than its order of historical development, this should provide it. This is not to say that there may not be situations where the historical order is important from the point of view of its cultural or pedagogical relevance.

As for teaching geometrical notions of perspective and projection, again there is much that can be done by the use of experiments and demonstrations that rest on the child's operational capacity to analyze concrete experience. We have watched children work with an apparatus in which rings of different diameter are placed at different positions between a candle and a screen with a fixed distance between them so that the rings cast shadows of varying sizes on the screen. The child learns how the cast shadow changes size as a function of the distance of the ring from the light source. By bringing to the child such concrete experience of light in revealing situations, we teach him maneuvers that in the end permit him to understand the general ideas underlying projective geometry.

These examples lead us to think that it is possible to draw up methods of teaching the basic ideas in science and mathematics to children considerably younger than the traditional age. It is at this earlier age that systematic instruction can lay a groundwork in the fundamentals that can be used later and with great profit at the secondary level.

The teaching of probabilistic reasoning, so very common and important a feature of modern science, is hardly developed in our educational system before college. The omission is probably due to the fact that school syllabi in nearly all countries follow scientific progress with a near-disastrous time lag. But it may also be due to the widespread belief that the understanding of random phenomena depends on the learner's grasp of the meaning of the rarity or commonness of events. And admittedly, such ideas are hard to get across to the young. Our research indicates that the understanding of random phenomena requires, rather, the use of certain concrete logical operations well within the grasp of the young child – provided these operations are free of awkward mathematical expression. Principal among these logical operations are disjunction ("either A *or* B is true") and combination. Games in which lots are drawn, games of roulette, and games involving a gaussian distribution of outcomes are all ideal for giving the child a basic grasp of the logical operation needed for thinking about probability. In such games, children first discover an entirely qualitative notion of chance defined as an uncertain event, contrasted with deductive certainty. The notion of probability as a fraction of certainty is discovered only later. Each of these discoveries can be made before the child ever learns the techniques of the calculus of probabilities or the formal expressions that normally go with probability theory. Interest in problems of a probabilistic nature could easily be awakened and developed before the introduction of any statistical processes or computation. Statistical manipulation and computation are only tools to be used *after* intuitive understanding has been established. If the array of computational paraphernalia is introduced first, then more likely than not it will inhibit or kill the development of probabilistic reasoning.

One wonders in the light of all this whether it might not be interesting to devote the first two years of school to a series of exercises in manipulating, classifying, and ordering objects in ways that highlight basic operations of logical addition, multiplication, inclusion, serial ordering, and the like. For surely these logical operations are the basis of more specific operations and concepts of all mathematics and science. It may indeed be the case that such an early science and mathematics 'pre-curriculum' might go a long way toward building up in the child the kind of intuitive and more inductive understanding that could be given embodiment later in formal courses in mathematics and science. The effect of such an approach would be, we think, to put more continuity into science and mathematics and also to give the child a much better and firmer comprehension of the concepts which, unless he has this early foundation, he will mouth later without being able to use them in any effective way."

A comparable approach can surely be taken to the teaching of social studies and literature. There has been little research done on the kinds of concepts that a child brings to these subjects, although there is a wealth of observation and anecdote. Can one teach the structure of literary forms by presenting the child with the first part of a story and then having him complete it in the form of a comedy, a tragedy, or a farce – without ever using such words? When, for example, does the idea of "historical trend" develop, and what are its precursors in the child? How does one make a child aware of literary style? Perhaps the child can discover the idea of style through the presentation of the same content written in drastically different styles, in the manner of Beerbohm's *Christmas Garland*. Again, there is no reason to believe that any subject cannot be taught to any child at virtually any age in some form.

Here one is immediately faced with the question of the economy of teaching. One can argue that it might be better to wait until the child is thirteen or fourteen before beginning geometry so that the projective and intuitive first steps can immediately be followed up by a full formal presentation of the subject. Is it worth-while to train the young inductively so that they may discover the basic order of knowledge before they can appreciate its formalism? In Professor Inhelder's memorandum, it was suggested that the first two grades might be given over to training the child in the basic logical operations that underlie instruction in mathematics and science. There is evidence to indicate that such rigorous and relevant early training has the effect of making later learning easier. Indeed the experiments on "learning set" seem to indicate just that – that one not only learns specifics but in so doing learns how to learn. So important is training per se that monkeys who have been given extensive training in problem-solving suffer considerably less loss and recover more quickly after induced brain damage than animals who had not been previously thus educated. But the danger of such early training may be that it has the effect of training out original but deviant ideas. There is no evidence available on the subject, and much is needed.

The act of learning

Learning a subject seems to involve three almost simultaneous processes. First there is *acquisition* of new information – often information that runs counter to or is a replacement for what the person has previously known implicitly or explicitly.

At the very least it is a refinement of previous knowledge. Thus one teaches a student Newton's laws of motion, which violate the testimony of the senses. Or in teaching a student about wave mechanics, one violates the student's belief in mechanical impact as the sole source of real energy transfer. Or one bucks the language and its built-in way of thinking in terms of "wasting energy" by introducing the student to the conservation theorem in physics which asserts that no energy is lost. More often the situation is less drastic, as when one teaches the details of the circulatory system to a student who already knows vaguely or intuitively that blood circulates.

A second aspect of learning may be called *transformation* – the process of manipulating knowledge to make it fit new tasks. We learn to "unmask" or analyze information, to order it in a way that permits extrapolation or interpolation or conversion into another form. Transformation comprises the ways we deal with information in order to go beyond it.

A third aspect of learning is *evaluation* – checking whether the way we have manipulated information is adequate to the task. Is the generalization fitting, have we extrapolated appropriately, are we operating properly? Often a teacher is crucial in helping with evaluation, but much of it takes place by judgments of plausibility without our actually being able to check rigorously whether we are correct in our efforts.

In the learning of any subject matter, there is usually a series of episodes, each episode involving the three processes. Photosynthesis might reasonably comprise material for a learning episode in biology, fitted into a more comprehensive learning experience such as learning about the conversion of energy generally. At its best a learning episode reflects what has gone before it and permits one to generalize beyond it.

A learning episode can be brief or long, contain many ideas or a few. How sustained an episode a learner is willing to undergo depends upon what the person expects to get from his efforts, in the sense of such external things as grades but also in the sense of a gain in understanding.

We usually tailor material to the capacities and needs of students by manipulating learning episodes in several ways: by shortening or lengthening the episode, by piling on extrinsic rewards in the form of praise and gold stars, or by dramatizing the shock of recognition of what the material means when fully understood. The unit in a curriculum is meant to be a recognition of the importance of learning episodes, though many units drag on with no climax in understanding. There is a surprising lack of research on how one most wisely devises adequate learning episodes for children at different ages and in different subject matters. There are many questions that need answers based on careful research, and to some of these we turn now.

There is, to begin with, the question of the balance between extrinsic rewards and intrinsic ones. There has been much written on the role of reward and punishment in learning, but very little indeed on the role of interest and curiosity and the lure of discovery. If it is our intention as teachers to inure the child to longer and longer episodes of learning, it may well be that intrinsic rewards in the form of quickened awareness and understanding will have to be emphasized far more in the detailed design of curricula. One of the least discussed ways of carrying a student through a hard unit of material is to challenge him with a chance to exercise his full powers, so that he may discover the pleasure of full and effective functioning. Good teachers know the power of this lure. Students should know what it feels like to be completely absorbed in a problem. They seldom experience this feeling in school. Given enough absorption in class, some students may be able to carry over the feeling to work done on their own.

There is a range of problems that have to do with how much emphasis should be placed on acquisition, transformation, and evaluation in a learning episode – getting facts, manipulating them, and checking one's ideas. Is it the case, for example, that it is best to give the young child a minimum set of facts first and then encourage him to draw the fullest set of implications possible from this knowledge? In short, should an episode for a young child contain little new information but emphasize what can be done to go beyond that bit on one's own? One teacher of social studies has had great success with fourth-graders through this approach: he begins, for example, with the fact that civilizations have most often begun in fertile river valleys – the only "fact." The students are encouraged in class discussion to figure out why this is the case and why it would be less likely for civilizations to start in mountainous country. The effect of this approach, essentially the technique of discovery, is that the child generates information on his own, which he can then check or evaluate against the sources, getting more new information in the process. This obviously is one kind of learning episode, and doubtless it has limited applicability. What other kinds are there, and are some more appropriate to certain topics and ages than others? It is not the case that "to learn is to learn is to learn," yet in the research literature there appears to be little recognition of differences in learning episodes.

With respect to the optimum length of a learning episode, there are a few common sense things one can say about it, and these are perhaps interesting enough to suggest fruitful research possibilities. It seems fairly obvious, for example, that the longer and more packed the episode, the greater the pay-off must be in terms of increased power and understanding if the person is to be encouraged to move to a next episode with zest. Where grades are used as a substitute for the reward of understanding, it may well be that learning will cease as soon as grades are no longer given – at graduation.

It also seems reasonable that the more one has a sense of the structure of a subject, the more densely packed and longer a learning episode one can get through without fatigue. Indeed, the amount of new information in any learning episode is really the amount that we cannot quite fit into place at once. And there is a severe limit, as we have already noted, on how much of such un-assimilated information we can keep in mind. The estimate is that adults can handle about seven independent items of information at a time. No norms are available for children – a deplorable lack.

There are many details one can discuss concerning the shaping of learning episodes for children, but the problems that have been mentioned will suffice to give their flavor. Inasmuch as the topic is central to an understanding of how one arranges a curriculum, it seems obvious that here is an area of research that is of the first importance.

The "spiral curriculum"

If one respects the ways of thought of the growing child, if one is courteous enough to translate material into his logical forms and challenging enough to tempt him to advance, then it is possible to introduce him at an early age to the ideas and styles that in later life make an educated man. We might ask, as a criterion for any subject taught in primary school, whether, when fully developed, it is worth an adult's knowing, and whether having known it as a child makes a person a better adult.

If the answer to both questions is negative or ambiguous, then the material is cluttering the curriculum.

If the hypothesis with which this section was introduced is true – that any subject can be taught to any child in some honest form – then it should follow that a curriculum ought to be built around the great issues, principles, and values that a society deems worthy of the continual concern of its members. Consider two examples – the teaching of literature and of science. If it is granted, for example, that it is desirable to give children an awareness of the meaning of human tragedy and a sense of compassion for it, is it not possible at the earliest appropriate age to teach the literature of tragedy in a manner that illuminates but does not threaten? There are many possible ways to begin: through a retelling of the great myths, through the use of children's classics, through presentation of and commentary on selected films that have proved themselves. Precisely what kinds of materials should be used at what age with what effect is a subject for research – research of several kinds. We may ask first about the child's conception of the tragic, and here one might proceed in much the same way that Piaget and his colleagues have proceeded in studying the child's conception of physical causality, of morality, of number, and the rest. It is only when we are equipped with such knowledge that we will be in a position to know how the child will translate whatever we present to him into his own subjective terms. Nor need we wait for all the research findings to be in before proceeding, for a skillful teacher can also experiment by attempting to teach what seems to be intuitively right for children of different ages, correcting as he goes. In time, one goes beyond to more complex versions of the same kind of literature or simply revisits some of the same books used earlier. What matters is that later teaching build upon earlier reactions to literature, that it seek to create an ever more explicit and mature understanding of the literature of tragedy. Any of the great literary forms can be handled in the same way, or any of the great themes – be it the form of comedy or the theme of identity, personal loyalty, or what not.

So too in science. If the understanding of number, measure, and probability is judged crucial in the pursuit of science, then instruction in these subjects should begin as intellectually, honestly, and as early as possible in a manner consistent with the child's forms of thought. Let the topics be developed and redeveloped in later grades. Thus, if most children are to take a tenth-grade unit in biology, need they approach the subject cold? Is it not possible, with a minimum of formal laboratory work if necessary, to introduce them to some of the major biological ideas earlier, in a spirit perhaps less exact and more intuitive?

Many curricula are originally planned with a guiding idea much like the one set forth here. But as curricula are actually executed, as they grow and change, they often lose their original form and suffer a relapse into a certain shapelessness. It is not amiss to urge that actual curricula be reexamined with an eye to the issues of continuity and development referred to in the preceding pages. One cannot predict the exact forms that revision might take; indeed, it is plain that there is now available too little research to provide adequate answers. One can only propose that appropriate research be undertaken with the greatest vigor and as soon as possible.

CHAPTER 6

THE ACT OF DISCOVERY

Harvard Educational Review (1961) 31, 21–32

Maimonides, in his *Guide for the Perplexed*,[1] speaks of four forms of perfection that men might seek. The first and lowest form is perfection in the acquisition of worldly goods. The great philosopher dismisses such perfection on the ground that the possessions one acquires bear no meaningful relation to the possessor: "A great king may one morning find that there is no difference between him and the lowest person." A second perfection is of the body, its conformation and skills. Its failing is that is does not reflect on what is uniquely human about man: "he could [in any case] not be as strong as a mule." Moral perfection is the third, "the highest degree of excellency in man's character." Of this perfection Maimonides says: "Imagine a person being alone, and having no connection whatever with any other person; all his good moral principles are at rest, they are not required and give man no perfection whatever. These principles are only necessary and useful when man comes in contact with others." "The fourth kind of perfection is the true perfection of man; the possession of the highest intellectual faculties...." In justification of his assertion, this extraordinary Spanish-Judaic philosopher urges: "Examine the first three kinds of perfection; you will find that if you possess them, they are not your property, but the property of others.... But the last kind of perfection is exclusively yours; no one else owns any part of it."

It is a conjecture much like that of Maimonides that leads me to examine the act of discovery in man's intellectual life. For if man's intellectual excellence is the most his own among his perfections, it is also the case that the most uniquely personal of all that he knows is that which he has discovered for himself. What difference does it make, then, that we encourage discovery in the learning of the young? Does it, as Maimonides would say, create a special and unique relation between knowledge possessed and the possessor? And what may such a unique relation do for a man – or for a child, if you will, for our concern is with the education of the young?

The immediate occasion for my concern with discovery – and I do not restrict discovery to the act of finding out something that before was unknown to mankind, but rather include all forms of obtaining knowledge for oneself by the use of one's own mind – the immediate occasion is the work of the various new curriculum projects that have grown up in America during the last six or seven years. For whether one speaks to mathematicians or physicists or historians, one encounters repeatedly an expression of faith in the powerful effects that come from permitting the student to put things together for himself, to be his own discoverer.

First, let it be clear what the act of discovery entails. It is rarely, on the frontier of knowledge or elsewhere, that new facts are "discovered" in the sense of being encountered as Newton suggested in the form of islands of truth in an uncharted sea of ignorance. Or if they appear to be discovered in this way, it is almost always thanks to some happy hypotheses about where to navigate. Discovery, like surprise, favors the well prepared mind. In playing bridge, one is surprised by a hand with no honors in it at all and also by hands that are all in one suit. Yet all hands in bridge are equiprobable: one must know to be surprised. So too in discovery. The history of science is studded with examples of men "finding out" something and not knowing it. I shall operate on the assumption that discovery, whether by a schoolboy going it on his own or by a scientist cultivating the growing edge of his field, is in its essence a matter of rearranging or transforming evidence in such a way that one is enabled to go beyond the evidence so reassembled to additional new insights. It may well be that an additional fact or shred of evidence makes this larger transformation of evidence possible. But it is often not even dependent on new information.

It goes without saying that, left to himself, the child will go about discovering things for himself within limits. It also goes without saying that there are certain forms of child rearing, certain home atmospheres that lead some children to be their own discoverers more than other children. These are both topics of great interest, but I shall not be discussing them. Rather, I should like to confine myself to the consideration of discovery and "finding-out-for-oneself" within an educational setting – specifically the school. Our aim as teachers is to give our student as firm a grasp of a subject as we can, and to make him as autonomous and self-propelled a thinker as we can – one who will go along on his own after formal schooling has ended. I shall return in the end to the question of the kind of classroom and the style of teaching that encourages an attitude of wanting to discover. For purposes of orienting the discussion, however, I would like to make an overly simplified distinction between teaching that takes place in the *expository mode* and teaching that utilizes the *hypothetical mode*. In the former, the decisions concerning the mode and pace and style of exposition are principally determined by the teacher as expositor; the student is the listener. If I can put the matter in terms of structural linguistics, the speaker has a quite different set of decisions to make than the listener: the former has a wide choice of alternatives for structuring, he is anticipating paragraph content while the listener is still intent on the words, he is manipulating the content of the material by various transformations, while the listener is quite unaware of these internal manipulations. In the hypothetical mode, the teacher and the student are in a more cooperative position with respect to what in linguistics would be called "speaker's decisions." The student is not a bench-bound listener, but is taking a part in the formulation and at times may play the principal role in it. He will be aware of alternatives and may even have an "as if" attitude toward these and, as he receives information he may evaluate it as it comes. One cannot describe the process in either mode with great precision as to detail, but I think the foregoing may serve to illustrate what is meant.

Consider now what benefit might be derived from the experience of learning through discoveries that one makes for oneself. I should like to discuss these under four headings: (1) The increase in intellectual potency, (2) the shift from extrinsic to intrinsic rewards, (3) learning the heuristics of discovering, and (4) the aid to memory processing.

1   *Intellectual potency.* If you will permit me, I would like to consider the difference between subjects in a highly constrained psychological experiment

involving a two-choice apparatus. In order to win chips, they must depress a key either on the right or the left side of the machine. A pattern of payoff is designed such that, say, they will be paid off on the right side 70% of the time, on the left 30%, although this detail is not important. What is important is that the payoff sequence is arranged at random, and there is no pattern. I should like to contrast the behavior of subjects who think that there *is* some pattern to be found in the sequence – who think that regularities are discoverable – in contrast to subjects who think that things are happening quite by *chance*. The former group adopts what is called an "event-matching" strategy in which the number of responses given to each side is roughly equal to the proportion of times it pays off: in the present case R70 : L30. The group that believes there is no pattern very soon reverts to a much more primitive strategy wherein *all* responses are allocated to the side that has the greater payoff. A little arithmetic will show you that the lazy all-and-none strategy pays off more if indeed the environment is random: namely, they win 70% of the time. The event-matching subjects win about 70% on the 70% payoff side (or 49% of the time there) and 30% of the time on the side that pays off 30% of the time (another 9% for a total take-home wage of 58% in return for their labors of decision). But the world is not always or not even frequently random, and if one analyzes carefully what the event-matchers are doing, it turns out that they are try-ing out hypotheses one after the other, all of them containing a term such that they distribute bets on the two sides with a frequency to match the actual occurrence of events. If it should turn out that there is a pattern to be discovered, their payoff would become 100%. The other group would go on at the middling rate of 70%.

What has this to do with the subject at hand? For the person to search out and find regularities and relationships in his environment, he must be armed with an expectancy that there will be something to find and, once aroused by expectancy, he must devise ways of searching and finding. One of the chief enemies of such expectancy is the assumption that there is nothing one can find in the environment by way of regularity or relationship. In the experiment just cited, subjects often fall into a habitual attitude that there is either nothing to be found or that they can find a pattern by looking. There is an important sequel in behavior to the two attitudes, and to this I should like to turn now.

We have been conducting a series of experimental studies on a group of some seventy school children over the last four years. The studies have led us to distinguish an interesting dimension of cognitive activity that can be described as ranging from *episodic empiricism* at one end to *cumulative constructionism* at the other. The two attitudes in the choice experiments just cited are illustrative of the extremes of the dimension. I might mention some other illustrations. One of the experiments employs the game of Twenty Questions. A child – in this case he is between 10 and 12 – is told that a car has gone off the road and hit a tree. He is to ask questions that can be answered by "yes" or "no" to discover the cause of the accident. After completing the problem, the same task is given him again, though he is told that the accident had a different cause this time. In all, the procedure is repeated four times. Children enjoy playing the game. They also differ quite markedly in the approach or strategy they bring to the task. There are various elements in the strategies employed. In the first place, one may distinguish clearly between two types of questions asked: the one is designed for locating constraints in the problem, constraints that will eventually give shape to an hypothesis; the other is the hypothesis as question. It is the difference between, "Was there anything wrong with the driver?" and "Was the driver rushing to the doctor's office for an appointment and the car got out of control?" There are children who precede hypotheses with efforts to locate constraint and there are those who, to use our local slang, are "pot-shotters," who string out hypotheses non-cumulatively one after the other. A second element of strategy is its connectivity of information gathering: the extent to which questions asked utilize or ignore or violate information previously obtained. The questions asked by children tend to be organized in cycles, each cycle of questions usually being given over to the pursuit of some particular notion. Both within cycles and between cycles one can discern a marked difference on the connectivity of the child's performance. Needless to say, children who employ constraint location as a technique preliminary to the formulation of hypotheses tend to be far more connected in their harvesting of information. Persistence is another feature of strategy, a characteristic compounded of what appear to be two components: a sheer doggedness component, and a persistence that stems from the sequential organization that a child brings to the task. Doggedness is probably just animal spirits or the need for achievement – what has come to be called *n-ach*. Organized persistence is a maneuver for protecting our fragile cognitive apparatus from overload. The child who has flooded himself with disorganized information from unconnected hypotheses will become discouraged and confused sooner than the child who has shown a certain cunning in his strategy of getting information – a cunning whose principal component is the recognition that the value of information is not simply in getting it but in being able to carry it. The persistence of the organized child stems from his knowledge of how to organize questions in cycles, how to summarize things to himself, and the like.

Episodic empiricism is illustrated by information gathering that is unbound by prior constraints, that lacks connectivity, and that is deficient in organizational persistence. The opposite extreme is illustrated by an approach that is characterized by constraint sensitivity, by connective maneuvers, and by organized persistence. Brute persistence seems to be one of those gifts from the gods that make people more exaggeratedly what they are.[2]

Before returning to the issue of discovery and its role in the development of thinking, let me say a word more about the ways in which information may get transformed when the problem solver has actively processed it. There is first of all a pragmatic question: what does it take to get information processed into a form best designed to fit some future use? Take an experiment by Zajonc[3] as a case in point. He gives groups of subjects information of a controlled kind, some groups being told that their task is to transmit the information to others, others that it is merely to be kept in mind. In general, he finds more differentiation and organization of the information received with the intention of being transmitted than there is for information received passively. An active set leads to a transformation related to a task to be performed. The risk, to be sure, is in possible overspecialization of information processing that may lead to such a high degree of specific organization that information is lost for general use.

I would urge now in the spirit of an hypothesis that emphasis upon discovery in learning has precisely the effect upon the learner of leading him to be a constructionist, to organize what he is encountering in a manner not only designed to discover regularity and relatedness, but also to avoid the kind of information drift that fails to keep account of the uses to which information might have to be put. It is, if you will, a necessary condition for learning the variety of techniques of problem solving, of transforming information for better use, indeed for learning how to go about the very task of learning. Practice in discovering for oneself teaches one to acquire information in a way that makes that information more readily viable in problem solving. So goes the hypothesis. It in still in need of testing. But is an hypothesis of such important human implications that we cannot afford not to test it – and testing will have to be in the schools.

2   *Intrinsic and extrinsic motives.* Much of the problem in leading a child to effective cognitive activity is to free him from the immediate control of environmental rewards and punishments. That is to say, learning that starts in response to the rewards of parental or teacher approval or the avoidance of failure can too readily develop a pattern in which the child is seeking cues as to how to conform to what is expected of him. We know from studies of children who tend to be early over-achievers in school that they are likely to be seekers after the "right way to do it" and that their capacity for transforming their learning into viable thought structures tends to be lower than children merely achieving at levels predicted by intelligence tests. Our tests on such children show them to be lower in analytic ability than those who are not conspicuous in overachievement.[4] As we shall see later, they develop rote abilities and depend upon being able to "give back" what is expected rather than to make it into something that relates to the rest of their cognitive life. As Maimonides would say, their learning is not their own.

The hypothesis that I would propose here is that to the degree that one is able to approach learning as a task of discovering something rather than "learning about" it, to that degree will there be a tendency for the child to carry out his learning activities with the autonomy of self-reward or, more properly by reward that is discovery itself.

To those of you familiar with the battles of the last half-century in the field of motivation, the above hypothesis will be recognized as controversial. For the classic view of motivation in learning has been, until very recently, couched in terms of a theory of drives and reinforcement: that learning occurred by virtue of the fact that a response produced by a stimulus was followed by the reduction in a primary drive state. The doctrine is greatly extended by the idea of secondary reinforcement: any state associated even remotely with the reduction of a primary drive could also have the effect of producing learning. There has recently appeared a most searching and important criticism of this position, written by Professor Robert White,[5] reviewing the evidence of recently published animal studies, of work in the field of psychoanalysis, and of research on the development of cognitive processes in children. Professor White comes to the conclusion, quite rightly I think, that the drive-reduction model of learning runs counter to too many important phenomena of learning and development to be either regarded as general in its applicability or even correct in its general approach. Let me summarize some of his principal conclusions and explore their applicability to the hypothesis stated above.

> I now propose that we gather the various kinds of behavior just mentioned, all of which have to do with effective interaction with the environment, under the general heading of competence. According to Webster, competence means fitness or ability, and the suggested synonyms include capability, capacity, efficiency, proficiency, and skill. It is therefore a suitable word to describe such things as grasping and exploring, crawling and walking, attention and perception, language and thinking, manipulating and changing the surroundings, all of which promote an effective – a competent – interaction with the environment. It is true of course, that maturation plays a part in all these developments, but this part is heavily overshadowed by learning in all the more complex accomplishments like speech or skilled manipulation. I shall argue that it is necessary to make competence a motivational concept; there is

competence motivation as well as competence in its more familiar sense of achieved capacity. The behavior that leads to the building up of effective grasping, handling, and letting go of objects, to take one example, is not random behavior that is produced by an overflow of energy. It is directed, selective, and persistent, and it continues not because it serves primary drives, which indeed it cannot serve until it is almost perfected, but because it satisfies an intrinsic need to deal with the environment.[6]

I am suggesting that there are forms of activity that serve to enlist and develop the competence motive, that serve to make it the driving force behind behavior.

I should like to add to White's general premise that the *exercise* of competence motives has the effect of strengthening the degree to which they gain control over behavior and thereby reduce the effects of extrinsic rewards or drive gratification.

The brilliant Russian psychologist Vigotsky[7] characterizes the growth of thought processes as starting with a dialogue of speech and gesture between child and parent; autonomous thinking begins at the stage when the child is first able to internalize these conversations and "run them off" himself. This is a typical sequence in the development of competence. So too in instruction. The narrative of teaching is of the order of the conversation. The next move in the development of competence is the internalization of the narrative and its "rules of generation" so that the child is now capable of running off the narrative on his own. The hypothetical mode in teaching by encouraging the child to participate in "speaker's decisions" speeds this process along. Once internalization has occurred, the child is in a vastly improved position from several obvious points of view – notably that he is able to go beyond the information he has been given to generate additional ideas that can either be checked immediately from experience or can, at least, be used as a basis for formulating reasonable hypotheses. But over and beyond that, the child is now in a position to experience success and failure not as reward and punishment, but as information. For when the task is his own rather than a matter of matching environmental demands, he becomes his own paymaster in a certain measure. Seeking to gain control over his environment, he can now treat success as indicating that he is on the right track, failure as indicating he is on the wrong one.

In the end, this development has the effect of freeing learning from immediate stimulus control. When learning in the short run leads only to pellets of this or that rather than to mastery in the long run, then behavior can be readily "shaped" by extrinsic rewards. When behavior becomes more long-range and competence-oriented, it comes under the control of more complex cognitive structures, plans and the like, and operates more from the inside out. It is interesting that even Pavlov, whose early account of the learning process was based entirely on a notion of stimulus control of behavior through the conditioning mechanism in which, through contiguity a new conditioned stimulus was substituted for an old unconditioned stimulus by the mechanism of stimulus substitution, that even Pavlov recognized his account as insufficient to deal with higher forms of learning. To supplement the account, he introduced the idea of the "second signalling system," with central importance placed on symbolic systems such as language in mediating and giving shape to mental life. Or as Luria[8] has put it, "the first signal system [is] concerned with directly perceived stimuli, the second with systems of verbal elaboration." Luria, commenting on the importance of the transition from first to second signal system, says: "It would be mistaken to suppose that verbal intercourse with adults merely changes the contents of the child's conscious activity without changing its form.... The word has a basic function not only because it indicates a corresponding object in the external world, but also because it abstracts, isolates the necessary signal, generalizes perceived signals and relates them to certain categories; it is this systematization of direct experience that makes the role of the word in the formation of mental processes so exceptionally important."[9,10]

It is interesting that the final rejection of the universality of the doctrine of reinforcement in direct conditioning came from some of Pavlov's own students. Ivanov-Smolensky[11] and Krasnogorsky[12] published papers showing the manner in which symbolized linguistic messages could take over the place of the unconditioned stimulus and of the unconditioned response (gratification of hunger) in children. In all instances, they speak of these as *replacements* of lower, first-system mental or neural processes by higher order or second-system controls. A strange irony, then, that Russian psychology that gave us the notion of the conditioned response and the assumption that higher order activities are built up out of colligations or structurings of such primitive units, rejected this notion while much of American learning psychology has stayed until quite recently within the early Pavlovian fold (see, for example, a recent article by Spence[13] in the *Harvard Educational Review* or Skinner's treatment of language[14] and the attacks that have been made upon it by linguists such as Chomsky[15] who have become concerned with the relation of language and cognitive activity). What is the more interesting is that Russian pedagogical theory has become deeply influenced by this new trend and is now placing much stress upon the importance of building up a more active symbolical approach to problem solving among children.

To sum up the matter of the control of learning, then, I am proposing that the degree to which competence or mastery motives come to control behavior, to that degree the role of reinforcement or "extrinsic pleasure" wanes in shaping behavior. The child comes to manipulate his environment more actively and achieves his gratification from coping with problems. Symbolic modes of representing and transforming the environment arise and the importance of stimulus-response-reward sequences declines. To use the metaphor that David Riesman developed in a quite different context, mental life moves from a state of outer-directedness in which the fortuity of stimuli and reinforcement are crucial to a state of inner-directedness in which the growth and maintenance of mastery become central and dominant.

3   Learning the heuristics of discovery. Lincoln Steffens,[16] reflecting in his *Autobiography* on his under graduate education at Berkeley, comments that his schooling was overly specialized on learning about the known and that too little attention was given to the task of finding out about what was not known. But how does one train a student in the techniques of discovery? Again I would like to offer some hypotheses. There are many ways of coming to the arts of inquiry. One of them is by careful study of its formalization in logic, statistics, mathematics, and the like. If a person is going to pursue inquiry as a way of life, particularly in the sciences, certainly such study is essential. Yet, whoever has taught kindergarten and the early primary grades or has had graduate students working with him on their theses – I choose the two extremes for they are both periods of intense inquiry – knows that an understanding of the formal aspect of inquiry is not sufficient. There appear to be, rather, a series of activities and attitudes, some directly related to a particular subject and some of them fairly generalized, that go with inquiry and research. These have to do with the *process* of trying to find out something and while they provide no guarantee that the *product* will be any *great* discovery, their absence is likely to lead to awkwardness or aridity or confusion. How difficult it is to describe these matters – the heuristics of inquiry. There is one set of attitudes or ways of doing that has to do with sensing the relevance of variables – how to avoid getting stuck with edge effects and getting instead to the big sources of variance. Partly this gift comes from intuitive familiarity with a range of phenomena, sheer "knowing the stuff." But it also comes out of a sense of what things among an ensemble of things "smell right" in the sense of being of the right order of magnitude or scope or severity.

The English philosopher Weldon describes problem solving in an interesting and picturesque way. He distinguishes between difficulties, puzzles, and problems. We solve a problem or make a discovery when we impose a puzzle form on to a difficulty that converts it into a problem that can be solved in such a way that it gets us where we want to be. That is to say, we recast the difficulty into a form that we know how to work with, then work it. Much of what we speak of as discovery consists of knowing how to impose what kind of form on various kinds of difficulties. A small part but a crucial part of discovery of the highest order is to invent and develop models or "puzzle forms" that can be imposed on difficulties with good effect. It is in this area that the truly powerful mind shines. But it is interesting to what degree perfectly ordinary people can, given the benefit of instruction, construct quite interesting and what, a century ago, would have been considered greatly original models.

Now to the hypothesis. It is my hunch that it is only through the exercise of problem solving and the effort of discovery that one learns the working heuristic of discovery, and the more one has practice, the more likely is one to generalize what one has learned into a style of problem solving or inquiry that serves for any kind of task one may encounter – or almost any kind of task. I think the matter is self-evident, but what is unclear is what kinds of training and teaching produce the best effects. How do we teach a child to, say, cut his losses but at the same time be persistent in trying out an idea; to risk forming an early hunch without at the same time formulating one *so* early and with so little evidence as to be stuck with it waiting for appropriate evidence to materialize; to pose good testable guesses that are neither too brittle nor too sinuously incorrigible; etc., etc. Practice in inquiry, in trying to figure out things for oneself is indeed what is needed, but in what form? Of only one thing I am convinced. I have never seen anybody improve in the art and technique of inquiry by any means other than engaging in inquiry.

4   Conservation of memory. I should like to take what some psychologists might consider a rather drastic view of the memory process. It is a view that in large measure derives from the work of my colleague, Professor George Miller.[17] Its first premise is that the principal problem of human memory is not storage, but retrieval. In spite of the biological unlikeliness of it, we seem to be able to store a huge quantity of information – perhaps not a full tape recording, though at times it seems we even do that, but a great sufficiency of impressions. We may infer this from the fact that recognition (i.e. recall with the aid of maximum prompts) is so extraordinarily good in human beings – particularly in comparison with spontaneous recall where, so to speak, we must get out stored information without external aids or prompts. The key to retrieval is organization or, in even simpler terms, knowing where to find information and how to get there.

Let me illustrate the point with a simple experiment. We present pairs of words to twelve-year-old children. One group is simply told to remember the pairs, that they will be asked to repeat them later. Another is told to remember them by producing a word or idea that will tie the pair together in a way that will make sense to them. A third group is given the mediators used by the second group when presented with the pairs to aid them in tying the pairs into working units.

The word pairs include such juxtapositions as "chair-forest," "sidewalk-square," and the like. One can distinguish three styles of mediators and children can be scaled in terms of their relative preference for each: *generic mediation* in which a pair is tied together by a superordinate idea: "chair and forest are both made of wood"; *thematic mediation* in which the two terms are imbedded in a theme or little story: "the lost child sat on a chair in the middle of the forest"; and *part-whole mediation* where "chairs are made from trees in the forest" is typical. Now, the chief result, as you would all predict, is that children who provide their own mediators do best – indeed, one time through a set of thirty pairs, they recover up to 95% of the second words when presented with the first ones of the pairs, whereas the uninstructed children reach a maximum of less than 50% recovered. Interestingly enough, children do best in recovering materials tied together by the form of mediator they most often use.

One can cite a myriad of findings to indicate that any organization of information that reduces the aggregate complexity of material by imbedding it into a cognitive structure a person has constructed will make that material more accessible for retrieval. In short, we may say that the process of memory, looked at from the retrieval side, is also a process of problem solving: how can material be "placed" in memory so that it can be got on demand?

We can take as a point of departure the example of the children who developed their own technique for relating the members of each word pair. You will recall that they did better than the children who were given by exposition the mediators they had developed. Let me suggest that in general, material that is organized in terms of a person's own interests and cognitive structures is material that has the best chance of being accessible in memory. That is to say, it is more likely to be placed along routes that are connected to one's own ways of intellectual travel.

In sum, the very attitudes and activities that characterize "figuring out" or "discovering" things for oneself also seem to have the effect of making material more readily accessible in memory.

Notes

1 Maimonides, *Guide for the Perplexed* (New York: Dover Publications, 1956).
2 I should also remark in passing that the two extremes also characterize concept attainment strategies as reported in *A Study of Thinking* by J. S. Bruner, J. J. Goodnow, G. A. Austin (New York: J. Wiley, 1956). Successive scanning illustrates well what is meant here by episodic empiricism; conservative focussing is an example of cumulative constructionism.
3 R. B. Zajonc (Personal communication, 1957).
4 J. S. Bruner and A. J. Caron, "Cognition, Anxiety, and Achievement in the Preadolescent," (Privately circulated, 1956).
5 R. W. White, "Motivation Reconsidered: The Concept of Competence," *Psychological Review*, LXVI (1959), 297–333.
6 Ibid., pp. 317–18.
7 L. S. Vigotsky, *Thinking and Speech* (Moscow, 1934).
8 A. L. Luria, "The Directive Function of Speech in Development and Dissolution," *Word*, XV (1959), 341–464.
9 Ibid., p. 12.
10 For an elaboration of the view expressed by Luria, the reader is referred to the forthcoming translation of L. S. Vigotsky's 1934 book being published by John Wiley and Sons and the Technology Press.
11 A. G. Ivanov-Smolensky, "Concerning the Study of the Joint Activity of the First and Second Signal Systems," *Journal of Higher Nervous Activity*, I (1951), 1.
12 N. D. Krasnogorsky, *Studies of Higher Nervous Activity in Animals and in Man*, Vol. I (Moscow, 1954).

13 K. W. Spence, "The Relation of Learning Theory to the Technique of Education," *Harvard Educational Review*, XXIX (1959), 84–95.

14 B. F. Skinner, *Verbal Behavior* (New York: Appleton-Century-Crofts, 1957).

15 N. Chomsky, *Syntactic Structure* (The Hague, The Netherlands: Mouton & Co., 1957).

16 L. Steffens, *Autobiography of Lincoln Steffens* (New York: Harcourt, Brace, 1931).

17 G. A. Miller, "The Magical Number Seven, Plus or Minus Two," *Psychological Review*, LXIII (1956), 81–97.

CHAPTER 7

THE COURSE OF COGNITIVE GROWTH

American Psychologist (1964) 19, 1–15

I shall take the view in what follows that the development of human intellectual functioning from infancy to such perfection as it may reach is shaped by a series of technological advances in the use of mind. Growth depends upon the mastery of techniques and cannot be understood without reference to such mastery. These techniques are not, in the main, inventions of the individuals who are "growing up;" they are, rather, skills transmitted with varying efficiency and success by the culture – language being a prime example. Cognitive growth, then, is in a major way from the outside in as well as from the inside out. Two matters will concern us. The first has to do with the techniques or technologies that aid showing human beings to represent in a manageable way the recurrent features of the complex environments in which they live. It is fruitful, I think, to distinguish three systems of processing information by which human beings construct models in their world: through action, through imagery, and through language. A second concern is with integration, the means whereby acts are organized into higher-order ensembles, making possible the use of larger and larger units of information for the solution of particular problems.

Let me first elucidate these two theoretical matters, and then turn to an examination of the research upon which they are based, much of it from the Center for Cognitive Studies at Harvard.

On the occasion of the One Hundredth Anniversary of the publication of Darwin's *The Origin of Species*, Washburn and Howell (1960) presented a paper at the Chicago Centennial celebration containing the following passage:

> It would now appear . . . that the large size of the brain in certain hominids was a relatively late development and that the brain evolved due to new selection pressures *after* pedalism and consequent upon the use of tools. The tool-using, ground-living, hunting way of life created the large human brain rather than a large brained man discovering certain new ways of life. [We] believe this conclusion is the most important result of the recent fossil hominid discoveries and is one which carries far-reaching implications for the interpretation of human behavior and its origins. . . . The important point is that size of brain, insofar as it can be measured by cranial capacity, has increased some threefold subsequent to the use and manufacture of implements. . . . The uniqueness of modern man is seen as the result of a technical-social life which tripled the size of the brain, reduced the face, and modified many other structures of the body
> (p. 49 f.)

This implies that the principal change in man over a long period of years – perhaps 500,000 thousand – has been alloplastic rather than autoplastic. That is to say, he has changed by linking himself with new, external implementation systems rather than by any conspicuous change in morphology – "evolution-by-prosthesis," as Weston La Barre (1954) puts it. The implement systems seem to have been of three general kinds – *amplifiers of human motor capacities* ranging from the cutting tool through the lever and wheel to the wide variety of modern devices; *amplifiers of sensory capacities* that include primitive devices such as smoke signaling and modern ones such as magnification and radar sensing, but also likely to include such "software" as those conventionalized perceptual shortcuts that can be applied to the redundant sensory environment; and finally *amplifiers of human ratiocinative capacities* of infinite variety ranging from language systems to myth and theory and explanation. All of these forms of amplification are in major or minor degree conventionalized and transmitted by the culture, the last of them probably the most since ratiocinative amplifiers involve symbol systems governed by rules that must, for effective use, be shared.

Any implement system, to be effective, must produce an appropriate internal counterpart, an appropriate skill necessary for organizing sensorimotor acts, for organizing percepts, and for organizing our thoughts in a way that matches them to the requirements of implement systems. These internal skills, represented genetically as capacities, are slowly selected in evolution. In the deepest sense, then, man can be described as a species that has become specialized by the use of technological implements. His selection and survival have depended upon a morphology and set of capacities that could be linked with the alloplastic devices that have made his later evolution possible. We move, perceive, and think in a fashion that depends upon techniques rather than upon wired-in arrangements in our nervous system.

Where representation of the environment is concerned, it too depends upon techniques that are learned – and these are precisely the techniques that serve to amplify our motor acts, our perceptions, and our ratiocinative activities. We know and respond to recurrent regularities in our environment by skilled and patterned acts, by conventionalized spatioqualitative imagery and selective perceptual organization, and through linguistic encoding which, as so many writers have remarked, places a selective lattice between us and the physical environment. In short, the capacities that have been shaped by our evolution as tool users are the ones that we rely upon in the primary task of representation – the nature of which we shall consider in more detail directly.

As for integration, it is a truism that there are very few single or simple adult acts that cannot be performed by a young child. In short, any more highly skilled activity can be decomposed into simpler components, each of which can be carried out by a less skilled operator. What higher skills require is that the component operations be combined. Maturation consists of an orchestration of these components into an integrated sequence. The "distractability," so-called, of much early behavior may reflect each act's lack of imbeddedness in what Miller, Galanter, and Pribram (1960), speak of as "plans." These integrated plans, in turn, reflect the routines and subroutines that one learns in the course of mastering the patterned nature of a social environment. So that integration, too, depends upon patterns that come from the outside in – an internalization of what Roger Barker (1963) has called environmental "behavior settings."

If we are to benefit from contact with recurrent regularities in the environment, we must represent them in some manner. To dismiss this problem as "mere memory" is to misunderstand it. For the most important thing about memory is not storage of past experience, but rather the retrieval of what is relevant in some usable form.

This depends upon how past experience is coded and processed so that it may indeed be relevant and usable in the present when needed. The end product of such a system of coding and processing is what we may speak of as a representation.

I shall call the three modes of representation mentioned earlier enactive representation, iconic representation, and symbolic representation. Their appearance in the life of the child is in that order each depending upon the previous one for its development, yet all of them remaining more or less intact throughout life – barring such early accidents as blindness or deafness or cortical injury. By enactive representation I mean a mode of representing past events through appropriate motor response. We cannot, for example, give an adequate description of familiar sidewalks or floor over which we habitually walk, nor do we have much of an image of what they are like. Yet we get about them without tripping or even looking much. Such segments of our environment – bicycle riding, tying knots, aspects of driving – get represented in our muscles, so to speak. Iconic representation summarizes events by the selective organization of percepts and of images, by the spatial temporal, and qualitative structures of the perceptual field and their transformed images. Images "stand for" perceptual events in the close but conventionally selective way that a picture stands for the object pictured. Finally, a symbol system represents things by design features that include remoteness and arbitrariness. A word neither points directly to its referent here and now, nor does it resemble it as a picture. The lexeme "Philadelphia" looks no more like the city so designated than does a nonsense syllable. The other property of language that is crucial is its productiveness in combination, far beyond what can be done with images or acts. "Philadelphia is a lavendar sachet in Grandmother's linen closet," or $(x + 2)^2 = x^3 + 4 + 4 = x(x + 4) + 4$.

An example or two of enactive representation underlines its importance in infancy and in disturbed functioning, while illustrating its limitations. Piaget (1954) provides us with an observation from the closing weeks of the first year of life. The child is playing with a rattle in his crib. The rattle drops over the side. The child moves his clenched hands before his face, opens it, looks for the rattle. Not finding it there, he moves his hand, closed again back to the edge of the crib, shakes it with movements like those he uses in shaking the rattle. There upon he moves his closed hand back toward his face, opens it, and looks. Again no rattle; and so he tries again. In several months, the child has benefited from experience to the degree that the rattle and action become separated. Whereas earlier he would not show signs of missing the rattle when it was removed unless he had begun reaching for it, now he cries and searches when the rattle is presented for a moment and hidden by a cover. He no longer repeats a movement to restore the rattle. In place of representation by action alone – where "existence" is defined by the compass of present action – it is now defined by an image that persists autonomously.

A second example is provided by the results of injury to the occipital and temporal cortex in man (Hanfmann, Rickers-Ovsiankina, and Goldstein, 1944). A patient is presented with a hard-boiled egg intact in its shell, and asked what it is. Holding it in his hand, he is embarrassed, for he cannot name it. He makes a motion as if to throw it and halts himself. Then he brings it to his mouth as if to bite it and stops before he gets there. He brings it to his ear and shakes it gently. He is puzzled. The experimenter takes the egg from him and cracks it on the table, handing it back. The patient then begins to peel the egg and announces what it is. He cannot identify objects without reference to the action he directs toward them.

The disadvantages of such a system are illustrated by Emerson's (1931) experiment in which children are told to place a ring on a board with seven rows and six columns of pegs, copying the position of a ring put on an identical board by the experimenter. Children ranging from 3 to 12 were examined in this experiment and in an extension of it carried out by Werner (1948). The child's board could be placed in various positions relative to the experimenter's: right next to it, 90 degrees rotated away from it, 180 degrees rotated, placed face to face with it so that the child has to turn full around to make his placement, etc. The older the child, the better his performance. But the younger children could do about as well as the oldest so long as they did not have to change their own position vis-a-vis the experimenter's board in order to make a match on their own board. The more they had to turn, the more difficult the task. They were clearly depending upon their bodily orientation toward the experimenter's board to guide them. When this orientation is disturbed by having to turn, they lose the position on the board. Older children succeed even when they must turn, either by the use of imagery that is invariant across bodily displacements, or, later, by specifying column and row of the experimenter's ring and carrying the symbolized self-instruction back to their own board. It is a limited world, the world of enactive representation.

We know little about the conditions necessary for the growth of imagery and iconic representation, or to what extent parental or environmental intervention affects it during the earliest years. In ordinary adult learning a certain amount of motoric skill and practice seems to be a necessary precondition for the development of a simultaneous image to represent the sequence of acts involved. If an adult subject is made to choose a path through a complex bank of toggle switches, he does not form an image of the path, according to Mandler (1962), until he has mastered and overpracticed the task by successive manipulation. Then, finally, he reports that an image of the path has developed and that he is now using it rather than groping his way through.

Our main concern in what follows is not with the growth of iconic representation, but with the transition from it to symbolic representation. For it is in the development of symbolic representation that one finds, perhaps, the greatest thicket of psychological problems. The puzzle begins when the child first achieves the use of productive grammar, usually late in the second year of life. Toward the end of the second year, the child is master of the single-word, agrammatical utterance, the - so-called holophrase. In the months following, there occurs a profound change in the use of language. Two classes of words appear – a pivot class and an open class – and the child launches forth on his career in combinatorial talking and, perhaps, thinking. Whereas before, lexemes like *allgone* and *mummy* and *sticky* and *bye-bye* were used singly, now, for example, *allgone* becomes a pivot word and is used in combination. Mother washes jam off the child's hands; he says *allgone sticky*. In the next days, if his speech is carefully followed (Braine, 1963), it will be apparent that he is trying out the limits of the pivot combinations, and one will even find constructions that have an extraordinary capacity for representing complex sequences – like *allgone bye-bye* after a visitor has departed. A recent and ingenious observation by Weir (1962) on her two and a half year-old son, recording his speech musings after he was in bed with lights out, indicates that at this stage there is a great deal of metalinguistic combinatorial play with words in which the child is exploring the limits of grammatical productiveness.

In effect, language provides a means, not only for representing experience, but also for transforming it. As Chomsky (1957) and Miller (1962) have both made clear in the last few years, the transformational rules of grammar provide a syntactic means of reworking the "realities" one has encountered. Not only, if you will, did the dog bite the man, but the man was bitten by the dog and perhaps the man was not bitten by the dog or was the man not bitten by the dog. The range of reworking that is made possible even by the three transformations of the passive, the negative, and the query is very striking indeed. Or the ordering device whereby the comparative mode makes it possible to connect what is *heavy* and what is *light* into the ordinal array of *heavy* and *less heavy* is again striking. Or, to take a final example, there is the discrimination that is made possible by the growth of attribute language such that the global dimension *big* and *little* can now be decomposed into *tall* and *short* on the one hand and *fat* and *skinny* on the other.

Once the child has succeeded in internalizing language as a cognitive instrument, it becomes possible for him to represent and systematically transform the regularities of experience with far greater flexibility and power than before. Interestingly enough, it is the recent Russian literature, particularly Vygotsky's (1962) book on language and thought and the work of his disciple, Luria (1961), and his students (Abramyan, 1958; Martsinovskaya, undated) that has highlighted these phenomena by calling attention to the so-called second-signal system which replaces classical conditioning with an internalized linguistic system for shaping and transforming experience itself.

If all these matters were not of such complexity and human import, I would apologize for taking so much time in speculation. We turn now to some new experiments designed to shed some light on the nature of representation and particularly upon the transition from its iconic to its symbolic form.

Let me begin with an experiment by Bruner and Kenney (1966) on the manner in which children between 5 and 7 handle a double classification matrix. The materials of the experiment are nine plastic glasses, arranged so that they vary in degrees of diameter and 3 degrees of height. They are set before the child initially, as in Figure 7.1, on a 3 × 3 grid marked on a large piece of cardboard. To acquaint

Matrix procedure

Scale in inches
0 1 2 3 4 5 6

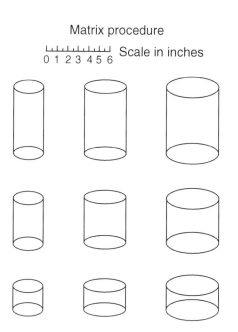

Figure 7.1 Array of glasses used in study of matrix ordering (Bruner and Kenney, 1966).

the child with the matrix, we first remove one, then two, and then three glasses from the matrix, asking the child to replace them. We also ask the children to describe how the glasses in the columns and rows are alike and how they differ. Then the glasses are scrambled and we ask the child to make something like what was there before by placing the glasses on the same grid that was used when the task was introduced. Now we scramble the glasses once more, but this time we place the glass that was formerly in the southwest corner of the grid in the southeast corner (it is the shortest, thinnest glass) and ask the child if he can make something like what was there before, leaving the one glass where we have just put it. That is the experiment.

The results can be quickly told. To begin with, there is no difference between ages 5, 6, and 7 either in terms of ability to replace glasses taken from the matrix or in building a matrix once it has been scrambled (but without the transposed glass). Virtually all the children succeed. Interestingly enough, *all* the children rebuild the matrix to match the original, almost as if they were copying what was there before. The only difference is that the older children are quicker.

Now compare the performance of the three ages in constructing the matrix with a single member transposed. Most of the 7-year-olds succeed in the transposed task, but hardly any of the youngest children. Figure 7.2 presents the results graphically. The youngest children seem to be dominated by an image of the original matrix. They try to put the transposed glass "back where it belongs," to rotate the cardboard so that "it will be like before," and sometimes they will start placing a few glasses neighboring the transposed glass correctly only to revert to the original arrangement. In several instances, 5- or 6-year-olds will simply try to reconstitute the old matrix, building right over the transposed glass. The 7-year-old, on the other hand, is more likely to pause, to treat the transposition as a problem, to talk

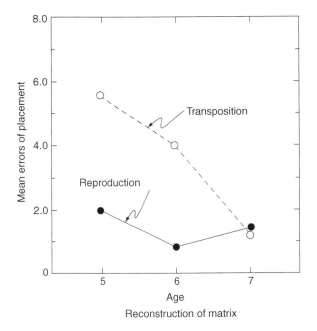

Figure 7.2 Mean number of errors made by children in reproducing and transposing a 3 × 3 matrix (Bruner and Kenney, 1966).

to himself about "where this should go." The relation of place and size is for him a problem that requires reckoning, not simply copying.

Now consider the language children use for describing the dimensions of the matrix. Recall that the children were asked how glasses in a row and in a column were alike and how they differed. Children answered in three distinctive linguistic modes. One was *dimensional*, singling out two ends of an attribute – for example, "That one is higher, and that one is shorter." A second was *global* in nature. Of glasses differing only in height the child says, "That one is bigger and that one is little." The same words could be used equally well for diameter or for nearly any other magnitude. Finally, there was *confounded* usage: "That one is tall and that one is little," where a dimensional term is used for one end of the continuum and a global term for the other. The children who used confounded descriptions had the most difficulty with the transposed matrix. Lumping all ages together, the children who used confounded descriptions were twice as likely to fail on the transposition task as those who used either dimensional or global terms (Figure 7.3). *But the language the children used had no relation whatsoever to their performance in reproducing the first untransposed matrix.* Inhelder and Sinclair[1] in a recent communication also report that confounded language of this kind is associated with failure on conservation tasks in children of the same age, a subject to which we shall turn shortly.

The findings of this experiment suggest two things. First, that children who use iconic representation are more highly sensitized to the spatial-qualitative organization of experience and less to the ordering principles governing such organization. They can recognize and reproduce, but cannot produce new structures based on rule. And second, there is a suspicion that the language they bring to bear on the task is insufficient as a tool for ordering. If these notions are correct, then certain

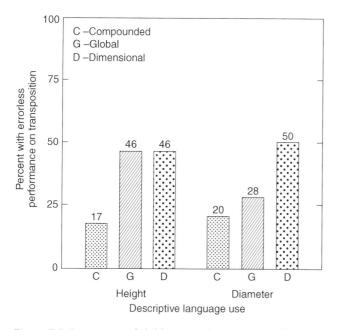

Figure 7.3 Percentage of children (aged 5–7) using different language patterns who reproduced transposed matrix errorlessly (Bruner and Kenney, 1966).

things should follow. For one thing, *improvement* in language should aid this type of problem solving. This remains to be investigated. But it is also reasonable to suppose that *activation* of language habits that the child has already mastered might improve performance as well – a hypothesis already suggested by the findings of Luria's students (e.g. Abramyan, 1958). Now, activation can be achieved by two means: One is by having the child "say" the description of something before him that he must deal with symbolically. The other is to take advantage of the remoteness of reference that is a feature of language, and have the child "say" his description in the absence of the things to be described. In this way, there would be less likelihood of a perceptual-iconic representation becoming dominant and inhibiting the operation of symbolic processes. An experiment by Françoise Frank (1966) illustrates this latter approach – the effects of saying before seeing.

Piaget and Inhelder (1962) have shown that if children between ages 4 and 7 are presented two identical beakers which they judge equally full of water, they will no longer consider the water equal if the contents of one of the beakers is now poured into a beaker that is either wider or thinner than the original. If the second beaker is thinner, they will say it has more to drink because the water is higher; if the second beaker is wider, they will say it has less because the water is lower. Comparable results can be obtained by pouring the contents of one glass into several smaller beakers (Figure 7.4). In Geneva terms, the child is not yet able to conserve liquid volume across transformations in its appearance. Consider how this behavior can be altered.

Françoise Frank first did the classic conservation tests to determine which children exhibited conservation and which did not. Her subjects were 4, 5, 6, and 7 years old. She then went on to other procedures, among which was the following (see Figure 7.5). Two standard beakers are partly filled so that the child judges them to contain equal amounts of water. A wider beaker of the same height is introduced and the three beakers are now, except for their tops, hidden by a screen. The experimenter pours from a standard beaker into the wider beaker. The

Figure 7.4 Two Geneva tests for conservation of liquid volume across transformations in its appearance (Piaget and Inhelder, 1962).

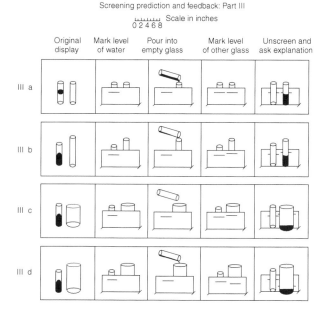

Figure 7.5 One procedure used in study of effect of language activation on conservation (Frank, 1966).

child, without seeing the water, is asked which has more to drink, or do they have the same amount, the standard or the wider beaker. The results are in Figure 7.6. In comparison with the unscreened pretest, there is a striking increase in correct equality judgments. Correct responses jump from 0% to 50% among the 4s, from 20% to 90% among the 5s, and from 50% to 100% among the 6s. With the screen present, most children justify their correct judgment by noting that "It's the same water," or "You only poured it."

Now the screen is removed. All the 4-year-olds change their minds. The perceptual display over-whelms them and they decide that the wider beaker has less water. But virtually all of the 5-year-olds stick to their judgment, often invoking the difference between appearance and reality – "It looks like more to drink, but it is only the same because it is the same water and it was only poured from there to there," to quote one typical 5-year-old. And all of the 6s and all the 7s stick to their judgment. Now, some minutes later, Frank does a posttest on the children using a tall thin beaker along with the standard ones, and no screen, of course. The 4s are unaffected by their prior experience: None of them is able to grasp the idea of invariant quantity in the new task. With the 5s, instead of 20% showing conservation, as in the pretest, 70% do. With both 6s and 7s, conservation increases from 50% to 90% (Figure 7.7). I should mention that control groups doing just a pretest and posttest show no significant improvement in performance.

A related experiment of Nair's (1963) explores the arguments children use when they solve a conservation task correctly and when they do not. Her subjects were all 5-year-olds. She transferred water from one rectangular clear plastic tank to another that was both longer and wider than the first. Ordinarily, a 5-year-old will say there is less water in the second tank. The water is, of course, lower in the

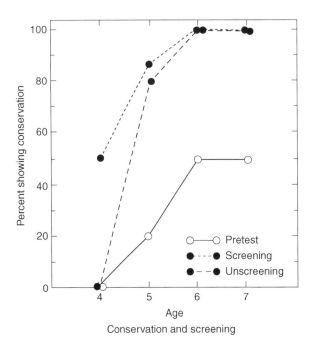

Figure 7.6 Percentage of children showing conservation of liquid volume before and during screening and upon unscreening of the displays (Frank, 1966).

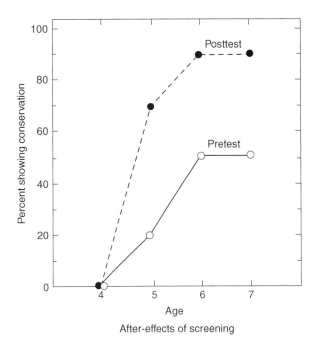

Figure 7.7 Percentage of children showing conservation of liquid volume in identical pretest and posttest run after completion of experiment (Frank, 1966).

second tank. She had a toy duck swimming in the first container, and when the water was poured into the new container, she told the child that "The duck was taking his water with him."

Three kinds of arguments were set forth by the children to support their judgments. One is perceptual – having to do with the height, width, or apparent "bigness" of the water. A second type has to do with action: The duck took the water along, or the water was only poured. A third one, "transformational" argument, invokes the reversibility principle: If you poured the water back into the first container, it would look the same again.[2] Of the children who thought the water was not equal in amount after pouring, 15% used nonperceptual arguments to justify their judgment. Of those who recognized the equality of the water, two-thirds used nonperceptual arguments. It is plain that if a child is to succeed in the conservation task, he must have some internalized verbal formula that shields him from the overpowering appearance of the visual displays much as in the Frank experiment. The explanations of the children who lacked conservation suggest how strongly oriented they were to the visual appearance of the displays they had to deal with.

Consider now another experiment by Bruner and Kenney (1966) also designed to explore the border between iconic and symbolic representation. Children aged 5, 6, and 7 were asked to say which of two glasses in a pair was fuller and which emptier. "Fullness" is an interesting concept to work with, for it involves in its very definition a ratio or proportion between the volume of a container and the volume of a substance contained. It is difficult for the iconically oriented child to see a half-full barrel and a half-filled thimble as equally full, since the former looms larger in every one of the attributes that might be perceptually associated with volume. It is like the old riddle of which is heavier, a pound of lead or a pound of feathers. To make a correct judgment of fullness or emptiness, the child must use a symbolic operation, somewhat like computing a ratio, and resist the temptation to use perceptual appearance – that is, unless he finds some happy heuristic to save him the labor of such a computation. Figure 7.8 contains the 11 pairs of glasses used, and they were selected with a certain malice aforethought.

There are four types of pairs. In Type I (Displays 4, 9a, and 9b), the glasses are of unequal volume, but equally, though fractionally, full. In Type II (Displays 2, 7a, and 7b) again the glasses are of unequal volume, but they are completely full. Type III (Displays 3, 8a, and 8b) consists of two glasses of unequal volume, one filled and the other part filled. Type IV consists of identical glasses, in one case equally filled, in another unequally (Displays 1 and 5).

All the children in the age range we have studied use pretty much the same criteria for judging *fullness*, and these criteria are based on directly observable sensory indices rather than upon proportion. That glass is judged fuller that has the greater apparent volume of water, and the favored indication of greater volume is water level; or where that is equated, then width of glass will do; and when width and water level are the same, then height of glass will prevail. But now consider the judgments made by the three age groups with respect to which glass in each pair is *emptier*. The older children have developed an interesting consistency based on an appreciation of the complementary relation of filled and empty space – albeit an incorrect one. For them "emptier" means the glass that has the largest apparent volume of unfilled space, just as "fuller" meant the glass that had the largest volume of filled space. In consequence, their responses seem logically contradictory. For the glass that is judged fuller also turns out to be the glass that is judged emptier – given a large glass and a small glass, both half full. The younger children, on the

Ratio procedure

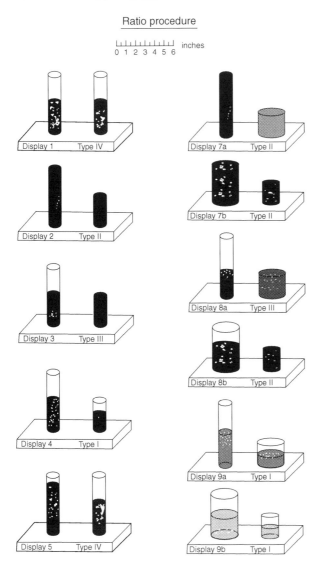

Figure 7.8 Eleven pairs of glasses to be judged in terms of which glass is fuller and which emptier (Bruner and Kenney, in press).

other hand, equate emptiness with "littleness": That glass is emptier that gives the impression of being smaller in volume of liquid. If we take the three pairs of glasses of Type I (unequal volumes, half filled) we can see how the judgments typically distribute themselves. Consider only the errors. The glass with the larger volume of empty space is called emptier by 27% of the erring 5-year-olds, by 53% of the erring 6-year-olds, and by 72% of erring 7-year-olds. But, the glass with the smallest volume of water is called emptier by 73% of the 5-year-olds who err, 47% of the 6s, and only 28% of the 7s Table 7.1. When the children are asked for their reasons for judging one glass as emptier, there is further confirmation: Most of the

Table 7.1 Percentage of erroneous judgments of which of two glasses is emptier based on two criteria for defining the concept

Criterion for "emptier" judgment	Age		
	5	6	7
Greater empty space	27%	53%	72%
Smaller volume of liquid	73%	47%	28%
	100%	100%	100%
Percentage correct	9%	8%	17%
N =	30	30	30

Note
Criteria are greater volume of empty space and lesser volume of water. From Bruner and Kenney (1966).

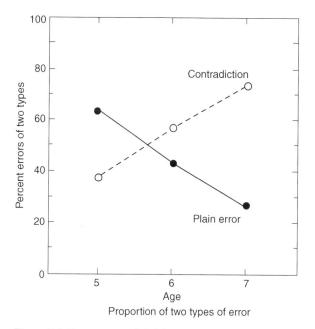

Proportion of two types of error

Figure 7.9 Percentage of children at three ages who make contradictory and plain errors in judging which of two glasses is fuller and which emptier. (A contradictory error is calling the same glass both fuller or emptier or calling them equally full but not equally empty or vice versa. A plain error is calling one glass fuller and the other emptier, lot incorrectly. From Bruner and Kenney, 1966.)

younger children justify it by pointing to "littleness" or "less water" or some other aspect of diminutiveness. And most of the older children justify their judgments of emptiness by reference to the amount of empty space in the vessel.

The result of all this is, of course, that the "logical structure" of the older children seems to go increasingly awry. But surely, though Figure 7.9 shows that contradictory errors steadily increase with age (calling the same glass fuller and emptier or equally full but not equally empty or vice versa), the contradiction is a by-product of the method of dealing with attributes. How shall we interpret these findings? – Let me suggest that what is involved is a translation difficulty in going from the perceptual or iconic realm to the symbolic. If you ask children of this age whether something can be fuller and also emptier, they will smile and think that you are playing riddles. They are aware of the contrastive nature of the two terms. Indeed, even the very young child has a good working language for the two poles of the contrast: "all gone" for completely empty and "spill" or "tippy top" for completely full. Recall too that from 5 to 7, there is perfect performance in judging which of two identical beakers is fuller and emptier. The difference between the younger and the older child is in the number of attributes that are being attended to in situations involving fullness and emptiness: The younger child is attending to one – the volume of water; the older to two – the volume of filled space and the volume of empty space. The young child is applying a single contrast pair – full-empty – to a single feature of the situation. The older child can attend to two features, but he does not yet have the means for relating them to a third, the volume of the container per se. To do so involves being able to deal with a relation in the perceptual field that does not have a "point-at-able" or ostensive definition. Once the third term is introduced – the volume of the glass – then the symbolic concept of proportion can come to "stand for" something that is not present perceptually. The older child is on the way to achieving the insight, in spite of his contradictions. And, interestingly enough, if we count the number of children who justify their judgments of fuller and emptier by pointing to *several* rather than a single attribute, we find that the proportion triples in both cases between age 5 and age 7. The older child, it would seem, is ordering his perceptual world in such a way that, shortly, he will be able to apply concepts of relationship that are not dependent upon simple ostensive definition. As he moves toward this more powerful "technology of reckoning," he is led into errors that seem to be contradictory. What is particularly telltale is the fact, for example, that in the Type III displays, younger children sometimes seem to find the judgment easier than older children – pointing to the fuller by placing their finger on the rim of the full member and pointing to the emptier with the remark that "It is not to the top." The older child (and virtually never the younger one) gets all involved in the judgment of "fuller by apparent filled volume" and then equally involved in the judgment of "emptier by apparent empty volume" (Table 7.2) and such are his efforts that he fails to note his contradiction when dealing with a pair like Display 8b.

Turn now to a quite different experimental procedure that deals with the related concept of equivalence – how seemingly different objects are grouped into equivalence classes. In the two experiments to be cited, one by Olver (1961), the other by Rigney (1962), children are given words or pictures to sort into groups or to characterize in terms of how they are alike. The two sets of results, one for words, the other for pictures, obtained for children between 6 and 14, can be summarized together.

Table 7.2 Percentage of children who justify judgments of "fuller" and "emptier" by mentioning more than a single attribute

Age	"Fuller" judgments (%)	"Emptier" judgments (%)	N
5	7.2	4.1	30
6	15.6	9.3	30
7	22.2	15.6	30

One may distinguish two aspects of grouping – the first has to do with the features or attributes that children use as a criterion for grouping objects: *perceptual features* (the color, size, pattern, etc.), *arbitrary functional features* (what I can do with the objects regardless of their usual use: You can make noise with a newspaper by crumpling it and with a book by slamming it shut, etc.), *appropriate functional features* (potato, peach, banana, and milk are characterized "You can eat them"). But grouping behavior can also be characterized in terms of the syntactical structure of the equivalence sets that the child develops. There are, first, what Vygotsky (1962) has called *heaps*: collections put together in an arbitrary way simply because the child has decided to put them together that way. Then there are *complexes*: The various members of a complex are included in the class in accordance with a rule that does not account uniformly for the inclusion of all the members. Edge matching is one such rule: Each object is grouped into a class on the basis of its similarity with a neighboring object. Yet no two neighboring pieces may be joined by the same similarity. Another type of complexive grouping is thematic: Here objects are put together by virtue of participating in a sentence or a little story. More sophisticated is a key ring in which one organizing object is related to all others but none of those to each other. And finally, considerably more sophisticated than heaps and complexes, there are *superordinate concepts*, in which one universal rule of inclusion accounts for all the objects in the set – all men and women over 21 are included in the class of voters provided they meet certain residence requirements.

The pattern of growth is revealing of many of the trends we have already discussed, and provides in addition a new clue. Consider first the attributes or features of objects that children at different ages use as a basis for forming equivalence groups. As Figure 7.10 indicates, the youngest children rely more heavily on perceptual

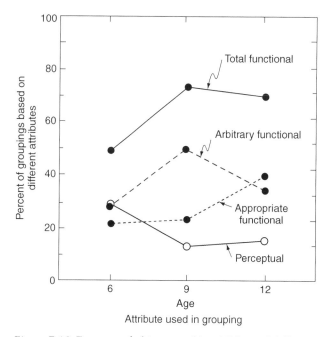

Figure 7.10 Features of objects used by children of different ages as a basis for placing the objects in equivalence groups (Olver, 1961).

attributes than do the others. As they grow older, grouping comes to depend increasingly upon the functional properties of things – but the transitional phase is worth some attention, for it raises anew the issue of the significance of egocentrism. For the first functional groupings to appear are of an arbitrary type – what "I" or "you" can do to objects that renders them alike, rather than what is the conventional use or function to which objects can be put. During this stage of "egocentric functionalism," there is a corresponding rise in the use of first- and second-person personal pronouns: "I can do thus and so to this object; I can do the same to this one," etc. Gradually, with increasing maturity the child shifts to an appropriate and less egocentric form of using functional groupings. The shift from perceptual to functional groupings is accompanied by a corresponding shift in the syntactical structure of the groups formed. Complexive groupings steadily windle; superordinate groupings rise, until the latter almost replace the former in late adolescence. It is difficult to tell which is the pacemaker in this growth – syntax or the semantic basis of grouping.

Rigney reports one other matter of some interest. Her young subjects formed groups of any size they wished, choosing pictures from a display board of several dozen little water colors. She observed that the most perceptually based groups and the ones most often based on complexive grouping principles were pairs. A count of these revealed that 61% of all the groups made by 6-year-olds were such pairs, 36% of those made by 8-year-olds, and only 25% of the groupings of 11-year-olds (Figure 7.11).

On the surface, this set of findings – Olver's and Rigney's alike – seems to point more to the decline of a preference for perceptual and iconic ways of dealing with objects and events, particularly with their grouping. But closer inspection suggests still another factor that is operating. In both cases, there is evidence of the

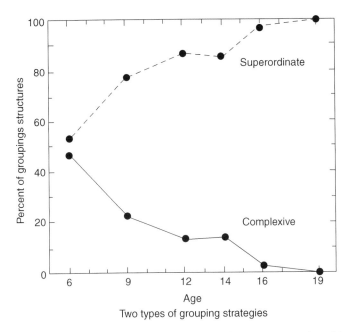

Figure 7.11 The use of two rules of equivalence grouping found in children of different ages (Olver, 1961).

development of hierarchical structure and rules for including objects in super-ordinate hierarchies. Hierarchical classification is surely one of the most evident properties of the structure of language – hierarchical grouping that goes beyond mere perceptual inclusion. Complexive structures of the kind described earlier are much more dominated by the sorts of associative principles by which the appearance of objects leads to their spontaneous grouping in terms of similarity or contiguity. As language becomes more internalized, more guiding as a set of rules for organizing events, there is a shift from the associative principles that operate in classical perceptual organization to the increasingly abstract rules for grouping events by the principles of inclusion, exclusion, and overlap, the most basic characteristics of any hierarchical system.

We have said that cognitive growth consists in part in the development of systems of representation as means for dealing with information. The growing child begins with a strong reliance upon learned action patterns to represent the world around him. In time, there is added to this technology a means for simultanizing regularities in experience into images that stand for events in the way that pictures do. And to this is finally added a technology of translating experience into a symbol system that can be operated upon by rules of transformation that greatly increase the possible range of problem solving. One of the effects of this development, or possibly one of its causes, is the power for organizing acts of information processing into more integrated and long-range problem solving efforts. To this matter we turn next.

Consider in rapid succession three related experiments. All of them point, I think, to the same conclusion.

The first is by Huttenlocher (1966), a strikingly simple study, performed with children between the ages of 6 and 12. Two light switches are before the child; each can be in one of two positions. A light bulb is also visible. The child is asked to tell, on the basis of turning only one switch, what turns the light on. There are four ways in which the presentations are made. In the first, the light is off initially and when the child turns a switch, the light comes on. In the second, the light is on and when the child turns a switch, it goes off. In the third, the light is on and when the child turns a switch, it stays on. In the fourth and final condition, the light is off and when the child turns a switch, it stays off. Now what is intriguing about this arrangement is that there are different numbers of inductive steps required to make a correct inference in each task. The simplest condition is the off-on case. The position to which the switch has just been moved is responsible for the light going on. Intermediate difficulty should be experienced with the on-off condition. In the on-off case, two connected inferences are required: The present position achieved is rejected and the original position of the switch that has been turned is responsible for lighting the bulb. An even larger number of consecutive acts is required for success in the on-on case: The present position of the turned switch is rejected, the original position as well and the present position of the *other* switch is responsible. The off-off case requires four steps: rejecting the present position of the turned switch, its original position, and the present position of the other switch, finally accepting the alternative position of the unturned switch. The natures of the individual steps are all the same. Success in the more complex cases depends upon being able to integrate them consecutively.

Huttenlocher's results show that the 6-year-olds are just as capable as their elders of performing the elementary operation involved in the one-step case: the on-off display. They, like the 9s and 12s, make nearly perfect scores. But in general, the more inferential steps the 6-year-old must make, the poorer his performance.

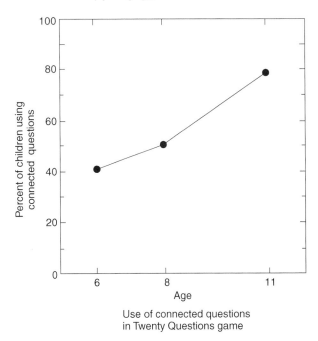

Use of connected questions
in Twenty Questions game

Figure 7.12 The proportion of children at different ages who use connected questions
in a Twenty Questions game (Mosher, 1962).

By age 12, on the other hand, there is an insignificant difference between the tasks requiring one, two, three, or four connected inferences.

An experiment by Mosher (1962) underlines the same point. He was concerned with the strategies used by children from 6 to 11 for getting information in the game of Twenty Questions. They were to find out by "yes-no" questions what caused a car to go off the road and hit a tree. One may distinguish between connected constraint-locating questions ("Was it night-time?" followed up appropriately) and direct hypothesis-testing questions ("Did a bee fly in the window and sting the man on the eye and make him go off the road and hit the tree?"). From 6 to 11, more and more children use constraint-locating, connected questioning (Figure 7.12). Let me quote from Mosher's account.

> We have asked children...after they have played their games, to tell us which of two questions they would rather have the answer to, if they were playing the games again – one of them a typical constraint-seeking question ("Was there anything wrong with the man?") and the other a typical discrete test of an hypothesis ("Did the man have a heart attack?"). All the eleven-year-olds and all the eight-year-olds choose the constraint-seeking question, but only 29% of the six-year-olds do
>
> (p. 6)

The questions of the younger children are all one-step substitutes for direct sense experience. They are looking for knowledge by single questions that provide the answer in a finished form. When they succeed they do so by a lucky question that hits an immediate, perceptible cause. When the older child receives a "yes" answer to one of his constraint-locating questions, he most often follows up by asking another. When, on the rare occasions that a younger child asks a constraint question and it is answered "yes," he almost invariably follows it up with a specific question to test a concrete hypothesis. The older child can accrete his information in a structure governed by consecutive inference. The younger child cannot.

Potter's (1966) study of the development of perceptual recognition bears on the same point. Ordinary colored photographs of familiar scenes are presented to children between 6 and 12, the pictures coming gradually into focus. Let me sum up one part of the results very briefly. Six-year-olds produce an abundance of hypotheses. But they rarely try to match new hypotheses to previous ones. "There is a big tower in the middle and a road over there and a big ice cream cone through the middle of the tower and a pumpkin on top." It is like a random collage. The 9-year-old's torrent of hypotheses, on the other hand, shows a sense of consistency about what is likely to appear with what. Things are in a context of likelihood, a frame of reference that demands internal consistency. Something is seen as a merry-go-round, and the child then restricts later hypotheses to the other things to be found in an amusement park. The adolescent operates under even more highly organized sequential constraints: He occasionally develops his initial hypotheses from what is implied by the properties of the picture, almost by intersection – "It is red and shiny and metallic: It must be a coffee-pot." Once such constraints are established, the order of hypotheses reflects even more the need to build up a consistent world of objects – even to the point of failing to recognize things that do not fit it.

What shall we make of these three sets of findings – that older children are able to cumulate information by asking questions in a directed sequence leading to a final goal, and that they are capable of recognizing visual displays in a manner governed by a dominating frame of reference that transcends momentary and isolated bits of information? Several points seem apparent. The first is that as children mature, they are able to use indirect information based on forms of information processing other than the act of pointing to what is immediately present. They seem, in short, to make remote reference to states and constraints that are not given by the immediate situation, to go beyond the information given. Second, and this is a matter that has already been discussed, they seem to be able to cumulate information into a structure that can be operated upon by rules that transcend simple association by similarity and contiguity. In the case of Twenty Questions, the rule is best described as implication – that knowing one thing implies certain other things and eliminates still others. In the experiments with the light switches, it is that if the present state does not produce the effect, then there is a system for tracing back to the other states that cause the light to go on. Where perceptual recognition is concerned, the rule is that a piece of information from one part of the display implies what other parts might be. The child, in sum, is translating redundancy into a manipulable model of the environment that is governed by rules of implication. It is this model of the environment that permits him to go beyond the information before him. I would suggest that it is this new array of cognitive equipment that permits the child to transcend momentaneity, to integrate longer sequences of events.

Let me urge, moreover, that such a system of processing environmental events depends upon the translation of experience into symbolic form. Such a translation is necessary in order for there to be the kind of remoteness of reference as is required when one deals with indirect information. To transcend the immediately perceptual, to get beyond what is vividly present to a more extended model of the environment, the child needs a system that permits him to deal with the nonpresent, with things that are remote in space, qualitative similarity, and time, from the present situation. Hockett (1959), in describing the design features of language includes this feature as crucial. He is referring to human speech as a system of communication. The same point can be made about language as an instrument of thought. That humans have the *capacity* for using speech in this way is only part of the point. What is critical is that the capacity is *not* used until it is coupled with the technology of language in the cognitive operations of the child.

The same can be said for the models of the environment that the child constructs to go beyond present information. This is not to say that nonverbal animals cannot make inferences that go beyond the present stimulus: Anticipatory activity is the rule in vertebrates. But the models that the growing child constructs seem not to be anticipatory, or inferential, or probabilistic-frequency models. They seem to be governed by rules that can more properly be called syntactical rather than associative.

My major concern has been to examine afresh the nature of intellectual growth. The account has surely done violence to the richness of the subject. It seems to me that growth depends upon the emergence of two forms of competence. Children, as they grow, must acquire ways of representing the recurrent regularities in their environment, and they must transcend the momentary by developing ways of linking past to present to future – representation and integration. I have suggested that we can conceive of growth in both of these domains as the emergence of new technologies for the unlocking and amplification of human intellectual powers. Like the growth of technology, the growth of intellect is not smoothly monotonic. Rather, it moves forward in spurts as innovations are adopted. Most of the innovations are transmitted to the child in some prototypic form by agents of the culture: ways of responding, ways of looking and imaging, and most important, ways of translating what one has encountered into language.

I have relied heavily in this account on the successive emergence of action, image, and word as the vehicles of representation, a reliance based both upon our observations and upon modern readings of man's alloplastic evolution. Our attention has been directed largely to the transition between iconic and symbolic representation.

In children between 4 and 12 language comes to play an increasingly powerful role as an implement of knowing. Through simple experiments, I have tried to show how language shapes, augments, and even supercedes the child's earlier modes of processing information. Translation of experience into symbolic form, with its attendant means of achieving remote reference, transformation, and combination, opens up realms of intellectual possibility that are orders of magnitude beyond the most powerful image forming system.

What of the integration of intellectual activity into more coherent and interconnected acts? It has been the fashion, since Freud, to see delay of gratification as the principal dynamism behind this development – from primary process to secondary process, or from assimilation to accommodation, as Piaget would put it today. Without intending to question the depth of this insight, let me suggest that delay of immediate gratification, the ability to go beyond the moment, also depends upon techniques, and again they are techniques of representation. Perhaps representation exclusively by imagery and perceptual organization has built into it one basic operation that ties it to the immediate present. It is the operation of pointing – ostensiveness, as logicians call it. (This is not to say that highly evolved images do not go beyond immediate time and given place. Maps and flow charts are iconic in nature, but they are images that translate prior linguistic and mathematical renderings into a visual form.) Iconic representation, in the beginning, is build upon a perceptual organization that is tied to the "point-at-able" spatioqualitative properties of events. I have suggested that, for all its limitations, such representation is an achievement beyond the earlier stage where percepts are not autonomous of action. But so long as perceptual representation dominates, it is difficult to develop higher-order techniques for processing information by consecutive inferential steps that take one beyond what can be pointed at.

Once language becomes a medium for the translation of experience, there is a progressive release from immediacy. For language, as we have commented, has the new and powerful features of remoteness and arbitrariness: It permits productive, combinatorial operations in the *absence* of what is represented. With this achievement, the child can delay gratification by virtue of representing to himself what lies beyond the present, what other possibilities exist beyond the clue that is under his nose. The child may be *ready* for delay of gratification, but he is no more able to bring it off than somebody ready to build a house, save that he has not yet heard of tools.

The discussion leaves two obvious questions begging. What of the integration of behavior in organisms without language? And how does language become internalized as a vehicle for organizing experience? The first question has to be answered briefly and somewhat cryptically. Wherever intergrated behavior has been studied – as in Lehrman's (1955) careful work on integrated instinctive patterns in the ringdove, it has turned out that a sustaining external stimulus was needed to keep the highly integrated behavior going. The best way to control behavior in subhuman species is to control the stimulus situation. Surely this is the lesson of Lashley's (1938) classic account of instinctive behavior. Where animal learning is concerned, particularly in the primates, there is, to be sure, considerable plasticity. But it too depends upon the development of complex forms of stimulus substitution and organization – as in Klüver's (1933) work on equivalence reactions in monkeys. If it should seem that I am urging that the growth of symbolic functioning links a unique set of powers to man's capacity, the appearance is quite as should be.

As for how language becomes internalized as a program for ordering experience, I join those who despair for an answer. My speculation, for whatever it is worth, is that the process of internalization depends upon interaction with others, upon the need to develop corresponding categories and transformations for communal action. It is the need for cognitive coin that can be exchanged with those on whom we depend. What Roger Brown (1958) has called the Original Word Game ends up by being the Human Thinking Game.

If I have seemed to underemphasize the importance of inner capacities – for example, the capacity *for* language or *for* imagery – it is because I believe that this part of the story is given by the nature of man's evolution. What is significant about the growth of mind in the child is to what degree it depends not upon capacity but upon the unlocking of capacity by techniques that come from exposure to the specialized environment of a culture. Romantic clichés, like "the veneer of culture" or "natural man," are as misleading if not as damaging as the view that the course of human development can be viewed independently of the educational process we arrange to make that development possible.

Acknowledgment

The assistance of R. R. Olver and Blythe Clinchy in the preparation of this chapter is gratefully acknowledged.

Notes

1   Bärbel Inhelder and Mimi Sinclair, personal communication, 1963.
2   Not one of the 40 children who participated in this experiment used the compensation argument – that though the water was lower it was correspondingly wider and was, therefore, the same amount of water. This type of reasoning by compensation is said by Piaget and Inhelder (1962) to be the basis of conservation.

References

Abramyan, L. A. Organization of the voluntary activity of the child with the help of verbal instruction. Unpublished diploma thesis, Moscow University, 1958. Cited by A. R. Luria, *The role of speech in the regulation of normal and abnormal behavior*. New York: Liveright, 1961.

Barker, R. G. On the nature of the environment. Kurt Lewin Memorial Address presented at American Psychological Association, Philadelphia, September 1963.

Braine, M. D. On learning the grammatical order of words. *Psychol. Rev.*, 1963, 70, 323–348.

Brown, R. *Words and things.* Glencoe, IL: Free Press, 1958.

Bruner, J. S. and Kenney, Helen. The development of the concepts of order and proportion in children. In J. S. Bruner, *Studies in cognitive growth*. New York: Wiley, 1966.

Chomsky, N. *Syntactic structures.* S'Gravenhage, Netherlands: Mouton, 1957.

Emerson, L. L. The effect of bodily orientation upon the young child's memory for position of objects. *Child Develpm.*, 1931, 2, 125–142.

Frank, Françoise. Perception and language in conservation. In J. S. Bruner, *Studies in cognitive growth*. New York: Wiley, 1966.

Hanfmann, Eugenia, Rickers-Ovsiankina, Maria, and Goldstein, K. Case Lanuti: Extreme concretization of behavior due to damage of the brain cortex. *Psychol. Monogr.*, 1944, 57(4, Whole No. 264).

Hockett, C. F. Animal "languages" and human language. In J. N. Spuhler, *The evolution of man's capacity for culture*. Detroit: Wayne State Univer. Press, 1959. pp. 32–39.

Huttenlocher, Janellen. The growth of conceptual strategies. In J. S. Bruner, *Studies in cognitive growth*. New York: Wiley, 1966.

Klüver, H. *Behavior mechanisms in monkeys.* Chicago, IL: Univer. Chicago Press, 1933.

La Barre, W. *The human animal.* Chicago, IL: Univer. Chicago Press, 1954.

Lashley, K. S. Experimental analysis of instinctive behavior. *Psychol. Rev.*, 1938, 45, 445–472.

Lehrman, D. S. The physiological basis of parental feeding behavior in the ring dove (*Streptopelia risoria*). *Behavior*, 1955, 7, 241–286.

Luria, A. R. *The role of speech in the regulation of normal and abnormal behavior.* New York: Liveright, 1961.

Mandler, G. From association to structure. *Psychol. Rev.*, 1962, 69, 415–427.

Martsinovskaya, E. N. Research into the reflective and regulatory role of the second signalling system of preschool age. Collected papers of the Department of Psychology, Moscow University, undated. Cited by A. R. Luria, *The role of speech in the regulation of normal and abnormal behavior*. New York: Liveright, 1961.

Miller, G. A. Some psychological studies of grammar. *Amer. Psychologist*, 1962, 17, 748–762.

Miller, G. A., Galanter, E., and Pribram, K. H. *Plans and the structure of behavior.* New York: Holt, 1960.

Mosher, F. A. Strategies for information gathering. Paper read at Eastern Psychological Association, Atlantic City, NJ, April 1962.

Nair, Patricia. An experiment in conservation. In Center for Cognitive Studies, *Annual Report*. Cambridge, MA: Author, 1963.

Olver, Rose R. A developmental study of cognitive equivalence. Unpublished doctoral dissertation, Radcliffe College, 1961.

Piaget, J. *The construction of reality in the child.* (Trans. by Margaret Cook) New York: Basic Books, 1954.

Piaget, J. and Inhelder, Bärbel. *Le développement des quantités physiques chez l'enfant.* (2nd rev. ed.) Neuchâtel, Switzerland: Delachaux & Niestlé, 1962.

Potter, Mary C. The growth of perceptual recognition. In J. S. Bruner, *Studies in cognitive growth.* New York: Wiley, 1966.

Rigney, Joan C. A developmental study of cognitive equivalence transformations and their use in the acquisition and processing of information. Unpublished honors thesis, Radcliffe College, Department of Social Relations, 1962.

Vygotsky, L. S. *Thought and language.* (Ed. and trans. by Eugenia Hanfmann and Gertrude Vakar) New York: Wiley, 1962.

Washburn, S. L. and Howell, F. C. Human evolution and culture. In S. Tax, *The evolution of man.* Vol. 2. Chicago, IL: Univer. Chicago Press, 1960.

Weir, Ruth H. *Language in the crib.* The Hague: Mouton, 1962.

Werner, H. *Comparative psychology of mental development.* (Rev. ed.) Chicago, IL: Follett, 1948.

CHAPTER 8

MAN
A course of study

ESI Quarterly Report (Spring–Summer 1965) 3–13,
Educational Services Incorporated

There is a dilemma in describing a course of study.

One must begin by setting forth the intellectual substance of what is to be taught, else there can be no sense of what challenges and shapes the curiosity of the student. Yet the moment one succumbs to the temptation to "get across" the subject, at that moment the ingredient of pedagogy is in jeopardy. For it is only in a trivial sense that one gives a course to "get something across," merely to impart information. There are better means to that end than teaching. Unless the learner also masters himself, disciplines his taste, and deepens his view of the world, the "something" that is got across is hardly worth the effort of transmission.

The more "elementary" a course and the younger its students, the more serious must be its pedagogical aim of forming the intellectual powers of those whom it serves. It is as important to justify a good mathematics course by the intellectual discipline it provides or the honesty it promotes as by the mathematics it transmits. Indeed, neither can be accomplished without the other.

We begin this article with an account of the substance or structure of a course in "social studies" now in the process of construction. A discussion of pedagogy follows. The aim of the exercise is to write a transitional first draft of the course, a common focus for those of us who have been trying to compose the course, trying to teach parts of it to children in Grade V. If the exercise is finally successful, we shall end with a completed course – with the materials, guides, films, and the other things that must be in the student's hands and on the teacher's shelf. There will be drafts in between. The exercise, we hope, will allow us to be clearer about what we are doing. In the final section we shall consider how we propose to get from a first draft such as this to a course that is ready for teaching.

Structure of the course

The content of the course is man: his nature as a species, the forces that shaped and continue to shape his humanity. Three questions recur throughout:

What is human about human beings?
How did they get that way?
How can they be made more so?

We seek exercises and materials through which our pupils can learn wherein man is distinctive in his adaptation to the world, and wherein there is discernible continuity between him and his animal forbears. For man represents that crucial point in evolution where adaptation is achieved by the vehicle of culture and only in a minor way by further changes in his morphology. Yet there are chemical tides that run in his blood that are as ancient as the reptiles. We make every effort at the outset to *tell* the children where we hope to travel with them. Yet little of such recounting gets through. It is much more useful, we have found, to pose the three questions directly to the children so that their own views can be brought into the open and so that they can establish some points of view of their own.

In pursuit of our questions we shall explore five matters, each closely associated with the evolution of man as a species, each defining at once the distinctiveness of man and his potentiality for further evolution. The five great humanizing forces are, of course, tool-making, language, social organization, the management of man's prolonged childhood, and man's urge to explain. It has been our first lesson in teaching that no pupil, however eager, can appreciate the relevance of, say, tool-making in human evolution without first grasping the fundamental concept of a tool, or what a language is, or a myth, or social organization. These are not obvious matters. So we are involved in teaching not only the role of tools or language in the emergence of man, but as a necessary precondition for doing so, setting forth the fundamentals of linguistics or the theory of tools. And it is as often the case as not that (as in the case of the "theory of tools") we must solve a formidable intellectual problem ourselves in order to be able to help our pupils do the same.

While one readily singles out these five massive contributors to man's humanization, under no circumstances can they be put into airtight compartments. Human kinship is distinctively different from primate mating patterns precisely because it is classificatory and rests on man's ability to use language. Or, if you will, tool use enhances the division of labor in a society which in turn affects kinship. And language itself is more clearly appreciated by reference to its acquisition in the uniquely human interaction between child and parent. Obviously, the nature of man's world view, whether formulated in myth or in science, depends upon, and is constrained by, the nature of human language. So while each domain can be treated as a separate set of ideas, as we shall see, success in teaching depends upon making it possible for children to have a sense of their interaction.

Language

Teaching the essentials of linguistics to children in the elementary grades has limits, but they are wider than we had expected. There are certain pedagogic precautions to be respected if ten-year-olds are to be captivated by the subject. It must not, to begin with, be presented as a normative subject – as an exercise in how things *should* be written or said. It must, moreover, be disassociated from such traditional "grammar" as the child has encountered. There is nothing so deadening as to have a child handle the "type and order" problem by "recognizing" one category of words as "nouns" and parroting, upon being asked what he means by a noun, that it is a "person, place, or thing." It is not that he is either "right" or "wrong," but rather that he is as remote from the issue as he would be if he attempted to account for grief over the assassination of a President by citing the Constitution on the division of powers. And finally, the discussion needs to remain close to the nature of language in use, its likely origin, and the functions to which it is put.

Whether it is true or not that a ten-year-old has a complete grammatical repertory, he is certainly capable of, and delighted in, recognizing all linguistic features when confronted with instances of them. The chief aid to such recognition is contrast – the opportunity to observe the oppositional features that are so much a feature of human language. What comes hard is to formulate these features conceptually; to go beyond the intuitive grasp of the native speaker to the more self-conscious understanding of the linguist. It is this task – getting children to look at and to ponder the things they can notice in their language long enough to understand them – that is most difficult and it should not be pushed to the point of tedium.

Our section on language includes a consideration of what communication is – by contrasting how humans and animals manage to send and receive messages. The early sessions have proved lively and in the course of them nearly every major issue of linguistics is raised and allowed to go begging. This preliminary exercise has the great virtue that it can be repeated on later occasions, when students have achieved varying levels of sophistication, with the result that they readily recognize how much progress they have made.

The opening session (or sessions, for students often want to continue the arguments over animals and humans) usually indicates which among several openings can be best pursued in later units. The instance which follows is influenced by far too little experience to be considered the general rule, but it is at least one example.

The discussion led naturally to the design features of a language. We designed a language game based on bee language, requiring the children to find hidden objects by using messages in this bee-like language. The children are encouraged to design similar languages and to improve on the design of the language used. They take to this readily and are eager to discuss and make clearer such design features as semanticity, voice-ear link, displacement, and cultural transmission. The game, of course, is a lead into the demonstration of bee language as presented in the von Frisch film (which is not altogether satisfactory). We were struck, however, at how much more interested the children were in talking about their own language than in discussing bee language or von Frisch's analysis of it. It is as if the bee linguistics were interesting as an introduction into the closer analysis of their own language.

Our next objective is to present the powerful ideas of arbitrariness, of productivity, and of duality of patterning, the latter the exclusive property of human language. We have approached arbitrariness by the conventional route of comparing how pictures, diagrams, charades, and words refer to things. There are nice jokes to be used, as in the example given by Hockett of the tiny word *whale* referring to a big thing, while the large word *microorganism* refers to a tiny one. With respect to productivity, we have had considerable initial success with two exercises. The first is with a language containing four types (how, what, when, where) with a limited number of tokens of each type (e.g., by hand, by weapon, by trap, as tokens of the "how" type) and with a highly constrained set of orders each referring to a different kind of food-related activity. By this means we readily establish the idea of *type* and *order* as two basic ideas. They readily grasp the idea of substitutivity of tokens within a type. (Indeed, given the interest in secret codes based on substitution of words or letters for code breaking, they need little instruction on this score.)

Once the ideas of type and order are established, we begin the following amusing exercises to illustrate the interchangeability of language frames. We present:

1	2	3	4	5
The	man	ate	his	lunch
A	lady	wore	my	hat
This	doctor	broke	a	bottle
My	son	drove	our	car

and the children are now asked to provide "matching" examples. They can do so readily. They soon discover that so long as they pick words in the order 1 2 3 4 5, from any place in each column, something "sensible" can be got – even if it is silly or not true like, "My doctor wore a car," or, "A lady ate a bottle," it is at least not "crazy" like, "Man the lunch his ate."

The students need no urging to construct new frames and to insert additional types into frames already set up (like a new first column the tokens of which include, *did, can, has,* etc.). Interesting discoveries are made – such as the relative openness of some positions and the closed nature of others. We hope to devise methods to help the children discover some of the deeper features of grammar, better to grasp what a language is – for example, that one can start with relatively simple sentence frames, "kernel sentences," and transform them progressively into negatives, queries, and passives or any two or even three of these, and that more complex forms can be returned to simpler forms by applying the transformations in reverse.

Finally, a game has been devised (a game involving signaling at sea) to illustrate duality of patterning, that most difficult feature of human language. It involves developing a language initially with a very limited set of building blocks (as with human languages, each of which combines intrinsically meaningless sound elements, phones, into a unique system that renders them into meaningful phonemes, a change in one of which will alter the meaning of a word so that, in English, *rob* and *lob* are different words, but not so in Japanese where /r/ and /l/ are allophones of the same phoneme just as plosive /p/ *(pin)* and non-plosive /p/ *(spin)* are "the same" for us but not for others). Three kinds of word blocks can be arranged in a frame, making twenty-seven possible "words" or lexemes. But there must be rules as to which combinations mean things and which do not. It is very quickly apparent to the children that the blocks as such "mean" nothing, but the frames do – or some do and some do not. We are in progress of going from this point toward other aspects of duality at this time.

It is a natural transition to go from syntax to the question of how language is acquired by young humans and other primates. We shall use the considerable resources provided by recent studies of language acquisition to show the manner in which syntax emerges from certain very elementary forms such as the pivot-plus-open-class and the head-plus-attribute. The idea of "writing a grammar" for any form of speech encountered will also be presented. In addition, the child-adult "expansion-idealization" cycle will be explored as an example of a powerful form of social grouping that is crucial for transmitting the language. For contrast, we hope to examine the problems of language development of Vicki, a chimpanzee raised by a family along with their own child of like age. The subtle problem of "traditional" and "hereditary" transmission is bound to emerge.

Finally, and with the benefit of their newly gained insight into the nature of language, we shall return to the question of the origins of human language and its role in shaping human characteristics. We hope first to cover the newly available materials on the universal characteristics of all human languages – first getting the children to make some informed guesses on the subject. Then we shall consider the role of language in the organization of the early human group and the effectiveness it might add to such group activities as hunting, given its design features and its universals. To go from this point to a consideration of myth and its nature is not a difficult step.

We have examined these matters in some detail here (though not closely enough). Our hope is to give the reader a concrete sense of how far we wish to go.

It is plain that the section on language can take as much of a year as one wishes. We are overproducing materials to give us some better idea of what is possible and how to combine what is possible. Some schools may want to devote much time to language, and we hope to make it possible for them to do so. But above all, we hope to provide enough variety so that a teacher can choose an emphasis of his own, whether it be to increase self-consciousness about language or to impart a livelier sense of some distinctively human aspect of human language. In the first stages of our work, the tendency is to concentrate more on "getting the subject right" – in this case linguistics – than on getting the whole course constructed. And just as there is a tension between the requirements of the subject itself and those imposed by the need to teach it to children, so is there a necessary tension between the parts of our course (the five topics) and the whole (the nature and evolution of man). We shall return to this matter in discussing the summer workshop in a later section.

The section on language has required the collaboration of a variety of linguists of different stripe – pure, anthropological, psychological – and of teachers, psychologists, film-makers, artists, and children. At that, it is hardly a quarter done. Gloria Cooper of Harvard has directed the unit, with the aid of David McNeill of Harvard, Mary Henle of the New School, John Mickey of Colorado State, Betsy Dunkman of the Newton Schools, and Florence Jackson of the New York City Schools.

Tool making

One starts with several truths about children and "tools." They have usually not used many of them, and in general, tools will not be of much interest. This may derive from the deeper truth that, in general, children (like their urban parents) think of tools as set pieces that are to be bought in hardware stores. And finally, children in our technologically mature society usually have little notion of the relation between tools and our way of life. Production takes place in factories where they have never been, its products are packaged to disguise the production process that brought them into being.

The tool unit is still under discussion. What follows are some of the leading ideas that animate the design of the unit.

We begin with a philosophical approach to the nature of tool-using. What is most characteristic of any kind of tool-using is not the tools themselves, but rather the program that guides their use. It is in this broader sense that tools take on their proper meaning as amplifiers of human capacities and implementers of human activity.

Seen as amplifiers, tools can fall into three general classes – amplifiers of sensory capacities, of motor capacities, and of ratiocinative capacities. Within each type there are many subspecies. There are sensory amplifiers like microscopes and ear horns that are "magnifiers," others, like spirit levels and bobs, that are "reference markers," etc. Some implement systems "stretch out" time (slow motion cinematography) and others condense it (time-lapse registration). In the realm of motor amplifiers, some tools provide a basis for binding, some for penetrating, some even for steadying – as when one of our pupils described a draughtsman's compass as a "steadying tool." And, of course, there are the "soft tools" of ratiocination such as mathematics and logic and the "hard tools" they make possible, ranging from the abacus to the high speed digital computer and the automaton.

Once we think of tools as imbedded in a program of use – as implementers of human activity – then it becomes possible to deal with the basic idea of substitutability, an idea as crucial to language as it is to tools. If one cannot find a certain word or phrase, a near equivalent can be substituted in its place. So too with tools: if a skilled carpenter happens not to have brought his chisel to the job, he can usually substitute something else in its place – the edge of a plane blade, a pocket knife, etc. In short, tools are not fixed, and the "functional fixedness" found by so many psychologists studying problem-solving comes finally because so much thinking about tools fixes them to the convention – a hammer is for nails and nothing but nails.

Our ultimate object in teaching about tools is, as noted before, not so much to explicate tools and their significance, but to explore how tools affected man's evolution. The evidence points very strongly to the central part in evolution played by natural selection favoring the user of spontaneous pebble tools over those proto-hominids who depended upon their formidable jaws and dentition. In time, survival depended increasingly on the capacities of the tool-user and tool-maker – not only his opposable forefinger and thumb, but the nervous system to go with them. Within a few hundred thousand years after the first primitive tool-using appears, man's brain size more than doubles. Evolution (or more simply, survival) favored the larger brained creatures capable of adapting by the use of tools, and brain size seems to have been roughly correlated with that capacity. There are many fascinating concomitants to this story. Better weapons meant a shift to carnivorousness. This in turn led to leisure – or at least less food-gathering – which in turn makes possible permanent or semipermanent settlement. Throughout, the changes produced lead to changes in way of life, changes in culture and social organization, changes in what it is possible to do.

All of these matters are now superbly documented in Leaky's excavations in Olduvai Gorge in East Africa. We have consulted with him and he has expressed eagerness to edit four films for us on tool-making and its subsequent effects on the emergence of a new way of life. These are scheduled for the fall of 1965. If we are successful in getting our pupils to speculate about the changes in a society that accompany changes in technology, we will at least have fulfilled one of the original aims of the Social Studies Program: to get across the idea that a technology requires a counterpart in social organization before it can be used effectively by a society.

There happen also to be new materials available on the burgeoning technology of the Magdalenian period when more decorative features appear and tool-makers begin to specialize. We are exploring this work to see whether it too can be used in the same spirit.

A few of the exercises being planned to the "tool section" give some flavor of the pedagogy. One unit calls for the taking of a "census of skills" – the tasks that children know how to perform, along with some effort to examine how they were learned (including tool skills). Another unit consists of trying to design an "all-purpose" tool so that the children can have some notion of the programmatic questions one asks in designing a tool and why specialized use has a role.

There will also be an opportunity (of which more in a later section) for the children to compare "tool play" of an Eskimo boy and Danai boy of New Guinea with the play of immature free-ranging baboons, macaques, and chimpanzees. We are also in process of obtaining films on the technique of manufacture of flint implements and hope also to obtain inexpensive enough materials to have our pupils try their hand at flint knapping and other modes of instrument making, guided possibly by films on the subject by the distinguished French archeologist, Dr Bordes.

There will also be some treatment in the course of tools to make tools as well as of tools that control various forms of natural power. A possible route into this discussion is an overview of the evolution of tool-making generally – from the first "spontaneous" or picked-up tools, to the shaped ones, to those shaped to a pattern, to modern conceptions of man-machine relations as in contemporary systems research. Indeed, if we do follow this approach we shall also explore the design of a game of tool design involving variables such as cost, time, gain, specificity of function, and skill required, with the object of making clear the programmatic nature of tools and the manner in which tools represent a selective extension of human powers.

Social organization

The section on social organization is still in preliminary planning, save in one respect where work is quite well advanced. The unit has as its objective to make children aware that there is a structure in a society and that this structure is not fixed once for all. It is an integrated pattern and you cannot change one part of the pattern without other parts of the society changing with it. The way a society arranges itself for carrying out its affairs depends upon a variety of factors ranging from its ecology at one end to the irreversible course of its history and world view at the other.

A first task is to lead children to recognize explicitly certain basic patterns in the society around them, patterns they know well in an implicit, intuitive way – the distinction between kin and others, between face-to-face groups and secondary groups, between reference groups and ones that have corporate being. These, we believe, are distinctions that children easily discover. We should also like the children to grasp the rather abstract fact that within most human groups beyond the immediate family, continuity depends not so much upon specific people, but upon "roles" filled by people – again, as with language and tool-use, there are structures with substitutability.

Such social organization is marked by reciprocity and exchange – cooperation is compensated by protection, service by fee, and so on. There is always giving and getting. There are, moreover, forms of legitimacy and sanction that define the limits of possible behavior in any given role. They are the bounds set by a society and do not depend upon the individual's choice. Law is the classic case, but not the only one. One cannot commit theft legally, but then too one cannot ignore friends with impunity and law has nothing to do with it.

A society, moreover, has a certain world view, a way of defining what is "real," what is "good," what is "possible." To this matter we turn in a later section, mentioning it here only to complete our catalogue of aspirations of ideas we hope to introduce in this part of the course.

We believe that these matters can be presented to children in a fashion that is gripping, close to life, and intellectually honest. The pedagogy is scarcely clear, but we are on the track of some interesting ways of operating. One difficulty with social organization is its ubiquity. Contrast may be our best way of saving social organization from obviousness – by comparing our own forms of social organization with those of baboon troops, of Eskimo, of Bushmen, of prehistoric man as inferred from excavated living floors in Europe and East Africa. But beyond this we are now developing a "family" of games designed to bring social organization into the personal consciousness of the children.

The first of these games, "Hunting," is designed to simulate conditions in an early human group engaged in hunting and is patterned on the life and ecology of the Bushmen of the Kalahari Desert. The elements of the game are Hunters, Prey, Weapons, Habitats, Messages, Predators, and Food. Without going into detail, the game simulates (in the manner of so-called Pentagon games used for increasing the sensitivities of generals) the problem of planning how far one wishes to go in search of various kinds of game, how resources need to be shared by a group to go beyond "varmint" hunting to larger game, how differentiation of labor can come about in weapon-making and weapon-using, how one must decide among different odds in hunting in one terrain or another. Given the form of the game (for which we are principally grateful to Dr Clark Abt), its content can be readily varied to fit the conditions of life of other hunting groups, such as the Eskimo, again with the object of contrast.

What has proved particularly interesting in our early work with the game is that it permits the grouping of a considerable amount of "real" material around it – accounts of the life of the Kalahari Bushmen (of which there is an extraordinarily rich record on film and in both literary and monographic form), their myths and art, the "forbiddingly" desert ecology that is their environment. And so too with the Eskimo; should we go ahead to construct an analogue game for them, for we are in possession of an equally rich documentation on the Netsilik Eskimo of Pelly Bay. Indeed, one of the documentary films made by the ESI Studio in collaboration with the Canadian Film Board and Dr Asen Balikci of the University of Montreal (one of seven half-hour films to be "cut" from our 100,000 feet of film) has already received international acclaim.

Finally, and again by contrast, there now exists a vast store of material on the social organization of higher primates – a considerable portion of which is also in film shot by a crew under Dr Irven DeVore of Harvard for ESI – that serves extremely well to provoke discussion on what is uniquely human about human social organization.

The group now at work on Social Organization consists of Edwin Dethlefsen of Harvard, Richard McCann, on leave from the Newton Schools, and Mrs Linda Braun of the ESI staff.

Child rearing

This unit has just begun to take shape at the time of writing. It is proceeding on three general themes in the hope of clarifying them by reference to particular materials in the areas of language, of social organization, of tool-making, and of childhood generally. The first general theme is the extent to which and the manner in which the long human childhood (assisted as it is by language) leads to the dominance of sentiment in human life, in contrast to instinctual patterns of gratification and response found to predominate at levels below man. That is to say, affect can now be aroused and controlled by symbols – human beings have an attitude about anger rather than just anger or not anger. The long process of sentiment formation requires both an extended childhood and access to a symbolized culture through language. Without sentiment (or values or the "second signal system" or whatever term one prefers) it is highly unlikely that human society or anything like it would be possible.

A second theme is organized around the human (perhaps primate) tendency toward mastery of skill for its own sake – the tendency of the human being, in his learning of the environment, to go beyond immediate adaptive necessity toward innovation. Recent work on human development has underlined this "push toward effectance," as it has been called. It is present in human play, in the increased variability of human behavior when things get under control. Just as William James commented three-quarters of a century ago that habit was the fly-wheel of society, we can now say that the innovative urge is the accelerator.

The third theme concerns the shaping of the man by the patterning of childhood – that while all humans are intrinsically human, the expression of their humanity is affected by what manner of childhood they have experienced.

The working out of these themes has only begun. One exercise now being tried out is to get children to describe differences between infancy, childhood, and adulthood for different species – using live specimens brought to class (in the case of non-human species) or siblings for humans. For later distribution, of course, the live specimens (and siblings) will be rendered on film. Yet the success of a session, say, with a ten-day-old, stud-tailed macaque suggests that the real thing should be used whenever possible.

Dr Balikci will be cutting a film on Eskimo childhood from the Netsilik footage, and comparable films on baboon and Japanese macaque childhood will also be in preparation. Beyond this there is still little to report. Dr Richard Jones of Brandeis is in charge of the unit, assisted by Miss Catherine Motz, on leave from Germantown Friends School, and Mrs Kathy Sylva and Mrs Phyllis Stein of ESI.

World view

The fifth unit in preparation concerns itself with man's drive to explicate and represent his world. While it concerns itself with myth, with art, with primitive legend, it is only incidentally designed to provide the stories, the images, the religious impulses, and the mythic romance of man's being. It would be more accurate to describe the unit as "beginning philosophy" in both senses of that expression – philosophy at the beginning and, perhaps, philosophy for young beginners.

Central to the unit is the idea that men everywhere are humans, however advanced or "primitive" their civilization. The difference is not one of more or less than human, but of how particular human societies express their human capacities. A remark by the French anthropologist, Levi-Strauss, puts it well.

> Prevalent attempts to explain alleged differences between the so-called primitive mind and scientific thought have resorted to qualitative differences between the working processes of the mind in both cases, while assuming that the entities which they were studying remained very much the same. If our interpretation is correct, we are led toward a completely different view – namely, that the kind of logic in mythical thought is as rigorous as that of modern science, and that the difference lies, not in the quality of the intellectual process, but in the nature of things to which it is applied. This is well in agreement with the situation known to prevail in the field of technology: What makes a steel ax superior to a stone ax is not that the first one is better made than the second. They are equally well made, but steel is quite different from stone. In the same way we may be able to show that the same logical processes operate in myth as in science, and that man has always been thinking equally well; the improvement lies, not in the alleged progress of man's mind, but in the discovery of new areas to which it may apply its unchanged and unchanging powers.

All cultures are created equal. One society – say, that of Eskimos – may have only a few tools, but they are used in a versatile way. The woman's knife does what our scissors do, but it also serves to scrape hides, and to clean and thin them. The man's knife is used for killing and skinning animals, carving wood and bone, cutting snow for building blocks for the igloo, chopping meat into bites. Such simple weapons are "the mother of tools," and by specialization a number of tools derive from them. What is "lost" in variety of tools is won in the versatility of uses; in brief, an Eskimo man and wife have tools for all their tasks and can carry most of these tools about with them at all times.

So too with symbolic systems. The very essence of being human is in the use of symbols. We do not know what the hierarchy of primacy is between speech, song, dance, and drawing; but, whichever came first, as soon as it stood for something else other than the act itself, man was born; as soon as it caught on with another man, culture was born, and as soon as there were two symbols, a system was born. A dance, a song, a painting, and a narrative can all symbolize the same thing. They do so differently. One way of searching for the structure of a world view is to take an important narrative and to see what it ultimately tells. A narrative, or at least a corpus of narratives, may be what philosophy used to be. It may reflect what is believed about the celestial bodies and their relation to man, it may tell how man came into being, how social life was founded, what is believed about death and about life after death, it may codify law and morals. In short, it may give expression to the group's basic tenets on astronomy, theology, sociology, law, education, even esthetics.

In studying symbolic systems, we want the students to understand myths rather than to learn them. We will give them examples from simple cultures for the same reason for which the anthropologist travels into an isolated society. Our hope is to lead the children to understand how man goes about explaining his world, making sense of it and that one kind of explanation is no more human than another.

We have selected for our starting point some hunting societies. An Eskimo society, a Bushman society, an Australian aboriginal society will certainly suffice to show what the life experience of hunting peoples is. From the scrutiny of the myths of these groups, it is immediately clear that you can tell a society by the narratives it keeps. The ecology, the economy, the social structure, the tasks of men and women, and the fears and anxieties are reflected in the stories, and in a way which the children can handle them. One good example of Eskimo narrative or Eskimo poetry, if skillfully handled in class, can show the child that the problems of an Eskimo are like our problems: to cope with his environment, to cope with his fellow men, and to cope with himself. We hope to show that wherever man lives, he manages not only to survive and to breed, but also to think and to express his thoughts. But we can also let the children enjoy the particulars of a given culture – the sense of an alien ecology, the bush, or ice and snow, and a participant understanding for alien styles.

We introduce an origin myth, things taking their present order, the sun shining over the paths of the Bushmen, and the Bushmen starting to hunt. But we should equip the children with some possible theories to make the discussion profitable, theories not in words, but in ways of reading and understanding a myth. If the narrative is to be called a myth, it should portray conditions radically different from the way things are now. It is possible to devise ways for children to analyze a plot. If done with one story variant only, such an analysis may yield something akin to a phrase-structure grammar; if done with a group of myths, something comparable to a transformational grammar may result. It is intriguing to see how stories change. Children know such things intuitively and can be helped to appreciate them more powerfully.

One last thing: why should such things be taught so early? Why not postpone them until the student can handle the "theory" itself, not only the examples? There is a reason: if such things are new to a twenty-year-old, there is not only a new view to learn, but an old established view to unlearn. We want the children to recognize that man is constantly seeking to bring reason into his world, that he does so with a variety of symbolic tools, and that he does so with a striking and fully rational humanity. The unit on world view is under the direction of Dr Elli Maranda, aided by Mr Pierre Maranda and assisted by Miss Bonnie McLane.

Pedagogy

The most persistent problem in social studies is to rescue the phenomena of social life from familiarity without, at the same time, making it all seem "primitive" and bizarre. Three techniques are particularly useful to us in achieving this end. The first is contrast, of which much has already been said. The second is through the use of "games" that incorporate the formal properties of the phenomena for which the game is an analogue. In this sense, a game is like a mathematical model – an artificialized but often powerful representation of reality. Finally, we use the ancient approach of stimulating self-consciousness about assumptions – going beyond mere admonition to think. We believe there is a learnable strategy for discovering one's unspoken assumptions.

Before considering each of these, a word is in order about a point of view quite different from ours. It holds that one should begin teaching social studies by presenting the familiar world of home, the street, and the neighborhood. It is a thoroughly commendable ideal; its only fault is its failure to recognize how difficult it is for human beings to see generality in what has become familiar. The "friendly postman" is indeed the vicar of federal powers, but to lead the child to the recognition of such powers requires many detours into the realm of what constitutes power, federal or otherwise, and how, for example, constituted power and willfully exercised force differ. We would rather find a way of stirring the curiosity of our children with particulars whose intrinsic drama and human significance are plain – whether close at hand or at a far remove. If we can evoke a feeling for bringing order into what has been studied, the task is well started.

A word first about contrast. We hope to use four principal sources of contrast: man *versus* higher primates, man *versus* prehistoric man, contemporary technological man *versus* "primitive" man, and man *versus* child. We have been gathering materials relevant to each of the contrasts – films, stories, artifacts, readings, pictures, and above all, ideas for pointing up contrasts in the interest of achieving clarity.

Indeed, we often hope to achieve for our pupils a sense of continuity by presenting them first with what seems like contrast and letting them live with it long enough to sense that what before seemed different is, in fact, closely akin to things they understand from their own lives. So it is particularly with our most extensive collection of material, a film record taken through the full cycle of the year of a family of Netsilik Eskimo. The ecology and the externals are full of contrast to daily life in an American or European setting. But there is enough material available to go into depth, to work into the year's cycle of a single family so that our pupils can get a sense of the integrity not only of a family, but of a culture. It is characteristic of Netsilik Eskimo, for example, that they make a few beautifully specialized tools and weapons, such as their fishing lester or spear. But it is also apparent that each man can make do with the stones he finds around him, that the Eskimo is a superbly gifted *bricoleur*. Whenever he needs to do something, improvised tools come from nowhere. A flat stone, a little fish oil, a touch of arctic cotton and he has a lamp. So while the Eskimo film puts modern technological man in sharp contrast, it also serves perhaps even better, to present the inherent, internal logic of any society. Each society has its own approach to technology, to the use of intelligence.

Games go a long way toward getting children involved in understanding language and social organization; they also introduce, as we have already noted, the idea of a theory of these phenomena. We do not know to what extent these games will be successful, but we shall give them a careful tryout. The alleged success of these rather sophisticated games in business management and military affairs is worth extrapolating!

As for stimulating self-consciousness about thinking, we feel that the best approach is through stimulating the art of getting and using information – what is involved in going beyond the information given and what makes it possible to take such leaps. Crutchfield has produced results in this sphere by using nothing more complicated than a series of comic books in which the adventures of a detective, aided by his nephew and niece, are recounted. The theme is using clues cleverly. As children explore the implications of clues encountered, their general reasoning ability increases, and they formulate more and better hypotheses. We plan to design materials in which children have an opportunity to do this sort of thinking with questions related to the course – possibly in connection with prehistoric materials where it will be most relevant. If it turns out to be the case that the clothing that people wore was made from the skins of the ibex, what can they "postdict" about the size of a hunting party and how would they look for data? Professor Leaky informs us that he has some useful material on this subject.

Children should be at least as self-conscious about their strategies of thought as they are about their attempts to commit things to memory. So too the "tools" of thought – what is explanation and "cause." One of those tools is language – perhaps the principal one. We shall try to encourage children to have a look at language in this light.

The most urgent need of all is to give our pupils the experience of what it is to use a theoretical model, with some sense of what is involved in being aware that one is trying out a theory. We shall be using a fair number of rather sophisticated theoretical notions, in intuitively rather than formally stated form, to be sure, but we should like to give children the experience of using alternative models. This is perhaps easiest to do in the study of language, but it can also be done elsewhere.

We shall, of course, try to encourage students to discover on their own. Children surely need to discover generalizations on their own. Yet we want to give them enough opportunity to do so to develop a decent competence at it and a proper confidence in their ability to operate on their own. There is also some need for the children to pause and review in order to recognize the connections within the structure they have learned – the kind of internal discovery that is probably of highest value. The cultivation of such a sense of connectedness is surely the hub of our curriculum effort.

If we are successful, we would hope to achieve five ideals:

1   To give our pupils respect for and confidence in the powers of their own mind.
2   To give them respect, moreover, for the powers of thought concerning the human condition, man's plight, and his social life.
3   To provide them with a set of workable models that make it simpler to analyze the nature of the social world in which they live and the condition in which man finds himself.

4   To impart a sense of respect for the capacities and plight of man as a species, for his origins, for his potential, for his humanity.
5   To leave the student with a sense of the unfinished, business of man's evolution.

The form of the course

It is one thing to describe the nature of a course in terms of its underlying discipline and its pedagogical aims, and quite another to render these hopes into a workable form for real teachers in real classes. Teachers are sufficiently constrained by their work loads so that it would be vain to hope they might read generally and widely enough in the field to be able to give form to the course in their own terms. The materials to be covered in this particular course, moreover, are so vast in scope as to be forbidding. The materials, in short, have got to be made usable and attractive not only to the highly gifted teacher, but to teachers in general, and to teachers who live with the ordinary fatigue of coping with younger pupils day by day. They cannot be overburdened with reading, nor can the reading be of such an order as to leave them with a feeling of impotence. At the same time, the material presented should be woven loosely enough to permit the teacher to satisfy his interests in forming a final product to be presented to children.

That much said, we can state what we mean by a *unit*, the elements of which the course is made. A unit is a body of materials and exercises that may occupy as much as several days of class time or as little as half a class period. In short, it can be played to the full and consume a considerable amount of the course content, or be taken *en passant*. Indeed, some units will surely be skipped and are intended only for those teachers who have a particular interest in a topic or a particular kind of exercise. There will be more units than can possibly be fitted into a year's course and teachers will be encouraged to put them together in a form that is commodious to their own intent.

In a manner of speaking, a collection of such units constitutes a course of study. But the image is unfortunate, connoting as it does so many beads strung together by some principle of succession. It is our hope that after a certain number of units have been got through, a unit can then be introduced to "recode" what has gone before, to exploit connection. Some units only review and present no new material.

A unit also sits on the teacher's ready shelf, and consists of six constituent elements.

1   Talks to teachers. These consist of lively accounts of the nature of the unit – particularly the nature of its mystery, what about it impels curiosity and wonder. Our experience in preparing these indicates the importance of staying close to the great men in the field, if possible to find a great article that can be presented in somewhat abridged form. The design of a language (taken from Hockett) or the nature of kinship (taken from Radcliffe-Brown) or how a thing should be called (Roger Brown) – these are examples. The genre needs further study and we are exploring the kind of writing required – something that is at once science and poetry. If it should turn out that a student finds "talks to teachers" worth reading, so much the better.

2   Queries and contrasts. In trying out materials to be taught, we have learned certain ways of getting ideas across or getting the students to think out matters on their own. Often these can be embodied in devices – pictures, reading, and diagrams. But sometimes they are best stated as hints to teachers about questions to use and contrasts to invoke.

"How could you improve the human hand?" turns out to be a useful question. So does the question, "What are the different ways something can 'stand for' something else, like a red light 'standing for' *stop?*"

We have already spoken of our tactical fondness for contrasts, and we are coming up with useful ones in our designing. One such is to have students contrast a cry of pain with the words, "It hurts." Another is to compare the usual words from which phonemes may be inferred – hit, hat, hate, hut, hot, etc. Or the difference to be found in the two allophones of the phoneme /p/ in the words *spit* and *pit* – the latter of which will blow out a match held to the lips, the former will not. Yet the two are regarded as the "same letter" or the "same sound" whereas *hot* and *hut* are "different."

3   *Devices.* This part of the unit contains the "stuff" – the material for students. Principal among the devices is, of course, reading material and we are, like others, struggling to get such material prepared. In good season we hope to understand this obscure matter better. Currently, we are operating, much as others have, to find, or cause to be written, material that is interesting, informative, and in a decent style.

But there are many devices beyond reading that are in need of developing for different units. One is the film loop for use with the Technicolor cartridge projectors that we use increasingly. We are putting together four-minute loops constructed from Eskimo and baboon footage, with the intention of *asking* questions or *posing* riddles. Too often, films have a way of producing passivity. Can we devise ones to do the opposite? Why does *Last Year at Marienbad* abrade the curiosity so well?

We are also exploring what can be done with games, as already noted, and with animation and graphics and maps. We shall get help where we can find it within ESI and outside.

4   *Model exercises.* From time to time in devising a unit it becomes plain that the problem we face is less in the subject matter and more in the intellectual habits of children in ordinary schools. We have commented on some of these problems already – the difficulty many children and not a few adults have in distinguishing necessary from necessary and sufficient conditions, the tendency of children to be lazy in using information, not exploiting its inferential power to nearly the degree warranted.

Model exercises are designed to overcome such intellectual difficulties. We think they are best kept imbedded in the very materials one is teaching. But it is often helpful to provide the teacher with additional special devices. We intend to use puzzles, conundrums, games – a kind of pedagogical first-aid kit.

5   *Documentaries.* These are accounts, or even tape recordings, of ordinary children at work with the materials in the unit. We would like the documentary to be both exemplary and at the same time typical enough to be within reach of a teacher in his own work.

Along with the documentary goes a more analytic description. The analytic documentary is designed to serve dual purposes. The first is to make it plainer both to ourselves and to teachers what in fact are the psychological problems involved in particular kinds of intellectual mastery that we hope to stimulate in children. In this sense, the analytic documentary is a further clarification of our pedagogical objectives. But in another sense, they represent an attempt on our part to accustom teachers to thinking in more general terms about the intellectual life of children. The second objective – call it educational – is to provide teachers with what might be a more useful educational psychology than the kind that is found conventionally in textbooks dedicated to that obscure subject.

It is our hope that as we proceed in our work there will be spin-offs in the form of general research problems that can be worked on by research centers not directly geared to the daily routines of curriculum building and curriculum testing. The work of such centers, as well as research in the regular literature on intellectual development, will constitute a continuing font from which we can draw material for the analytic documentaries.

6 *Supplementary materials.* The final section of the unit "kit" consists of such supplementary materials as paperbacks (and lists of related paperbacks), additional film and game materials, and such other devices as might attract the attention of either a diligent student or an aspiring teacher. Without question, it will become clearer what is needed by way of supplement once we have gone further into providing what will be our standard fare.

A final word about the unit materials. We hope to issue them in such a form that each year's experience can be added to the previous year's kit. That is to say, we believe that as new experience is gained in teaching the course, new editions of the kits should be made available to all our teachers. We intend to gather the wisdom of teachers who try out the course so that it may be made available later to others, to gather in new materials for teaching, new documentaries, new analyses of the scholarly literature, and fresh attempts through our talks to teachers to lend a still more compelling mystery to those topics that deserve to be taught. Indeed, it is probably obvious by now that the six-sectioned unit kit, stretched from one end of the teacher's shelf to the other, is our proposed substitute for that normally most unhelpful genre, the teacher's manual.

Teacher training

No plans for teacher training have yet been established, save that we hope within the next two years to bring together for a summer session a group of master teachers to help advise us about proper steps. Our staff now includes several highly gifted and experienced teachers, all now brooding over this very issue.

Tryout and shaping

The "course," such as it is, will be "taught" to three classes this coming summer (1965) at the Underwood School in Newton. The classes will be fourth, fifth, and sixth grades, with the object of discovering at what level to pitch the material, how to take account of the slow and fast learners, and so on. But teaching is in this case part of a summer workshop effort to get material written, drawn, readied. It will also provide an opportunity to do the kind of intensive interviewing of children to determine what they are making of the material and how their grip may be strengthened.

In short, the summer ahead is a first effort to do an intensive summer workshop on the course.

CHAPTER 9

THE PERFECTIBILITY OF INTELLECT

P. H. Oeshser (ed.), *Knowledge among Men: Eleven Essays on Science, Culture and Society Commemorating the 200th Anniversary of the Birth of James Smithson* (1966), New York: Simon & Schuster

I shall concern myself in what follows with the vexed problem of the perfectibility of man's intellect. Let me consider the matter in the light of four constraints on the exercise of intellect. The first is the nature of knowing itself, as we observe it in intact human beings attempting to gain knowledge. The second derives from the evolution of intellect in primates, including man. The third constraint is imposed by the growth of intellect from childhood to such perfection as man may reach. The fourth has to do with the nature of knowledge as it becomes codified and organized in the society of learned men. It is too broad a task I have set for myself, but unavoidably so, for the question before us suffers distortion if its perspective is reduced. Better to risk the dangers of a rough sketch.

Let me confess that I, indeed any student of human intellect, can hardly pretend that what I say of the reach and range of human intellect is innocent of social, political, and moral consequences. For however one poses the problem, whatever one finds must inevitably affect or at least question our concept of what is humanly possible in the cultivation of mind. The issue of the perfectibility of intellect stirs passionate debate. Beware those who urge that the debate is without purpose, that the results of scientific inquiry carry self-evident implications with them. For it is a debate that requires continual renewal lest our educational enterprise fail to fulfill its function either as an agency for empowering human minds or as a reflector of the values of the culture. What the student of human intellect can do is to refresh the debate with estimates of what is possible and estimates of what is the cost of the possible.

The nature of knowing

Consider first the nature of human intellect as we understand it after a half century of investigation – investigation often more orderly than startling, yet of a nature that yields a steady knowledge. In most recent years, the quest has yielded more surprising turns as we have undertaken the job of forging compatible links between man's intellect and the computers that are its servants.

Perhaps the most pervasive feature of human intellect is its limited capacity at any moment for dealing with information. There is a rule that states that we have about seven slots, plus or minus two, through which the external world can find translation into experience. We easily become overwhelmed by complexity or clutter. Cognitive mastery in a world that generates stimuli far faster than we can sort them depends upon strategies for reducing the complexity and the clutter. But reduction must be selective, attuned to the things that "matter." Some of the modes of reduction require, seemingly, no learning – as with our adaptation mechanisms. What does not change ceases to register: steady states in their very nature cease to stimulate. Stabilize the image on the retina by getting rid of fine tremor, and the visual world fades away. There is another type of selectivity that reflects man's deepest intellectual trait and is heavily dependent on learning. Man constructs models of his world, not only templates that represent what he encounters and in what context, but also ones that permit him to go beyond them. He learns the world in a way that enables him to make predictions of what comes next by matching a few milliseconds of what is now experienced to a stored model and reading the rest from the model. We see a contour and a snatch of movement. "Ah yes, that's the night watchman checking the windows..." Or a patient sits before a physician complaining that vision in one eye is unaccountably dim. Both doctor and patient are involved in kindred activities. If the doctor diagnoses a scotoma, a deadened area on the retina, he does so by a process analogous to the process that leads the patient not to see a "hole" in his visual field, but a dimming, for the victim of a scotoma completes the hole by extrapolating what the rest of the eye is taking in. It is in the nature of the selectivity governed by these models that we come increasingly to register easily on those things in the world that we expect; indeed we assume that the expected is there on the basis of a minimum of information. There is compelling evidence that so long as the environment conforms to the expected patterns within reasonable limits, alerting mechanisms in the brain are quietened. But once expectancy is violated, once the world ceases strikingly to correspond to our models of it (and it must be rather striking, for we ride roughshod over minor deviations), then all the alarms go off and we are at full alertness, thanks to our neural reticular system. So man can not only deal with information before him, but go far beyond the information given – with all that this implies both for swiftness of intellect and for fallibility. Almost by definition, the exercise of intellect, involving as it must the use of short cuts and of leaps from partial evidence, always courts the possibility of error. It is the good fortune of our species that not only are we highly adept at correction (given sufficient freedom from time pressure), but also have learned to institutionalize ways of, keeping error within tolerable limits.

The models or stored theories of the world that are so useful in inference are strikingly generic and reflect man's ubiquitous tendency to categorize. William James remarked that the life of mind begins when the child is first able to proclaim, "Aha, thingumbob again." We organize experience to represent not only the particulars that have been experienced, but the classes of events of which the particulars are exemplars. We go not only from part to whole, but irresistibly from the particular to the general. At least one distinguished linguist has argued in recent times that this generic tendency of human intellect must be innately human, for without it one could not master the complex web of categorial or substitution rules that constitutes the syntax of language – any language. Both in achieving the economy with which human thought represents the world and in effecting swift correction for error, the categorizing tendency of intelligence is central – for it yields a structure of thought that becomes hierarchically organized with growth, forming branching structures in which it is relatively easy to search for alternatives. The blunders occur, of course, where things that must be together for action or for understanding happen to be organized in different hierarchies. It is a form of error that is as familiar in science as in everyday life.

I do not mean to imply, of course, that man structures his knowledge of the world only by the categorial rules of inclusion, exclusion, and overlap, for clearly he traffics in far greater complexity, too. Witness the almost irresistible urge to see cause and effect. Rather, the categorial nature of thought underlines its rule-bound nature. The eighteenth-century assumption that knowledge grows by a gradual accretion of associations built up by contact with events that are contiguous in time, space, or quality does not fit the facts of mental life. There are spheres where such associative laws operate within limits, as, say, with material that is strange and meaningless (the psychologist's nonsense syllables, for example), but for the most part organization is a far more active process of imposing order – as by forming a hypothesis and then checking it to be sure.

In the main, we do the greater part of our work by manipulating our representations or models of reality rather than by acting directly on the world itself. Thought is then vicarious action, in which the high cost of error is strikingly reduced. It is characteristic of human beings and no other species that we can carry out this vicarious action with the aid of a large number of intellectual prosthetic devices that are, so to speak, tools provided by the culture. Natural language is the prime example, but there are pictorial and diagrammatic conventions as well, theories, myths, modes of reckoning, and ordering. We are even able to employ devices to fulfill functions not given man through evolution, devices that bring phenomena into the human range of registering and computing: phenomena too slow to follow or too fast, too small or too large, too numerous or too few. Today, indeed, we develop devices to determine whether the events we watch conform to or deviate from expectancy in comprehensible ways. My colleague George Miller (1965) put it well, speaking about computers: "Mechanical intelligence will not ultimately replace human intelligence, but rather, by complementing our human intelligence, will supplement and amplify it. We will learn to supply by mechanical organs those functions that natural evolution has failed to provide."

The range of man's intellect, given its power to be increased from the outside in, can never be estimated without considering the means a culture provides for empowering mind. Man's intellect then is not simply his own, but is communal in the sense that its unlocking or empowering depends upon the success of the culture in developing means to that end. There is a sense in which, as Professor Lévi-Strauss has taught us, human intellect does not vary in power as a function of the means and technology available to it. For the use of amplifiers of mind requires, admittedly, a commonly shared human capacity, and each society fashions and perfects this capacity to its needs. But there is, I believe, a respect in which a lack of means for understanding one matter places out of reach other matters that are crucial to man's condition whatever his culture.

Let me add one final point. Human beings have three different systems, partially translatable one into the other, for representing reality. One is through action. We know some things by knowing how to do them: to ride bicycles, tie knots, swim, and so on. A second way of knowing is through imagery and those products of mind that, in effect, stop the action and summarize it in a representing ikon. While Napoleon could say that a general who thinks in images is not fit to command, it is still true that a thousand words scarcely exhaust the richness of a single image. Finally, there is representation by symbol, of which the typecase is language with its rules for forming sentences not only about what exists in experience but, by its powerful combinatorial techniques, for forming equally good ones about what might or might not exist. Each of these modes has its own skills, its own prosthetic aids, its own virtues and defects, and we shall encounter them again before we are done.

The evolution of primate intelligence

The evolution of primate intelligence is only now beginning to be understood. The evidence today is that the full evolution of human intelligence required for its movement the presence of bipedalism and tool use in early hominids. It is subsequent to these developments that we find a sharp increase in man's cranial capacity and in the size of his cerebral cortex. But the logic of the situation and indirect evidence argues that the development of tool using itself required some prior capacity, however minimal. I have recently observed a film shot in a natural park in East Africa in which a chimpanzee is using a straw, properly wetted in spittle, to insert into a termite hill to extract these insects. A baboon is watching. When his turn comes he tears the termite hill apart. Tool using of the kind found in early hominids is quite plainly a program in which tools are substituted for manual operations in much the same way that the carpenter can substitute a chisel for his forgotten plane, or a knife or even a saw blade. The evidence indicates that the change in tools used in East Africa after the first stabilization of a chopping tool was not very rapid. What was probably more important was the range of programs or activities into which this tool was substituted.

But having said that much, it is well to note that it was not a large-brained hominid that developed the technical-social way of life of the human, but rather the tool-using, cooperative pattern that gradually changed man's morphology by favoring the tool user over the heavy-jawed, smaller brained creature who depended upon his morphology alone. I must comment in passing upon the emergence of tools made to pattern, in contrast to spontaneous tools. It is at this point in human evolution, place it at some multiple of 10^5 years ago, that man comes to depend upon a culture and its technical pool in order to be able to fill his ecological niche. The biologist Peter Medawar (1963) commented that it is at about this point that human evolution becomes sufficiently elaborated to merit being called Lamarckian and reversible, rather than Darwinian and irreversible. For what is now being transmitted, over and beyond the human gene pool, is a set of acquired characteristics passed on in the cultural pool of a people. The reversibility, of course, is attested to by many splendid ruins, ruins manned by descendants with genes indistinguishable from their ancestors.

It is folly to speculate about the birth date of language. It seems likely, however, that the capacity that made possible the development of human language, the abstractive, rule-producing gift, must also have had something to do with the programmatic nature of tool using with its rules of substitution. It is not plain how we shall ever be able to reconstruct the matter.

One further feature of the evolution of intelligence relates to impulse control. We have had, in the past decade, several impressive overviews of the evolution of mammalian sexuality, from the familiar laboratory rat, through the ubiquitous macaque monkey, through the great apes, to man. The picture that emerges in the transition from lower mammals through primates is one of decreasing control by the hormonal system and an increasing part played by early experience through intervention of the cerebral cortex. Even before the emergence of higher apes, hominids, and early man, there was a striking increase in control of sexual activity by the central nervous system. With man and his ability to symbolize, the role of the central nervous system is further increased. For what is most striking in the change in sexuality from higher primates to humans is the emergence of what anthropologists speak of as classificatory kinship. In place of the higher apes' sexual dominance and restricting tradition of remaining within a range, the human species seems early to have developed a pattern involving reciprocal exchange of women outward to neighboring groups, an exchange used in the formation of mutual alliances. The role of this more stable and reciprocal kinship pattern in the upbringing of young must now concern us.

Human beings have a more prolonged and dependent childhood than other primates. Present opinion concerning the origin of this condition is somewhat as follows. As hominids became increasingly bipedal, with the free hands necessary for tool using, there was not only an increase in the size of the brain, but also a requirement of a stronger pelvic girdle to withstand the impacting strain of upright walking. The increased strength of the pelvic girdle came through a gradual closing down of the birth canal, and an obstetrical paradox was produced: a larger brain, but a smaller birth canal for the neonate to pass through. The resolution seems to have been achieved through the cerebral immaturity of the human infant, not only permitting the newborn to pass through the reduced canal, but assuring a prolonged childhood during which the ways and skills of the culture could be transmitted. There are reasonable arguments to be advanced in favor of the view that the direction of evolution in the nervous system of primates from the lowly tree shrews through lemurs and tarsiers and monkeys on to the higher apes and man has been in the direction not only of more cerebral cortex and more tissue for the distance receptors, but also toward the evolutionary selection of immature forms. This tendency to neoteny, as it is called, is particularly notable in man, to the extent that the human brain more closely resembles the fetal brain of the gorilla in some respects than the adult brain of that great ape. And so, to take one index, the human brain is about a quarter of adult size at birth; in rhesus monkeys and gibbons, the job is about finished after six months. And so it is argued that human infancy with its more malleable dependency can be viewed as a prolongation of the fetal period of the earlier primates.

It is not simply the length and dependency of childhood that increases in man, but also the mode of raising young to the requirements of communal life. Let me describe very briefly some salient differences in the free learning patterns of immature baboons and the children of a hunting-gathering group in a roughly comparable ecology – the !Kung Bushmen. Baboons have a highly developed social life in their troops, with well-organized and stable dominance patterns. They live within a range, protecting themselves from predators by joint action of the strongly built, adult males. It is striking that the behavior of baboon juveniles is shaped principally by play with their peer group, play that provides opportunity for the spontaneous expression and practice of the component acts that, in maturity, will be orchestrated into the behavior either of the dominant male or of the infant-protective female. All this seems to be accomplished with little participation by any mature animals in the play of the juveniles. We know from a variety of experiments how devastating a disruption in development can be produced in subhuman primates raised in a laboratory by interfering with their opportunity for peer-group play and social interaction.

Among hunting-gathering humans, on the other hand, there is *constant* interaction between adult and child, or adult and adolescent, or adolescent and child. !Kung adults and children play and dance together, sit together, participate in minor hunting together, join in song, and story telling together. At very frequent intervals, moreover, children are party to rituals presided over by adults – minor, as in the first haircutting, or major, as when a boy kills his first kudu buck and goes through the proud but painful process of scarification. Children, besides, are constantly playing imitatively with the rituals, implements, tools, and weapons of the adult world. Young juvenile baboons, on the other hand, virtually never play with things or imitate directly large and significant sequences of adult behavior.

Note, however, that among the !Kung one virtually never sees an instance of "teaching" taking place outside the situation where the behavior to be learned is relevant. Nobody "teaches" in our prepared sense of the word. There is nothing like school, nothing like lessons. Indeed, among the !Kung there is very little "telling." Most of what we would call instruction is through showing. In the end, everybody in the culture knows nearly all there is to know about how to get on with life as a man or as a woman.

The change in the instruction of children in more complex societies is twofold. First of all, there is knowledge and skill in the culture far in excess of what any one individual knows. And so increasingly there develops an economical technique of instructing the young based heavily on *telling* out of context rather than *showing* in context. The result of "teaching the culture" can, at its worst, lead to the ritual, rote nonsense that has led generations of critics to despair. But school imposes indirect demands that may be one of the most important departures from indigenous practice. It takes learning, as we have noted, out of the context of immediate action just by dint of putting it into a school. This very extirpation makes learning become an act in itself, freed from the immediate ends of action, preparing the learner for that form of reckoning that is remote from payoff and conducive to reflectiveness. In school, moreover, one must "follow the lesson" which means one must learn to follow either the abstraction of written speech – abstract in the sense that it is divorced from the concrete situation to which the speech might originally have been related – or the abstraction of language delivered orally but out of the context of an on-going action. Both of these are highly abstract uses of language.

It is no wonder, then, that many recent studies report large differences between "primitive" children who are in schools and their brothers who are not: differences in perception, abstraction, time perspective, and so on.

The growth of intellect

Let me now describe very briefly some of the major aspects of intellectual growth as we observe it in the growing child. The first and most general thing that can be said is that it does not flow smoothly but rather in spurts of rapid growth followed by consolidation. The spurts in growth seem to be organized around the emergence of certain capacities, including intellectual capacities. These latter have about them the character of prerequisites: one thing must be mastered before the child can go on to the next. Many of them are directed to two ends: the maintenance of invariance and the transcending of momentariness in registration and response. Let me say a word about each.

By invariance, we mean the recognition of kinship and continuity in things that are transformed either in location or appearance or in the response they evoke. The child must first learn to distinguish that objects have a persistent identity beyond the identity endowed upon them by the action one takes toward them. He then learns that an object persists beyond one's visual or tactile contact with it so that out of sight is not out of mind and a new appearance is not a new thing. He must then travel the long road of decentration, as Piaget (who has taught us so much about mental development) calls it: being able to represent things not only from the egocentric axis, but from other vantage points, personally as well as geometrically. In time, the child moves (at least in our culture) from a representation of the world through action to a representation based very heavily upon the appearance of things. Water poured from a standard beaker into one that is longer and thinner is now said by the four-year-old to be more water because it is "taller than before." In time, the child recognizes that there is constancy across change in appearance. What he is doing in the process of mastering invariance is, of course, constructing increasingly stable models of the world, increasingly comprehensive ones capable of reducing the surface complexity of the world to the limits of his capacity for dealing with information. In good season, and always with help from the culture, the child develops models or modes of representation that are far more symbolic or linguistic in nature. The growth of invariance, then, takes place with development of the enactive, ikonic, and symbolic representations we examined earlier. Students of the developmental process agree in broad outline about this progress, though the details and the terminology differ as one travels west from Moscow to Geneva to Paris to Cambridge to Boulder to Berkeley.

With respect to transcending momentariness, let me illustrate by citing a child, age five, who said of the larger of two half-filled beakers that it was fuller than the other, a moment later that it was also emptier, and then a moment later in answer to a question that it could not be both fuller and emptier. He worked with a consistent logic and saw no contradiction. The logic was self-sufficient for each episode and the three in question were not put together to make possible the recognition of contradiction. The bigger glass was fuller because it appeared to have more water; the bigger was also emptier because it appeared to have more empty space; a vessel could not be both emptier and fuller because, to cite the product of the child's *Sprachgefühl*, "that's silly." Again, development provides models that permit the child to sense coherence over larger and larger segments of experience, time- and space-binding representations that permit wider ranges of connection.

Save in the artificial setting of the school, dominated as it is by telling and a lack of guiding feedback, there is an extraordinary property of self-reward about the act of learning during growth. The satisfaction of curiosity seems to be self-rewarding among all primates. So, too, the development of competence. More uniquely human, finally, is that mysterious process whereby human beings pattern themselves on another and gain satisfaction by maintaining the supposed standard of their model. The three self-rewarding processes provide a motor for growth that is stalled only by repeated failure or by an inability to determine how one is progressing at a task. This does not mean, of course, that what a child learns is what is most empowering of his capacities but, rather, what happens to be available. It is here that the innovation of school and teacher can be critically important.

The nature of codified knowledge

Consider now the nature of codified knowledge as it might affect our views about the perfectibility of intellect. The past half century has surely been one of the richest as well as the most baffling in the history of our effort to understand the nature of knowledge. Advances in the foundation of mathematics and logic, in the philosophy of science, in the theory of information processing, in linguistics, and in psychology – all of these have led to new formulations and new conjectures.

Perhaps the greatest change, stemming principally from the revolutions in physics, is in our conception of what a theory is. For Newton, inquiry was a voyage on the sea of ignorance to find the islands of truth. We know now that theory is more than a general description of what happens or a statement of probabilities of what might or might not happen – even when it claims to be nothing more than that, as in some of the newer behavioral sciences. It entails, explicitly or implicitly, a model of what it is that one is theorizing about, a set of propositions that, taken in ensemble, yield occasional predictions about things. Armed with a theory, one is guided toward what one will treat as data, is predisposed to treat some data as more relevant than others. A theory is also a way of stating tersely what one already knows without the burden of detail. In this sense it is a canny and economical way of keeping in mind a vast amount while thinking about a very little.

Discussing the organization of thought, Whitehead remarks in *The Aims of Education*, "Mankind found itself in possession of certain concepts respecting nature – for example, the concept of fairly permanent material bodies – and proceeded to determine laws which related the corresponding percepts in nature. But the formulation of laws changed the concepts, sometimes gently by an added precision, sometimes violently. At first this process was not much noticed or at least was felt to be a process curbed within narrow bounds, not touching fundamental ideas. At the stage where we now are, the formulation of the concepts can be seen to be as important as the formulation of the empirical laws connecting the events in the universe as thus conceived by us." What is perhaps most important about this way of viewing theory is the attitude it creates toward the use of mind. We now see the construction of theory as a way of using the mind, the imagination, of standing off from the activities of observation and inference and creating a shape of nature.

It can also be said of knowledge that, though it is constrained by the very mode of its expression, it can be expressed in various modes. There is a continuity between knowing how to operate a seesaw, being able to describe a balance beam and cause it to balance with weights placed differentially on either side, knowing that three ounces at six inches from the center of the balance will be equal to six ounces at three inches or two ounces at nine inches or eighteen ounces at one inch, and finally, knowing Newton's conception of moments. This partial isomorphism between more and less abstract ways of knowing something, though it gives the appearance of great obviousness, has implications that are all too easily overlooked.

Let me comment on a point that preoccupied J. Robert Oppenheimer: the connexity of knowledge. There is an implosion of knowledge just as there is an explosion. As observations have become more numerous, the ways in which they may be integrated and connected by powerful theories have also increased. Where the danger lies, of course, is in the possibility that fewer men will come to know the larger and more comprehensive domains to which such theories can be related. But there is reason to question such an eventuality. For it may be that the technologies now being devised for storing, relating, and retrieving information may change the very texture of the intellectual community. Crude though its present conception may be, the idea of a society of scholars connected to a data base through computational devices and programs that can quickly retrieve related information, suggests that we may have automatic servants and assistants vital to the pursuit of connection. We can begin to envisage ways of making knowledge less inert and discrete than it is now, placed as it is on the shelves of libraries or within the pages of our journals. What is required is a means of constantly rearranging and reordering knowledge in a fashion to reflect the theoretical advances and hypotheses current in the intellectual community that uses the knowledge.

The disciplines of learning represent not only codified knowledge but ways of thought, habits of mind, implicit assumptions, short cuts, and styles of humor that never achieve explicit statement. Concentrations of these ways of thought probably account for the phenomenal productivity in ideas and men of, say, the Cavendish

Laboratory under Rutherford or Copenhagen under Bohr. For these ways of thought keep knowledge lively, keep the knower sensitive to opportunity and anomaly. I draw attention to this matter, for studies in the history of knowledge suggest that deadening and banalization are also characteristics of knowledge once it becomes codified.

Perfecting the power of thought

I have concentrated on right-handed knowledge and given short shrift to the left hand – to the disciplines of art, of poetry, of history, of drama, and of metaphysics. Several implications follow from the account that I have given that bear not only upon the perfectibility of man's intellect but also upon the process of its perfecting. Let me in conclusion, then, comment upon a few of these.

In speaking of the nature of intellectual functioning, its evolution, its growth, and its codified products, I have placed heavy emphasis upon the role of models or theories that human beings build to render the varieties of experience into some manageable and economical form. Man creates theories before he creates tools. His capacity and skill for catching the invariances of the world around him probably underlie not only his success as a tool user and tool maker but also his use of that powerful instrument for expression and thought: human language. His myths, his art, his ritual, his sciences are all expressions of this deep-lying tendency to explicate and condense, to seek steady meaning in capricious experience.

Many scholars in this country and abroad have been involved this past decade in what has come popularly to be called the "curriculum revolution," the effort to start children younger and more effectively on the way to grasping the more powerful ideas embodied in the learned disciplines. And indeed it is a revolution in at least one obvious respect: the union of men at the frontiers of knowledge with those charged with instructing the young, the two working jointly on the conversion of learning into a form comprehensible and nutritious to the young. The effort is also recentering the work of psychologists and others concerned with the development of children, though we are only beginning to understand the means whereby intellectual development can be assisted. It is in this activity that I see á fresh approach to the perfectibility of intellect.

Once granted that a principal task of intellect is in the construction of explanatory models for the ordering of experience, the immediate problem then becomes one of converting the most powerful ways of knowing into a form that is within the grasp of a young learner. Let curriculum consist of a series of prerequisites in knowledge and in skill, to be mastered with a built-in reward in increased competence as the learner goes from one step to the next. Such a view assumes that for any knowledge or empowering skill that exists in the culture there is a corresponding form that is within the grasp of a young learner at the stage of development where one finds him – that any subject can be taught to anybody at any age in some form that is both interesting and honest. Once mastered in that appropriate form, the learner can go on to more powerful, more precise forms of knowing and of using knowledge. It is already reasonably clear that this can be done in mathematics and science – though we are very, very far from doing it well. But it is also the case that reading simpler poetry brings more complex poetry into reach, or that reading a poem once makes a second reading more rewarding.

The conception of a curriculum as an effort to go more deeply and more powerfully and more precisely into a body of knowledge before one risks traveling more widely carries with it a self-limiting but benign constraint. One must choose the subjects one teaches from domains of knowledge robust and deep enough to permit such revisits.

And invention is required if one is to proceed in this way. How to convert knowledge into the form that is within the grasp of a learner, so that he may be tempted on? Recall the three modes of knowing, characteristic of human cognitive operations – by action, by image, and by symbol. One approach to the task that has proved moderately successful is to begin a sequence of learning with an enactive representation – learning inertial physics by operating levers, learning music by composing and playing in a highly simplified musical notation, and so on. One goes beyond that to intuitive, image-laden forms, as with intuitive geometry or the kind of visual aids by which formal logic can be rendered in Venn diagrams, and finally to the increasingly abstract symbolic modes of a field of learning.

A more difficult task is to instill early in the learner what in effect is a balance between impatience with the trivial as proof against clutter and an open spirit toward what might be but is not obviously relevant. Here again, the experience of those who have worked on constructing curriculum suggests that one plunge right in. Short of that, it is difficult to accomplish anything. One starts concretely trying to give some feeling for the way of thought that is a discipline and one often succeeds. Again, it is as with musical instruction where one gives the learner the simplest possible Mozart rather than a scale so that as early as possible he may sense what music is.

Above all, what emerges from the past decade of experimenting with instruction is the importance of increasing the child's power of thought by inventing for him modes of access to the empowering techniques of the culture. The nature of a school as an instrument for doing this is very unclear. The perfecting of intellect begins earlier than we thought and goes communally from the outside in as well as growing from within. Perhaps the task of converting knowledge into a form fit for this function is, after all, the final step in our codification of knowledge. Perhaps the task is to go beyond the learned scholarship, scientific research, and the exercise of disciplined sensibility in the arts to the transmission of what we have discovered. Surely no culture will reach its full potential unless it invents ever better means for doing so.

References

Medawar, P. Onwards from Spencer: evolution and evolutionism. *Encounter*, 1963, *21*, 35–43.

Miller, G. A. Computers, communication, and cognition. *Advancement of Science*, January 1965, *21*, 417–430.

Whitehead, A. N. *The aims of education and other essays*, 1929. New York: Macmillan.

CHAPTER 10

THE WILL TO LEARN

Toward a Theory of Instruction (1966), New York: W.W. Norton & Company Inc

The single most characteristic thing about human beings is that they learn. Learning is so deeply ingrained in man that it is almost involuntary, and thoughtful students of human behavior have even speculated that our specialization as a species is a specialization for learning. For, by comparison with organisms lower in the animal kingdom, we are ill equipped with prepared reflex mechanisms. As William James put it decades ago, even our instinctive behavior occurs only once, thereafter being modified by experience. With a half century's perspective on the discoveries of Pavlov, we know that man not only is conditioned by his environment, but may be so conditioned even against his will.

Why then invoke the idea of a "will to learn"? The answer derives from the idea of education, a human invention that takes a learner beyond "mere" learning. Other species begin their learning afresh each generation, but man is born into a culture that has as one of its principal functions the conservation and transmission of past learning. Given man's physical characteristics, indeed, it would be not only wasteful but probably fatal for him to reinvent even the limited range of technique and knowledge required for such a species to survive in the temperate zone. This means that man cannot depend upon a casual process of learning; he must be "educated." The young human must regulate his learning and his attention by reference to external requirements. He must eschew what is vividly right under his nose for what is dimly in a future that is often incomprehensible to him. And he must do so in a strange setting where words and diagrams and other abstractions suddenly become very important. School demands an orderliness and neatness beyond what the child has known before; it requires restraint and immobility never asked of him before; and often it puts him in a spot where he does not *know* whether he knows and can get no indication from anybody for minutes at a time as to whether he is on the right track. Perhaps most important of all, school is away from home with all that fact implies in anxiety, or challenge, or relief.

In consequence of all this the problem of "the will to learn" becomes important, indeed exaggerated. Let us not delude ourselves: it is a problem that cannot be avoided, though it can be made manageable, I think. We shall explore what kinds of factors lead to satisfaction in "educated" learning, to pleasure in the practice of learning as it exists in the necessarily artificial atmosphere of the school. Almost all children possess what have come to be called "intrinsic" motives for learning. An intrinsic motive is one that does not depend upon reward that lies outside the activity it impels. Reward inheres in the successful termination of that activity or even in the activity itself.

Curiosity is almost a prototype of the intrinsic motive. Our attention is attracted to something that is unclear, unfinished, or uncertain. We sustain our attention until the matter in hand becomes clear, finished, or certain. The achievement of clarity or merely the search for it is what satisfies. We would think it preposterous if somebody thought to reward us with praise or profit for having satisfied our curiosity. However pleasant such external reward might be, and however much we might come to depend upon it, the external reward is something added. What activates and satisfies curiosity is something inherent in the cycle of activity by which we express curiosity. Surely such activity is biologically relevant, for curiosity is essential to the survival not only of the individual but of the species. There is considerable research that indicates the extent to which even nonhuman primates will put forth effort for a chance to encounter something novel on which to exercise curiosity. But it is clear that unbridled curiosity is little more than unlimited distractibility. To be interested in everything that comes along is to be interested in nothing for long. Studies of the behavior of three-year-olds, for example, indicate the degree to which they are dominated from the outside by the parade of vivid impressions that pass their way. They turn to this bright color, that sharp sound, that new shiny surface. Many ends are beyond their reach, for they cannot sustain a steady course when the winds shift. If anything, they are "too curious." They live by what psychologists have long called the laws of primary attention: attention dominated by vividness and change in the environment. There has been much speculation about the function of this early and exhausting tempo of curiosity. One neuro-psychologist, Donald Hebb, has suggested that the child is drinking in the world, better to construct his neural "models" of the environment. And it is plain that a stunted organism is produced by depriving an infant of the rich diet of impressions on which his curiosity normally feeds with such extravagance. Animals raised in homogenized environments show crippling deficits in their later ability to learn and to transfer what they have learned. Children "kept in the attic" by misguided or psychotic parents show the same striking backwardness. Indeed, even the children who have suffered the dull, aseptic environment of backward foundling homes often show a decline in intelligence that can be compensated only by vigorous measures of enrichment. So surely, then, an important early function is served by the child's omnivorous capacity for new impressions. He is sorting the world, storing those things that have some recurrent regularity and require "knowing," discriminating them from the parade of random impressions.[1]

But if attention is to be sustained, directed to some task and held there in spite of temptations that come along, then obviously constraints must be established. The voluntary deployment of curiosity, so slowly and painfully mastered, seems to be supported in part by the young child's new-found capacity to "instruct himself," literally to talk to himself through a sustained sequence. And in part the steadying force seems to be the momentum of concrete overt acts that have a way of sustaining the attention required for their completion by shutting off irrelevant impressions. In time, and with the development of habitual activities, and of language, there emerges more self-directed attention, sometimes called derived primary attention. The child is held steady not so much by vividness as by the habitual round of activity that now demands his attention. Little enough is known about how to help a child become master of his own attention, to sustain it over a long, connected sequence. But while young children are notoriously wandering in their attention, they can be kept in a state of rapt and prolonged attentiveness by being told compelling stories. There may be something to be learned from this observation. What makes the internal sequence of a story even more compelling than the distractions that lie outside it? Are there comparable properties inherent in other activities? Can these be used to train a child to sustain his curiosity beyond the moment's vividness?

Observe a child or group of children building a pile of blocks as high as they can get them. Their attention will be sustained to the flashing point until they reach the climax when the pile comes crashing down. They will return to build still higher. The drama of the task is only its minor virtue. More important is the energizing lure of uncertainty made personal by one's own effort to control it. It is almost the antithesis of the passive attraction of shininess and the vivid. To channel curiosity into more powerful intellectual pursuits requires precisely that there be this transition from the passive, receptive, episodic form of curiosity to the sustained and active form. There are games not only with objects, but with ideas and questions – like Twenty Questions – that provide such a disciplining of the channeling of curiosity. Insofar as one may count on this important human motive – and it seems among the most reliable of the motives – then it seems obvious that our artificial education can in fact be made less artificial from a motivational standpoint by relating it initially to the more surfacy forms of curiosity and attention, and then cultivating curiosity to more subtle and active expression. I think it is fair to say that most of the success in contemporary curriculum building has been achieved by this route. When success comes, it takes the form of recognition that beyond the few things we know there lies a domain of inference: that putting together the two and two that we have yields astonishing results. But this raises the issue of competence, to which we must turn next.

For curiosity is only one of the intrinsic motives for learning. The drive to achieve competence is another. Professor Robert White puts the issue well:

> According to Webster, competence means fitness or ability, and the suggested synonyms include capability, capacity, efficiency, proficiency, and skill. It is therefore a suitable word to describe such things as grasping and exploring, crawling and walking, attention and perception, all of which promote an effective – a competent – interaction with the environment. It is true, of course, that maturation plays a part in all these developments, but this part is heavily overshadowed by learning in all the more complex accomplishments like speech or skilled manipulation. I shall argue that it is necessary to make competence a motivational concept; there is *competence motivation* as well as competence in its more familiar sense of achieved capacity. The behavior that leads to the building up of effective grasping, handling, and letting go of objects, to take one example, is not random behavior that is produced by an overflow of energy. It is directed, selective, and persistent, and it continues not because it serves primary drives, which indeed it cannot serve until it is almost perfect, but because it satisfies an intrinsic need to deal with the environment.[2]

Observations of young children and of the young of other species suggest that a good deal of their play must be understood as practice in coping with the environment. Primatologists describe, for example, how young female baboons cradle infant baboons in their arms long before they produce their own offspring. In fact, baboon play can be seen almost entirely as the practice of interpersonal skills. Unlike human children, baboons never play with objects, and this, the anthropologists believe, is connected with their inability to use tools when they grow up. And there is evidence that early language mastery, too, depends on such early preparation. One linguist recently has shown how a two-year-old goes on exploring the limits of language use even after the lights are out, parents removed, communication stopped, and sleep imminent.[3]

The child's metalinguistic play is hard to interpret as anything other than pleasure in practicing and developing a new skill. Although competence may not "naturally" be directed toward school learning, it is certainly possible that the great access of energy that children experience when they "get into a subject they like" is made of the same stuff.

We get interested in what we get good at. In general, it is difficult to sustain interest in an activity unless one achieves some degree of competence. Athletics is the activity par excellence where the young need no prodding to gain pleasure from an increase in skill, save where prematurely adult standards are imposed on little leagues formed too soon to ape the big ones. A custom introduced some years ago at the Gordonstoun School in Scotland has become legendary. In addition to conventionally competitive track and field events within the school, there was established a novel competition in which boys pitted themselves against their own best prior record in the events. Several American schools have picked up the idea and, while there has been no "proper evaluation," it is said that the system creates great excitement and enormous effort on the part of the boys.

To achieve the sense of accomplishment requires a task that has some beginning and some terminus. Perhaps an experiment can serve again as a parable. There is a well-known phenomenon known to psychologists by the forbidding name of the Zeigarnik Effect. In brief, tasks that are interrupted are much more likely to be returned to and completed, and much more likely to be remembered, than comparable tasks that one has completed without interruption. But that puts the matter superficially, for it leaves out of account one factor that is crucial. The effect holds only if the tasks that the subject has been set are ones that have a structure – a beginning, a plan, and a terminus. If the tasks are "silly" in the sense of being meaningless, arbitrary, and without visible means for checking progress, the drive to completion is not stimulated by interruption.

It seems likely that the desire to achieve competence follows the same rule. Unless there is some meaningful unity in what we are doing and some way of telling how we are doing, we are not very likely to strive to excel ourselves. Yet surely this too is only a small part of the story, for everybody does not want to be competent in the same activities, and some competencies might even be a source of embarrassment to their possessors. Boys do not thrill to the challenge of sewing a fine seam (again, in our culture), nor girls to becoming competent street fighters. There are competencies that are appropriate and activating for different ages, the two sexes, different social classes. But there are some things about competence motives that transcend these particulars. One is that an activity (given that it is "approved"), must have some meaningful structure to it if it requires skill that is a little bit beyond that now possessed by the person – that it be learned by the exercise of effort. It is probably the combination of the two that is critical.

Experienced teachers who work with the newer curricula in science and mathematics report that they are surprised at the eagerness of students to push ahead to next steps in the course. Several of the teachers have suggested that the eagerness comes from increased confidence in one's ability to understand the material. Some of the students were having their first experience of understanding a topic in some depth, of going somewhere in a subject. It is this that is at the heart of competence motives, and surely our schools have not begun to tap this enormous reservoir of zest.

While we do not know the limits within which competence drives can be shaped and channeled by external reward, it seems quite likely that they are strongly open to external influence. But channelization aside, how can education keep alive and nourish a drive to competence – whether expressed in farming, football, or mathematics? What sustains a sense of pleasure and achievement in mastering things for their own sake – what Thorstein Veblen referred to as an instinct for workmanship? Do competence motives strengthen mainly on their exercise, in whatever context they may be exercised, or do they depend also upon being linked to drives for status, wealth, security, or fame?

There are, to begin with, striking differences among cultures and between strata within any particular society with respect to the encouragement given to competence drives. David McClelland, for example, in writing about the "achieving society," comments upon the fact that in certain times and places one finds a flowering of achievement motivation strongly supported by the society and its institutions and myths alike.[4] Emphasis upon individual responsibility and initiative, upon independence in decision and action, upon perfectibility of the self – all of these things serve to perpetuate more basic competency motives past childhood.

But cultures vary in their evaluation of *intellectual* mastery as a vehicle for the expression of competence. Freed Bales, for example, in comparing Irish and Jewish immigrant groups in Boston, remarks that the Jewish, much more than the Irish, treat school success and intellectuality as virtues in their own right as well as ways of upward mobility.[5] The reasons can be found in history. Herzog and Zborowski, in their book on eastern European Jewish communities, suggest that the barrier erected against Jews' entering other professions may have helped foster the cultivation of intellectual excellence as a prized expression of competence.[6]

A culture does not "manage" these matters consciously by the applications of rewards and reproofs alone. The son of the rabbi in the eastern European *stetl* was not punished if he wished to become a merchant rather than a Talmudic scholar, and, indeed, if he chose to become the latter he typically went through long, extrinsically unrewarding, and arduous training to do so. More subtle forces are at work, all of them fairly familiar but too often overlooked in discussing education. One of them is "approval." The professional man is more "respected" than the manual worker. But that scarcely exhausts the matter. Respected by whom? Contemporary sociologists speak of the approval of one's "reference group" – those to whom one looks for guides to action, for the definition of the possible, for ultimate approbation. But what leads *this* individual to look to *that* particular reference group?

What appears to be operative is a process we cavalierly call identification. The fact of identification is more easily described than explained. It refers to the strong human tendency to model one's "self" and one's aspirations upon some other person. When we feel we have succeeded in "being like" an identification figure, we derive pleasure from the achievement and, conversely, we suffer when we have "let him down." Insofar as the identification figure is also "a certain kind of person" – belongs to some group or category – we extend our loyalties from an individual to a reference group. In effect, then, identification relates one not only to individuals, but to one's society as well.

While this account is oversimplified, it serves to underline one important feature of identification as a process – its self-sustaining nature. For what it accomplishes is to pass over to the learner the control of punishment and reward. Insofar as we now carry our standards with us, we achieve a certain independence from the immediate rewards and punishments meted out by others.

It has been remarked by psychologists that identification figures are most often those who control the scarce psychological resources that we most desire – love, approval, sustenance. Let me skip this issue for a moment and return to it later.

The term identification is usually reserved for those strong attachments where there is a considerable amount of emotional investment. But there are "milder" forms of identification that are also important during the years of childhood and after. Perhaps we should call those who serve in these milder relationships "competence models." They are the "on the job" heroes, the reliable ones with whom we can interact in some way. Indeed, they control a rare resource, some desired competence, but what is important is that the resource is attainable by interaction. The "on the job" model is nowhere better illustrated than in the manner in which the child learns language from a parent. The tryout-correction-revision process continues until the child comes to learn the rules whereby sentences are generated and transformed appropriately. Finally he develops a set of productive habits that enable him to be his own sentence maker and his own corrector. He "learns the rules of the language." The parent is the model who, by interaction, teaches the skill of language.

In the process of teaching a skill the parent or teacher passes on much more. The teacher imparts attitudes toward a subject and, indeed, attitudes toward learning itself. What results may be quite inadvertent. Often, in our schools, for example, this first lesson is that learning has to do with remembering things when asked, with maintaining a certain undefined tidiness in what one does, with following a train of thought that comes from outside rather than from within and with honoring right answers. Observant anthropologists have suggested that the basic values of the early grades are a stylized version of the feminine role in the society, cautious rather than daring, governed by a ladylike politeness.

One recent study by Pauline Sears underlines the point.[7] It suggests that girls in the early grades, who learn to control their fidgeting earlier and better than boys, are rewarded for excelling in their "feminine" values. The reward can be almost too successful, so that in later years it is difficult to move girls beyond the orderly virtues they learned in their first school encounters. The boys, more fidgety in the first grade, get no such reward and as a consequence may be freer in their approach to learning in later grades. Far more would have to be known about the other conditions present in the lives of these children to draw a firm conclusion from the findings, but it is nonetheless suggestive. There are surely many ways to expand the range of competence models available to children. One is the use of a challenging master teacher, particularly in the early grades. And there is film or closed-circuit television, opening up enormously the range of teachers to whom the student can be exposed. Filmed teaching has, to be sure, marked limits, for the student cannot interact with an image. But a kind of pseudo interaction can be attained by including in the television lesson a group of students who are being taught right on the screen, with whom the student can take common cause. Team teaching provides still another approach to the exemplification of a range of competences, particularly if one of the teachers is charged specially with the role of gadfly. None of the above is yet a tried practice, but pedagogy, like economics and engineering, often must try techniques to find not only whether they work, but how they may be made to work.

I would like to suggest that what the teacher must be, to be an effective competence model, is a day-to-day working model with whom to interact. It is not so much that the teacher provides a model to *imitate*. Rather, it is that the teacher can become a part of the student's internal dialogue – somebody whose respect he wants, someone whose standards he wishes to make his own. It is like becoming a speaker of a language one shares with somebody. The language of that interaction becomes a part of oneself, and the standards of style and clarity that one adopts for that interaction become a part of one's own standards.

Finally, a word about one last intrinsic motive that bears closely upon the will to learn. Perhaps it should be called reciprocity. For it involves a deep human need to respond to others and to operate jointly with them toward an objective. One of the important insights of modern zoology is the importance of this intraspecies reciprocity for the survival of individual members of the species. The psychologist Roger Barker[8] has commented that the best way he has found to predict the behavior of the children whom he has been studying in great detail in the midst of their everyday activities is to know their situations. A child in a baseball game behaves baseball; in the drugstore the same child behaves drugstore. Situations have a demand value that appears to have very little to do with the motives that are operative. Surely it is not simply a "motive to conform"; this is too great an abstraction. The man who is regulating his pressure on the back of a car, along with three or four others, trying to "rock it out," is not so much conforming as "fitting his efforts into an enterprise." It is about as primitive an aspect of human behavior as we know.

Like the other activities we have been discussing, its exercise seems to be its sole reward. Probably it is the basis of human society, this response through reciprocity to other members of one's species. Where joint action is needed, where reciprocity is required for the group to attain an objective, then there seem to be processes that carry the individual along into learning, sweep him into a competence that is required in the setting of the group. We know precious little about this primitive motive to reciprocate, but what we do know is that it can furnish a driving force to learn as well. Human beings (and other species as well) fall into a pattern that is required by the goals and activities of the social group in which they find themselves. "Imitation" is not the word for it, since it is usually not plain in most cases what is to be imitated. A much more interesting way of looking at what is involved is provided by the phenomenon of a young child learning to use the pronouns "I" and "you" correctly. The parent says to the child, "You go to bed now." The child says, "No, you no go to bed." We are amused. "Not *me* but *you*," we say. In time, and after a surprisingly brief period of confusion, the child learns that "you" refers to himself when another uses it, and to another person when he uses it – and the reverse with "I." It is a prime example of reciprocal learning. It is by much the same process that children learn the beautifully complicated games they play (adult and child games alike), that they learn their role in the family and in school, and finally that they come to take their role in the greater society.

The corpus of learning, using the word now as synonymous with knowledge, is reciprocal. A culture in its very nature is a set of values, skills, and ways of life that no one member of the society masters. Knowledge in this sense is like a rope, each strand of which extends no more than a few inches along its length, all being intertwined to give a solidity to the whole. The conduct of our educational system has been curiously blind to this interdependent nature of knowledge. We have "teachers" and "pupils," "experts" and "laymen." But the community of learning is somehow overlooked.

What can most certainly be encouraged – and what is now being developed in the better high schools – is something approximating the give and take of a seminar in which discussion is the vehicle of instruction. This is reciprocity. But it requires recognition of one critically important matter: you cannot have both reciprocity and the demand that everybody learn the same thing or be "completely" well rounded in the same way all the time. If reciprocally operative groups are to give support to learning by stimulating each person to join his efforts to a group, then we shall need tolerance for the specialized roles that develop – the critic, the innovator, the second helper, the cautionary. For it is from the cultivation of these interlocking roles that the participants get the sense of operating reciprocally in a group. Never mind that this pupil for this term in this seminar has a rather specialized task to perform. It will change. Meanwhile, if he can see how he contributes to the effectiveness of the group's operations on history or geometry or whatnot, he is likely to be the more activated. And surely one of the roles that will emerge is that of auxiliary teacher – let it, encourage it. It can only help in relieving the tedium of a classroom with one expert up here and the rest down there.

At the risk of being repetitious, let me restate the argument. It is this. The will to learn is an intrinsic motive, one that finds both its source and its reward in its own exercise. The will to learn becomes a "problem" only under specialized circumstances like those of a school, where a curriculum is set, students confined, and a path fixed. The problem exists not so much in learning itself, but in the fact that what the school imposes often fails to enlist the natural energies that sustain spontaneous learning – curiosity, a desire for competence, aspiration to emulate a model, and a deep-sensed commitment to the web of social reciprocity. Our concern has been with how these energies may be cultivated in support of school learning. If we know little firmly, at least we are not without reasonable hypotheses about how to proceed. The practice of education does, at least, produce interesting hypotheses. After all, the Great Age of Discovery was made possible by men whose hypotheses were formed before they had developed a decent technique for measuring longitude.

You will have noted by now a considerable de-emphasis of "extrinsic" rewards and punishments as factors in school learning. There has been in these pages a rather intentional neglect of the so-called Law of Effect, which holds that a reaction is more likely to be repeated if it has previously been followed by a "satisfying state of affairs." I am not unmindful of the notion of reinforcement. It is doubtful, only, that "satisfying states of affairs" are *reliably* to be found outside learning itself – in kind or harsh words from the teacher, in grades and gold stars, in the absurdly abstract assurance to the high school student that his lifetime earnings will be better by 80 percent if he graduates. External reinforcement may indeed get a particular act going and may even lead to its repetition, but it does not nourish, reliably, the long course of learning by which man slowly builds in his own way a serviceable model of what the world is and what it can be.

Notes

1   For a further account of the functions of early curiosity, see J. S. Bruner, "The Cognitive Consequences of Early Sensory Deprivation," *Psychosomatic Medicine*, 21.2:89–95 (1959).

2   R. W. White, "Motivation Reconsidered: The Concept of Competence," *Psychological Review*, 66:297–333 (1959).

3   Ruth H. Weir, *Language in the Crib* (The Hague: Mouton, 1962).

4   David C. McClelland, *The Achieving Society* (Princeton, NJ: Van Nostrand, 1961).

5   R. Freed Bales, "The 'Fixation Factor' in Alcohol Addiction: A Hypothesis Derived from a Comparative Study of Irish and Jewish Social Norms," unpublished doctoral dissertation, Harvard University, 1944.

6   Mark Zborowski and Elizabeth Herzog, *Life Is with People: The Jewish Little-Town of Eastern Europe* (New York: International Universities Press, 1952).

7   Pauline Sears, "Attitudinal and Affective Factors Affecting Children's Approaches to Problem Solving," in J. S. Bruner, ed., *Learning about Learning* (Washington, DC: US Office of Education, 1966).

8   Roger Barker, "On the Nature of the Environment," *Journal of Social Issues*, 19.4:17–38 (1963).

CHAPTER 11

THE GROWTH OF MIND

The Relevance of Education (1971), New York: W. W. Norton & Company Inc

What is most unique about man is that his growth as an individual depends upon the history of his species – not upon a history reflected in genes and chromosomes but, rather, reflected in a culture external to man's tissue and wider in scope than is embodied in any one man's competency. Perforce, then, the growth of mind is always growth assisted from the outside. And since a culture, particularly an advanced one, transcends the bounds of individual competence, the limits for individual growth are by definition greater than what any single person has previously attained. For the limits of growth depend on how a culture assists the individual to use such intellectual potential as he may possess.

Amplifying skills and knowledge

What a culture does to assist the development of the powers of mind of its members is, in effect, to provide amplification systems to which human beings, equipped with appropriate skills, can link themselves. There are, first, the amplifiers of action – hammers, levers, digging sticks, wheels – but more important, the programs of action into which such implements can be substituted. Second, there are amplifiers of the senses, ways of looking and noticing that can take advantage of devices ranging from smoke signals and hailers to diagrams and pictures that stop the action or microscopes that enlarge it. Finally and most powerfully, there are amplifiers of the thought processes, ways of thinking that employ language and formation of explanation, and later use such languages as mathematics and logic and even find automatic servants to crank out the consequences. A culture is, then, a deviser, a repository, and a transmitter of amplification systems and of the devices that fit into such systems.

But it is reasonably clear that there is a major difference between the mode of transmission in a technical society, with its schools, and an indigenous one, where cultural transmission is in the context of action. It is not just that an indigenous society, when its action pattern becomes disrupted, falls apart – at a most terrifying rate – as in uncontrolled urbanization in some parts of Africa. Rather, it is that the institution of a school serves to convert knowledge and skill into more symbolical, more abstract, more verbal form. It is this process of transmission – admittedly very new in human history – that is so poorly understood and to which, finally, we shall return.

There are certain obvious specifications that can be stated about how a society must proceed in order to equip its young. It must convert what is to be known – whether a skill or a belief system or a connected body of knowledge – into a form capable of being mastered by a beginner. The more we know of the process of growth, the better we shall be at such conversion. The failure of modern man to understand mathematics and science may be less a matter of stunted abilities than our failure to understand how to teach such subjects. Second, given the limited amount of time available for learning, there must be a due regard for saving the learner from needless learning. There must be some emphasis placed on economy and transfer and the learning of general rules. All societies must (and virtually all do) distinguish those who are clever from those who are stupid – though few of them generalize this trait across all activities. Cleverness in a particular activity almost universally connotes strategy, economy, heuristics, and highly generalized skills. A society must also place emphasis upon how one derives a course of action from what one has learned. Indeed, in an indigenous society it is almost impossible to separate what one does from what one knows. More advanced societies often have not found a way of dealing with the separation of knowledge and action – probably a result of the emphasis they place upon "telling" in their instruction. All societies must maintain interest among the young in the learning process, a minor problem when learning is in the context of life and action, but harder when it becomes more abstracted. Once these matters are in hand, a society assures that its necessary skills and procedures remain intact from one generation to the next – which does not always happen, as witnessed by Easter Islanders, Incas, Aztecs, and Mayas.[1]

Psychologists have too easily assumed that learning is learning is learning – that the early version of what was taught did not matter much, one thing being much like another and reducible to a pattern of association, to stimulus-response connections, or to our favorite molecular componentry. We denied there was a problem of development beyond the quantitative one of providing more experience, and with a denial, closed our eyes to the pedagogical problem of how to represent knowledge, how to sequence it, how to embody it in a form appropriate to young learners. We expended more passion on the part-whole controversy than on what whole or what part of it was to be presented first. I should except Piaget (1954), Köhler (1940), and Vygotsky (1962) from these complaints – all until recently unheeded voices.

The psychologist's neglect of the economy of learning stems, ironically, from the heritage of Ebbinghaus (1913), who was vastly interested in savings. Nonsense syllables, random mazes failed to take into account how we reduce complexity and strangeness to simplicity and the familiar, how we convert what we have learned into rules and procedures, how, to use Bartlett's (1932) term of over thirty years ago, we turn around on our own schemata to reorganize what we have mastered into more manageable form.

Nor have psychologists taken naturally to the issue of knowledge and action. Its apparent mentalism has repelled us. Tolman (1948), who bravely made the distinction, was accused of leaving his organisms wrapt in thought. But he recognized the problem and if he insisted on the idea that knowledge might be organized in cognitive maps, it was in recognition (as a great functionalist) that organisms go somewhere on the basis of what they have learned. I believe we are getting closer to the problem of how knowledge affects action and vice versa, and offer in testimony of my conviction the provocative book by Miller, Galanter, and Pribram (1960), *Plans and the Structure of Behavior.*

Where the maintenance of the learner's interest is concerned, I emphasize what my colleague Gordon Allport (1946) had long warned. We have been so concerned with the model of driven behavior, with drive reduction and the *vis a tergo* that, again, until recently, we have tended to overlook the question of what keeps learners interested in the activity of learning, in the achievement of competence beyond bare necessity and first payoff. The work of R. W. White (1959) on effectance motivation, of Harlow and his colleagues (Butler, 1954; Harlow, 1953) on curiosity, and of Heider (1958) and Festinger (1962) on consistency begins to redress the balance. But it is only a beginning.

I have tried to examine briefly what a culture must do in passing on its amplifying skills and knowledge to a new generation and, even more briefly, how psychologists have dealt or failed to deal with the problems. I think the situation is fast changing – with a sharp increase in interest in the conversion problem, the problems of economy of learning, the nature of interest, the relation of knowledge and action. We are, I believe, at a major turning point where psychology will once again concern itself with the design of methods of assisting cognitive growth, be it through the invention of a rational technology of toys, of ways of enriching the environment of the crib and nursery, of organizing the activity of a school, or of devising a curriculum whereby we transmit an organized body of knowledge and skill to a new generation to amplify their powers of mind.

Constructing a course of study

There is strikingly little knowledge available about the "third way" of training the skills of the young: the first being the play practice of component skills in prehuman primates, the second the teaching-in-context of indigenous societies, and the third being the abstracted, detached method of the school.

Let me now become highly specific. Let me consider a particular course of study, one given in a school of the kind that exists in Western culture. My and my colleagues' experience in constructing an upper elementary social sciences course, "Man: A Course of Study," may serve to highlight the kinds of problems and conjectures one encounters in studying how to assist the growth of intellect in this "third way." The "we" I employ in this context is no editorial fiction but rather a group of anthropologists, zoologists, linguists, theoretical engineers, artists, designers, camera crews, teachers, children, and psychologists. The project was carried out at the Education Development Center (formerly Educational Services, Incorporated), with grants from the National Science Foundation and the Ford Foundation.

There is a dilemma in describing a course of study. One begins by setting forth the intellectual substance of what is to be taught. Yet if such a recounting tempts one to "get across" the subject, the ingredient of pedagogy is in jeopardy. For only in a trivial sense is a course designed to "get something across," merely to impart information. There are better means to that end than teaching. Unless the learner develops his skills, disciplines his taste, deepens his view of the world, the "something" that is got across is hardly worth the effort of transmission.

The more "elementary" a course and the younger its students, the more serious must be its pedagogical aim of forming the intellectual powers of those whom it serves. It is as important to justify a good mathematics course by the intellectual discipline it provides or the honesty it promotes as by the mathematics it transmits. Indeed, neither can be accomplished without the other. The content of this particular course is man: his nature as a species, the forces that shaped and continue to shape his humanity. Three questions recur throughout: What is human about human beings? How did they get that way? How can they be made more so?

In pursuit of our questions we explore five matters, each closely associated with the evolution of man as a species, each defining at once the distinctiveness of man and his potentiality for further evolution. The five great humanizing forces are, of course, tool making, language, social organization, the management of man's prolonged childhood, and man's urge to explain. It has been our first lesson in teaching that no pupil, however eager, can appreciate the relevance of, say, tool making or language in human evolution without first grasping the fundamental concept of a tool or what a language is. These are not self-evident matters, even to the expert. So we are involved in teaching not only the role of tools or language in the emergence of man but, as a necessary precondition for doing so, setting forth the fundamentals of linguistics or the theory of tools. And it is as often the case as not that (as in the case of the "theory of tools") we must solve a formidable intellectual problem ourselves in order to be able to help our pupils do the same.

While one readily singles out five sources of man's humanization, under no circumstances can they be put into airtight compartments. Human kinship is distinctively different from primate mating patterns precisely because it is classificatory and rests on man's ability to use language. Or, if you will, tool use enhances the division of labor in a society which in turn affects kinship. So while each domain can be treated as a separate set of ideas, their teaching must make it possible for the children to have a sense of their interaction. We have leaned heavily on the use of contrast, highly controlled contrast, to help children achieve detachment from the all too familiar matrix of social life: the contrasts of man versus higher primates, contemporary technological man versus "primitive" man, and man versus child. The primates are principally baboons, and the "primitive" peoples mostly the Netsilik Eskimos of Pelly Bay. The materials collected for our purposes are on film, in story, in ethnography, in pictures and drawings, and principally in ideas embodied in exercises.

We had high aspirations. We hoped to achieve five goals:

1   To give our pupils respect for and confidence in the powers of their own minds.
2   To give them respect, moreover, for the powers of thought concerning the human condition, man's plight, and his social life.
3   To provide them with a set of workable models that make it simpler to analyze the nature of the social world in which they live and the condition in which man finds himself.
4   To impart a sense of respect for the capacities and plight of man as a species, for his origins, for his potential, for his humanity.
5   To leave the student with a sense of the unfinished business of man's evolution.

One last word about the course of study that has to do with the quality of the ideas, materials, and artistry – a matter that is at once technological and intellectual. We felt that the making of such a curriculum deserved the best talent and technique available in the world. Whether artist, ethnographer, film maker, poet, teacher – nobody we asked refused us.

The psychology of a subject matter

Let me now try to describe some of the major problems one encounters in trying to construct a course of study. I shall not try to translate the problems into refined theoretical form, for they do not as yet merit such translation. They are more difficulties than problems. I choose them because they are vividly typical of what one encounters in such enterprises.

One special point about these difficulties. They are born of trying to achieve an objective and are as much policy bound as theory bound. It is like the difference between building an economic theory about monopolistic practices and constructing policies for controlling monopoly. Let me remind you that modern economic theory has been reformulated, refined, and revived by having a season in policy. I am convinced that the psychology of assisted growth – that is, pedagogy – will have to be forged in the policy crucible of curriculum making before it can reach its full descriptive power as theory. Economics was first through the cycle from theory to policy to theory to policy; it is happening now to psychology, anthropology, and sociology.

Now on to the difficulties. The first is what might be called *the psychology of a subject matter*. A learned discipline can be conceived as a way of thinking about certain phenomena. Mathematics is one way of thinking about order without reference to what is being ordered. The behavioral sciences provide one or perhaps several ways of thinking about man and his society – about regularities, origins, causes, effects. They are probably special (and suspect) because they permit man to look at himself from a perspective that is outside his own skin and beyond his own preferences – at least for awhile.

Underlying a discipline's "way of thought," there is a set of connected, varyingly implicit, generative propositions. In physics and mathematics, most of the underlying generative propositions like the conservation theorems, or the axioms of geometry, or the associative, distributive, and commutative rules of analysis are by now very explicit indeed. In the behavioral sciences we must be content with more implicitness. We traffic in inductive propositions: for example, the different activities of a society are interconnected such that if you know something about the technological response of a society to an environment, you will be able to make some shrewd guesses about its myths or about the things it values, etc. We use the device of a significant contrast – as when, in linguistics, we describe the restricting tradition of a baboon troop to always stay within a given range – in order to help us recognize the system of reciprocal exchange of a human group, the former somehow provoking awareness of the latter.

There is nothing more central to a discipline than its way of thinking. There is nothing more important in its teaching than to provide the child the earliest opportunity to learn that way of thinking – the forms of connection, the attitudes, hopes, jokes, and frustrations that go with it. In a word, the best introduction to a subject is the subject itself. At the very first breath, the young learner should, we think, be given the chance to solve problems, to conjecture, to quarrel as these are done at the heart of the discipline. But, you will ask, how can this be arranged?

Here again the problem of conversion. There exist ways of thinking characteristic of different stages of development. We are acquainted with Inhelder and Piaget's (1954) account of the transition from preoperational, through concrete operational, to propositional thought in the years from preschool through, say, high school. If you have an eventual pedagogical objective in mind, you can translate the way of thought of a discipline into its Piagetian (or other) equivalent appropriate to a given level of development and take the child onward from there. The Cambridge Mathematics Project of the Education Development Center argues that if the child is to master the calculus early in his high school years, he should start work early with the idea of limits, the earliest work being manipulative, later going on to images and diagrams, and finally moving on to the more abstract notation needed for delineating the more precise idea of limits.

In "Man: A Course of Study," there are also versions of the subject appropriate to a particular age that can at a later age be given a more powerful rendering. We tried to choose topics with this in mind: The analysis of kinship that begins with children using sticks and blocks and colors and whatnot to represent their own families, goes on to the conventional kinship diagrams by a meandering but, as you can imagine, interesting path, and then can move on to more formal and powerful componential analysis. So, too, with myth. For our early tryouts, we began with the excitement of a powerful myth (like the Netsilik Nuliajik myth), then had the children construct some myths of their own, then examine what a set of Netsilik myths have in common, which takes us finally to Lévi-Strauss's (1963) analysis of contrastive features in myth construction. A variorum text of a myth or corpus of myths put together by sixth graders can be quite an extraordinary document.

This approach to the psychology of a learned discipline illuminates another problem raised earlier: the maintenance of interest. There is, in this approach, a reward in understanding that grows from the subject matter itself. It is easier to engineer this satisfaction in mathematics, for understanding is so utter in a formal discipline – a balance beam balances or it does not; therefore there is an equality or there is not. In the behavioral sciences the payoff in understanding cannot be so obviously and startlingly self-revealing. Yet, one can design exercises in the understanding of man, too – as when children figure out the ways in which, given limits of ecology, skills, and materials, Bushmen hunt different animals, and then compare their predictions with the real thing on film.

Stimulating thought in a school

Now consider a second problem: *how to stimulate thought in the setting of a school.* We know from experimental studies like those of Bloom and Broder (1950), and of Goodnow and Pettigrew (1955), that there is a striking difference in the acts of a person who thinks that the task before him represents a problem to be solved rather than being controlled by random forces. School is a particular subculture where these matters are concerned. By school age, children have come to expect quite arbitrary and, from their point of view, meaningless demands to be made upon them by adults – the result, most likely, of the fact that adults often fail to recognize the task of conversion necessary to give their questions some intrinsic significance for the child. Children, of course, will try to solve problems if they recognize them as such. But they are not often either predisposed to or skillful in problem finding, in recognizing the hidden conjectural feature in tasks set them. But we know now that children in school can quite quickly be led to such problem finding by encouragement and instruction.

The need for this instruction and encouragement and its relatively swift success relates, I suspect, to what psychoanalysts refer to as the guilt-ridden over suppression of primary process and its public replacement by secondary process. Children, like adults, need reassurance that it is all right to entertain and express highly subjective ideas, to treat a task as a problem where you *invent* an answer rather than *finding* one out there in the book or on the blackboard. With children in elementary school, there is often a need to devise emotionally vivid special games, story-making episodes, or construction projects to reestablish in the child's mind his right not only to have his own private ideas but to express them in the public setting of a classroom.

But there is another, perhaps more serious difficulty: the interference of intrinsic problem solving by extrinsic. Young children in school expend extraordinary time and effort figuring out what it is that the teacher wants – and usually coming to the conclusion that she or he wants tidiness or remembering or doing things at a certain time in a certain way. This I refer to as extrinsic problem solving. There is a great deal of it in school.

There are several quite straightforward ways of stimulating problem solving. One is to train teachers to want it, and that will come in time. But teachers can be encouraged to like it, interestingly enough, by providing them and their children with materials and lessons that *permit* legitimate problem solving and permit the teacher to recognize it. For exercises with such materials, create an atmosphere by treating things as instances of what *might* have occurred rather than simply as what did occur. Let me illustrate by a concrete instance. A fifth-grade class was working on the organization of a baboon troop – on this particular day, specifically on how they might protect against predators. They saw a brief sequence of film in which six or seven adult males go forward to intimidate and hold off three cheetahs. The teacher asked what the baboons had done to keep the cheetahs off, and there ensued a lively discussion of how the dominant adult males, by showing their formidable mouthful of teeth and making threatening gestures, had turned the trick. A boy tentatively raised his hand and asked whether cheetahs always attacked together. Yes, though a single cheetah sometimes followed behind a moving troop and picked off an older, weakened straggler or an unwary, straying juvenile. "Well, what if there were four cheetahs and two of them attacked from behind and two from in front? What would the baboons do then?" The question could have been answered empirically – and the inquiry ended. Cheetahs *do not* attack that way, and so we do not know what baboons *might* do. Fortunately, it was not. For the question opens up the deep issues of what might be and why it is not. Is there a necessary relation between predators and prey that share a common ecological niche? Must their encounters have a "sporting chance" outcome? It is such conjecture, in this case quite unanswerable, that produces rational, self-consciously problem-finding behavior so crucial to the growth of intellectual power. Given the materials, given some background and encouragement, teachers like it as much as the students.

I should like to turn now to the *personalization of knowledge*. A generation ago, the progressive movement urged that knowledge be related to the child's own experience and brought out of the realm of empty abstractions. A good idea was translated into banalities about the home, then the friendly postman and trashman, then the community, and so on. It is a poor way to compete with the child's own dramas and mysteries. Two decades ago, my colleague Clyde Kluckhohn (1949) wrote a prize-winning popular book on anthropology, with the entrancing title *Mirror for Man*. In some deep way, there is extraordinary power in "that mirror which other civilizations still hold up to us to recognize and study...[the] image of ourselves." The psychological bases of the power are not obvious. Is it as in discrimination learning, where increasing the degree of contrast helps in the learning of a discrimination, or as in studies of concept attainment where a negative instance demonstrably defines the domain of a conceptual rule? Or is it some primitive identification? All these miss one thing that seems to come up frequently in our interviews with the children. It is the experience of discovering kinship and likeness in what at first seemed bizarre, exotic, and even a little repellant.

Consider two examples, both involving film of the Netsilik. In the films, a single nuclear family – Itimangnark, Kingnuk, and their four-year-old Umiapik – is followed through the year. Spring sealing, summer fishing at the stone weir, fall caribou hunting, early winter fishing through the ice, winter at the big ceremonial igloo.

Children report that at first the three members of the family look weird and uncouth. In time they look normal, and eventually, as when Kingnuk finds sticks around which to wrap her braids, the girls speak of how pretty she is. That much is superficial – or so it seems. But consider a second episode.

It has to do with Umiapik who, with his father's help, devises a snare and catches a gull. There is a scene in which he stones the gull to death. Our children watched, horror struck. One girl, Kathy, blurted out, "He's not even human, doing that to the seagull." The class was silent. Then another girl, Jennine, said quietly: "He's got to grow up to be a hunter. His mother was smiling when he was doing that." And then an extended discussion about how people have to do things to learn and even do things to learn how to feel appropriately. "What would you do if you had to live there? Would you be as smart about getting along as they are with what they've got?" said one boy, going back to the accusation that Umiapik was inhuman to stone the bird.

I am sorry it is so difficult to say it clearly. What I am trying to say is that to personalize knowledge one does not simply link it to the familiar. Rather, one makes the familiar an instance of a more general case and thereby produces awareness of it. What the children were learning about was not seagulls and Eskimos but about their own feelings and preconceptions that, up to then, were too implicit to be recognizable to them.

Consider finally the problem of *self-conscious reflectiveness*. It is an epistemological mystery why traditional education has so often emphasized extensiveness and coverage over intensiveness and depth. We have already observed that memorizing was usually perceived by children as one of the high-priority tasks, but rarely did children sense an emphasis upon ratiocination with a view toward redefining what had been encountered, reshaping it, reordering it. The cultivation of reflectiveness, or whatever you choose to call it, is one of the great problems one faces in devising curriculum. How does one lead children to discover the powers and pleasures that await the exercise of retrospection?

Let me suggest one answer that has grown from what we have done. It is the use of the "organizing conjecture." We have used three such conjectures – what is human about human beings, how they got that way, how they could become more so. They serve two functions, one of them the very obvious though important one of putting perspective back into the particulars. The second is less obvious and considerably more surprising. The questions often seemed to serve as criteria for determining where they were getting, how well they were understanding, whether anything new was emerging. Recall Kathy's cry: "He's not human doing that to the seagull." She was hard at work in her rage on the conjecture what makes human beings human.

There, in brief, are four problems that provide some sense of what a psychologist encounters when he takes a hand in assisting the growth of mind in children in the special setting of a school. The problems look quite different from those we encounter in formulating classical developmental theory with the aid of typical laboratory research. They also look very different from those that one would find in an indigenous society, describing how children picked up skills and knowledge and values in the context of action and daily life. We clearly do not have a theory of the school that is sufficient to the task of running schools – just as we have no adequate theory of toys or of readiness building or whatever the jargon is for preparing children to do a better job the next round. It only obscures the issue to urge that some day our classical theories of learning will fill the gap. They show no sign of doing so.

I hope that psychologists will not allow themselves to be embarrassed by their present ignorance. It has been a long time since they have looked at what is involved in imparting knowledge through the vehicle of the school – if ever they did look at it squarely. Let us delay no longer.

But I am deeply convinced that the psychologist cannot alone construct a theory of how to assist cognitive development and cannot alone learn how to enrich and amplify the powers of a growing human mind. The task belongs to the whole intellectual community: the behavioral scientists and the artists, scientists, and scholars who are the custodians of skill, taste, and knowledge in our culture. The special task of psychologists is to convert skills and knowledge to forms and exercises that fit growing minds – and it is a task ranging from how to keep children free from anxiety and how to translate physics for the very young child into a set of playground maneuvers that, later, the child can turn around upon and convert into a sense of inertial regularities. Psychology is peculiarly prey to parochialism. Left to their own devices, psychologists tend to construct models of a man who is neither a victim of history, a target of economic forces, nor even a working member of a society. I am still struck by Roger Barker's (1963) ironic truism that the best way to predict the behavior of a human being is to know where he is: In a post office he behaves post office, at church he behaves church.

Psychology, and you will forgive me if the image seems a trifle frivolous, thrives on polygamy with her neighbors. Its marriage with the biological sciences has produced a cumulation of ever more powerful knowledge. So, too, its joint undertakings with anthropology and sociology. Joined together with a variety of disciplines, psychologists have made lasting contributions to the health sciences and, I judge, will make even greater contributions now that the emphasis is shifting to the problems of alleviating stress and arranging for a community's mental health. What I find lacking is an alignment that might properly be called the growth sciences. The field of pedagogy is one participant in the growth sciences. Any field of inquiry devoted to assisting the growth of effective human beings, fully empowered with zest, with skill, with knowledge, with taste is surely a candidate for this sodality. My friend Philip Morrison once suggested to his colleagues at Cornell that his department of physics grant a doctorate not only for work in theoretical, experimental, or applied physics, but also for work in pedagogical physics. The limits of the growth sciences remain to be drawn. They surely transcend the behavioral sciences cum pediatrics. It is plain that, if we are to achieve the effectiveness of which we as human beings are capable, there will one day have to be such a field.

Note

1   I have purposely left out of the discussion the problems of impulse regulation and socialization of motives, topics that have received extended treatment in the voluminous literature on culture and personality. The omission is dictated by emphasis rather than evaluation. Obviously, the shaping of character by culture is of great importance for an understanding of our topic as it bears, for example, upon culture-instilled attitudes toward the uses of mind. Since the psychologist's emphasis is upon human potential and its amplification by culturally patterned instrumental skills, I mention the problem of character formation in passing and in recognition of its importance in a complete treatment of the issues under discussion.

Bibliography

Allport, G. W. Effect: A secondary principle of learning. *Psychological Review*, 1946, 53, 335–347.

Barker, R. On the nature of the environment. *Journal of Social Issues*, 1963, *19*, 17–38.

Bartlett, F. C. *Remembering*. Cambridge: Cambridge University Press, 1932.

Bloom, B. and Broder, L. Problem solving processes of college students. *Supplementary Educational Monograph, No. 73*. Chicago: University of Chicago Press, 1950.

Bruner, J. S. Man: A course of study. *Educational Services Inc. Quarterly Report*, Spring–Summer, 1965, 3–13.

Butler, R. A. Incentive conditions which influence visual exploration. *Journal of Experimental Psychology*. 1954, *48*, 19–23.

Ebbinghaus, H. *Memory: A contribution to experimental psychology*. Dover Publications, 1913.

Festinger, L. *A theory of cognitive dissonance*. Stanford: Stanford University Press, 1962.

Goodnow, J. J. and Pettigrew, T. Effect of prior patterns of experience on strategies and learning sets. *Journal of Experimental Psychology*, 1955, *49*, 381–389.

Harlow, H. F. Mice, monkeys, men, and motives. *Psychological Review*, 1953, *60*, 23–32.

Heider, F. *The psychology of interpersonal relations*. New York: Wiley, 1958.

Kluckhohn, C. *Mirror for man*. New York: Whittlesey House, 1949.

Köhler, W. *Dynamics in psychology*. New York: Liveright, 1940.

Levi-Strauss, C. The structural study of myth. In *Structural anthropology*. (Trans. by Claire Jacobson and B. Grundfest Scharpf.) New York: Basic Books, 1963, pp. 206–231.

Miller, G. A., Galanter, E., and Pribram, K. H. *Plans and the structure of behavior*. New York: Holt, 1960.

Piaget, J. *The construction of reality in the child*. New York: Basic Books, 1954.

Tolman, E. C. Cognitive maps in rats and men. *Psychological Review*, 1948, *55*(4), 189–204.

Vygotsky, L. *Thought and language*. (Ed. & trans. by Eugenia Hanfmann & Gertrude Vakar.) Cambridge, Mass.: MIT Press, and New York: Wiley, 1962.

White, R. W. Motivation reconsidered: The concept of competence. *Psychological Review*, 1959, *66*, 297–333.

CHAPTER 12

NATURE AND USES OF IMMATURITY

K. Connolly and J. S. Bruner (eds), *The Growth of Competence* (1972), London: Academic Press

To understand the nature of any species fully, we need to know more than the ways of its adults. We need to know how its young are brought from initial, infantile inadequacy to mature, species-typical functioning. Variation in the uses of immaturity tells much about how adaptation to habitat is accomplished, as well as what is likely to happen given a change in habitat. The nature and uses of immaturity are themselves subject to evolution, and their variations are subject to natural selection, much as any morphological or behavioural variant would be.

One of the major speculations about primate evolution is that it is based on the progressive selection of a distinctive pattern of immaturity. It is this pattern of progressive selection that has made possible the more flexible adaptation of our species. Too often this pattern is over-explained by noting that human immaturity is less dominated by instinct and more governed by learning.

Because our ultimate concern is with the emergence of human adaptation, our first concern must be the most distinctive feature of that adaptation. This feature is man's trait, typical of his species, of 'culture using', with all of the intricate set of implications that follow. Man adapts (within limits) by changing the environment, by developing not only amplifiers and transformers for his sense organs, muscles, and reckoning powers, as well as banks for his memory, but also by changing literally the properties of his habitat. Man, so the truism goes, lives increasingly in a man-made environment. This circumstance places special burdens on human immaturity. For one thing, adaptation to such variable conditions depends heavily on opportunities for learning, in order to achieve knowledge and skills that are not stored in the gene pool. But not all that must be mastered can be learned by direct encounter. Much must be 'read out' of the culture pool, things learned and remembered over several generations: knowledge about values and history, skills as varied as an obligatory natural language or an optional mathematical one, as mute as using levers or as articulate as myth telling. Yet, though there is the gene pool, and though there exist direct experience and the culture as means for shaping immaturity, none of these directly prepare for the novelty that results when man alters his environment. That flexibility depends on something else.

Yet, it would be a mistake to leap to the conclusion that because human immaturity makes possible high flexibility in later adjustment, anything is possible for the species. Human traits were selected for their survival value over a four–five-million-year period, with a great acceleration of the selection process during the last half of that period. There were crucial, irreversible changes during that final man-making period – recession of formidable dentition, doubling of brain volume, creation of what Washburn and Howell (1960) have called a 'technical-social way of life', involving tool and symbol use. Note, however, that *hominidization* consisted principally of adaptations to conditions in the Pleistocene. These pre-adaptations, shaped in response to earlier demands of the habitat, are part of man's evolutionary inheritance. This is not to say that close beneath the skin of man is a naked ape, that 'civilization' is only a 'veneer'. The technical-social way of life is a deep feature of the species adaptation.

But we would err if we assumed *a priori* that man's inheritance places no constraint on his power to adapt. Some of the pre-adaptations can be shown to be presently maladaptive. Man's inordinate fondness for fats and sweets no longer serves his individual survival well. And human obsession with sexuality is plainly not fitted for survival of the species now, however well it might have served to pop-ulate the upper Pliocene and the Pleistocene. But note that the species responds typically to these challenges by technical innovation rather than by morphological or behavioural change. This is not to say that man is not capable of controlling or, better, transforming behaviour. Whatever its origin, the incest taboo is a phenome-nally successful technique for the control of certain aspects of sexuality – although its beginning among the great apes (Van Lawick-Goodall, 1968) suggests that it may have a base that is rooted partly in the biology of propinquity, a puzzling issue. The technical innovation is contraception, which dissociates sexuality from reproduction. What we do not know, of course, is what kinds and what range of stresses are produced by successive rounds of such technical innovation. Dissociating sexuality and reproduction, for example, may produce changes in the structure of the family by redefining the sexual role of women, which in turn may alter the authority pattern affecting the child, etc. Continuous, even accelerating, change may be inherent in such adaptation. If this is so, then there is an enormous added pressure on man's uses of immaturity for instruction. We must prepare the young for unforeseeable change – a task made the more difficult if Severe constraints imposed by human pre-adaptations to earlier conditions of life have created rigidities.

Evolution of educability

LeGros Clark's (1963) *echelle des etres* of the primates runs from tree shrews through the prosimian lorisiformes, lemuriformes, and related forms, through the New World and Old World monkeys, through the hylobates such as the gibbon, through the great apes, through the early hominids like Australopithecus and *Homo habilis* and other small-brained predecessors, terminating in the modern form of *Homo sapiens* with his $1\,300\,\text{cm}^3$ brain. Closing the gap between great apes and modern man is, of course, a complex and uncertain undertaking, partic-ularly where behaviour is concerned, for all that remains are paleontological and archaeological fragments, and little by way of a behaviour record. But there are inferences that can be made from these fragments, as well as from the evolution of primate behaviour up to the great apes. Enough is known to suggest hypotheses, though no conclusions. Such an *echelle des etres* is bound to be only a metaphor since contemporary species are only approximations to those that existed in the evolutionary tree. But it can tell us something about change in the primate order. We propose to use it where we can to make inferences, not so much about pre-adaptations to earlier conditions that characterize our species, but rather more to assess crucial changes that have been recurring in immaturity. My interest is in the evolution of educability.

But you will know by my credentials that I am not primarily a student of prehuman primates. I have brought the materials of primate evolution together to understand better the course of human infancy and childhood, its distinctiveness or species typicality. I propose to go back and forth, so to speak, between primate phylogeny and human ontogeny, not to establish any shallow parallel between the two, but in the hope that certain contrasts will help us see more clearly. If indeed the fish will be the last to discover water, perhaps we can help ourselves by looking at some other species.

Specifically, I should like to look at several issues whose resolution might be of particular help. The first of these has to do with the nature and evolution of social organization within a species and how this may affect the behaviour of the immature. The second has to do with the structure of skill and how the evolution of primate skill almost inevitably leads to tool using. We must then pause to consider the nature of tool using and its consequences. That matter in turn leads us directly to the roles of both play and imitation in the evolution of educability. Inevitably, we shall deal with that distinctly human trait, language: what it is and how its emergence drastically alters the manner in which we induct young into the species.

My emphasis throughout is principally on the evolution of intellect – problem solving, adaptation to habitat, and the like. But it will soon be apparent that, to use the jargon (Bloom, 1956), one cannot easily separate the cognitive from the conative and the affective. I have been told that the Chinese character for *thinking* combines the character for *head* and the character for *heart*. It is a pity it does not also include the character for *others* as well, for then it would be appropriate to what will concern us. At the end of this chapter, I try to deal with the question of what can be done to better equip the young for coping.

Any species depends, as we know from the work of the last half century (e.g. Mayr, 1963), on the development of a system of mutuality – a set of mechanisms for sharing a habitat or territory, a system of signalling that is effective against predators, dominance relations that are effective without being pre-empting (Chance, 1967), a system of courtship with matching mating releasers (Tinbergen, 1953), etc. There is, at the lower end of the primate line, a considerable amount of rather fixed or linear structure about such mutuality. Behaviour repertoires are limited in prosimians and in monkeys, and the combinatorial richness in their behaviour is not great (see Jolly, 1966), though one can make a case for their goodness of fit to habitat conditions (as Hinde, 1971, recently has). Even where there is, within a given species, an increased variety in behaviour produced by enriched or more challenging environments – as in the contrast between urban and forest-dwelling rhesus monkeys (Singh, 1969) or among Japanese macaques tempted by new foods introduced in their terrain (Itani, 1958) – the difference is not toward variability or loosening of social structure, but toward the incorporation of new patterns into the species-typical social pattern. Action patterns that are altogether fixed prevail; and *play*, that special form of violating fixity, is limited in variety, early and short lived, and irreversibly gone by adulthood – a matter to which I shall return.

There are notably fixed limits for the young of these species; and as the animal grows from infant to juvenile to adult – transitions usually marked by conspicuous changes in appearance and coat colour – social induction into the group is effected rapidly, usually by the quick response of a young animal to the threat of attack by an older animal in the troop. The sharply defined oestrous receptivity of the adult female almost assures that the young animal will be rejected and made virtually self-sufficient within a year. It is this sharply defined receptivity that also creates a scarcity economy in sexual access and leads to such a close link between male dominance and sexual access – perhaps the most notable source of linear, tight social structure virtually throughout the monkeys and prosimians. The comfort-contact system of mother and infant, involving not only initial nursing but also hair holding and grasping by the young for protection in flight and for sheer comfort, is obviously of great importance in prosimians, New World, and Old World monkeys. But as Dolhinow and Bishop (1970) have remarked, we must be careful about exaggerating it. Harlow's (e.g. 1959) pioneering studies do show that a macaque made solely dependent on a terry-cloth and wire-mesh mother surrogate is more backward than one dependent on a real mother. Yet, for all that, twenty minutes of play daily with peers in a play cage obliterates the difference between the three groups – another of Harlow's (Harlow and Harlow, 1962) findings. Note by way of contrast that a three-year-old chimpanzee deprived of a mother modelling the skilled act of fishing for termites seems not to be able to master the act later, even if among peers who are succeeding.

Loosening the primate bond

Probably the first step toward loosening the initially tight primate bond is the development of what Chance (1967) has referred to as an 'attentional structure' within the group. Rather than behaviour patterns leading to constant interaction and mutual release of agonistic patterns, there is instead a deployment of attention in which the dominant animal is watched, his behaviour is anticipated, and confrontation is avoided. One of the major things that induction into a tightly organized Old World monkey group means, then, is an enormous investment in attention to the requirements of the troop – mating, dominance, food foraging, etc. There is, so to speak, little attentional capacity left for anything else.

The great apes represent a crucial break away from this pattern toward a far more relaxed one, and as we shall see in a moment, the effect on the young is striking. All three of the great ape species are virtually free of predators. None of them defends a territory. None of them has a troop structure nearly as well defined and rigidly maintained as, say, the least rigid Old World species, if such as phrase makes sense. In the gorilla, the orang-utan, and the chimpanzee, male dominance does not preclude copulation between a subdominant male and a female in the presence of the dominant male. It is even difficult, in fact, in the case of chimpanzee and orang-utan to define a dominant male in the monkey sense (cf. e.g. Goodall, 1965; Reynolds, 1965; Schaller, 1964). Indeed the route to dominance may even involve a superior technological skill. Note the increased deference paid to a male in the Gombe Stream Reserve who had learned to produce an intimidating din by banging two discarded tin cans together (Van Lawick-Goodall, 1968). Thus, too, while oestrus marks the period of maximum receptivity in which the female initiates sexual activity, her availability to a male may in fact continue even into the first two months of pregnancy (Reynolds, 1965). Doubtless the achievements of a 600–700 cm^3 brain in great apes also contributes to the further evolution of cerebral control of sexual behaviour of which Beach (1965) has written. The spacing of infants is over three years apart, on the average, and the bond between mother and infant, particularly in the chimpanzee, remains active for as long as five years (Van Lawick-Goodall, 1968).

One concomitant of the change is the decline in fixed patterns of induction into the group. There is much less of what might be called training by threat from adults or actual punishment by adults of a juvenile who has violated a species-typical pattern. The prolonged infant–mother interaction includes now a much larger element of play between them often initiated by the mother and often used to divert an infant from a frustration-arousing situation.

What appears to be happening is that, with the loosening of fixed bonds, a system of reciprocal exchange emerges, the structure of which is at first difficult to describe. In any case, the system makes it possible for chimpanzee and gorilla groups to encounter groups of conspecifics in their range without fighting; indeed in the case of the more flexibly organized chimpanzees, such encounters may even include sexual relations between groups and an exchange of members (Reynolds, 1965; Van Lawick-Goodall, 1968). There can be little doubt that primate evolution is strongly and increasingly characterized by such reciprocal exchange. The trend probably predates the emergence of hominids. In a recent article, Trivers (1971) said,

> During the Pleistocene, and probably before, a hominid species would have met the preconditions for the evolution of reciprocal altruism: long life span, low dispersal rate; life in small, mutually dependent, stable, social groups (Lee and DeVore, 1968; Campbell, 1966); and a long period of parental care. It is very likely that dominance relations were of the relaxed, less linear form characteristic of the baboon (Hall and DeVore, 1965).
>
> (p. 45)

As Gouldner (1960) reminded us a decade ago and as new studies on remaining hunter-gatherers reassert (Lee and DeVore, 1968), there is no known human culture that is not marked by reciprocal help in times of danger and trouble, by food sharing, by communal nurturance for the young or disabled, and by the sharing of knowledge and implements for expressing skill. Levi-Strauss (1963) posited such exchanges as the human watershed and classified them into three types: one involving the exchange of symbols and myths and knowledge; another involving the exchange of affectional and affiliative bonds, including the exchange of kin women in marriage to outside groups for political alliances, with this rare resource preserved by an incest taboo; and finally an exchange system for goods and service. The pressures in such primate groups would surely select traits consonant with reciprocity, leading to self-domestication by the selection of those capable of 'fitting in'. The incessant aggressiveness of the linear pattern would wane gradually.

What accompanies these changes is a marked transformation in ways of managing immaturity. The maternal buffering and protection of the young not only lengthens materially but undergoes qualitative changes. Several of these have been mentioned: a much prolonged period dominated by play; increased participation in play by adults, especially, though not exclusively, by the mother; decline in the use of punishment and threat as modes of inducting the young into the pattern of species-typical interactions. The most important, I believe, is the appearance of a pattern involving an enormous amount of observation of adult behaviour by the young, with incorporation of what has been learned into a pattern of play (Dolhinow and Bishop, 1970; Hamburg, 1968; Hayes and Hayes, 1952; Köhler, 1926; Reynolds, 1965; Rumbaugh, 1970; Van Lawick-Goodall, 1968; Yerkes and Yerkes, 1929).[1] Though psychologists are chary about using the term imitation because of the difficulty of defining it, virtually all primatologists comment on the enormous increase in imitation found in chimpanzees in contrast to Old World monkeys (where there is genuine doubt whether imitation in any commonsense meaning of the term occurs at all). After its first appearance at about seventeen months of age, this pattern of observing and imitating takes up much of the time of infants and young juveniles – watching social interaction, watching the care of the young, watching copulation, watching agonistic displays, watching instrumental or tool behaviour. Such observation requires free attention on the part of the young; and, indeed, the incorporation of observed behaviour in play occurs most usually during the more relaxed periods in the life of the group. It was Köhler (1926), in his classic *The mentality of apes*, who commented initially on the intelligent rather than the mechanical or slavish nature of imitative behaviour in anthropoids – how the sight of another animal solving a problem is used not to mimic but as a basis for guiding the observer's own problem solving or goal striving. He used the term 'serious play' (p. 157), and the literature since the early 1920s bears him out (e.g. Dolhinow and Bishop, 1970; Hamburg, 1968). In a word, the chimpanzee adult serves not only as a buffer or protector or 'shaper' for the young but as a model – though there is no indication of any intentional modelling or of behaviour that is specifically 'demonstrational'.

To summarize briefly, the emergence of a more flexible form of social bonding in primate groups seems to be accompanied by the emergence of a new capacity for learning by observation. Such learning indeed may be necessary if not sufficient for transmission of culture. But that gets ahead of the argument still to be made; for there is still an enormous gap to be accounted for between the behaviour of a grouping of great apes, however flexible, and the mode of structuring of a human society, no matter how simple it may be.

Observational learning

There are many facets to observational learning (I cautiously continue to avoid the term *imitation*). There is ample evidence that many mammals considerably less evolved than primates can benefit from exposure to another animal carrying out a task; for example, the classic study of cats by Herbert and Harsh (1944) demonstrates improvement in escape from a puzzle box by cats who have seen other animals escape – and the more so if the cats observed were still inexpert at the task. Whether they are learning the possibility of getting out of the box, the means for doing so (by displacing a bar), or whatever, observation helps. So too with *Macaca fuscata*, the Japanese macaque, where the young animals learn to eat what the mother eats by eating what she leaves (Itani, 1958; Kawamura, 1959); or the naive, cage-reared *patas* monkey transported to a habitat and released in a natural troop, who learns from the group by following it in search of food.

But this is quite different from the sort of 'serious play' to which Köhler (1926) referred. Consider an example:

> I would call the following behavior of a chimpanzee imitation of the 'serious play' type. On the playground a man has painted a wooden pole in white color. After the work is done he goes away leaving behind a pot of white paint and a beautiful brush. I observe the only chimpanzee who is present, hiding my face behind my hands, as if I were not paying attention to him. The ape for a while gives much attention to me before approaching the brush and the paint because he has learned that misuse of our things may have serious consequences. But very soon, encouraged by my attitude, he takes the brush, puts it into the pot of color and paints a big stone which happens to be in the place, beautifully white. The whole time the ape behaved completely seriously. So did others when imitating the washing of laundry or the use of a borer.
>
> (pp. 156–157)

I consider such behaviour to be dependent on two important prerequisites, both amenable to experimental analysis:

The first is the ability to differentiate or abstract oneself from a task, to turn around on one's own performance and, so to speak, see oneself, one's own performance as differentiated from another. This involves self-recognition in which one, in some way, is able to model one's *own* performance on some selected feature of another's performance. This phenomenon in linguistics is known as *deixis*: as in learning that when I say *I*, it is not the same as when you say *I*, or that *in front* of me is not the same as *in front* of you or *in front* of the car (cf. Miller and Johnson-Laird[2]). It is a deep problem in language learning, and though it seems cumbersome and abstract in a discussion of hominid evolution, it may be amenable to demonstration. Indeed, I believe that the excellent study by Gallup (1970) indicates that there is a large gap between such Old World monkeys as the stump-tailed macaque and the chimpanzee: the latter can recognize his mirror image and guide self-directed behaviour by it (e.g. inspecting by touch a spot on the forehead seen in the mirror); the former cannot. The macaque, as a matter of fact, seems able only to attack or threaten its mirror image or to ignore it. These findings are surely not proof of the emergence of deictic capacities in the ape, but they do suggest a crucial trend for guiding one's own behaviour by feedback other than, so to speak, from action proper. Learning by observation is one instance of that class.

The second prerequisite for observation learning is a form of skill I now examine: *construction of an action pattern by the appropriate sequencing of a set of constituent subroutines to match a model* (Lashley, 1951). Observing the development of skilled, visually directed manipulatory activity in human infants and children, one is struck repeatedly by the extent to which such activity grows from the mastery of specific acts, the gradual perfecting of these acts into what may be called a modular form, and the combining of these into higher order, longer range sequences. Flexible skilled action may almost be conceived of as the construction of a sequence of constituent acts to achieve an objective (usually a change in the environment) while taking into account local conditions. As the Russian neurophysiologist Bernstein (1967) has put it, one can almost conceive of an initial skilled act as a motoric hypothesis concerning how to change the environment along a desired parameter. The flexibility of skill consists not only of this constructive feature but also of the rich range of 'paraphrases' that are possible: for a skilled operator, there are many different ways of skinning a cat; and the word paraphrase is not amiss, for there is in this sense something language-like about skill, the kind of substitution rules that permit the achievement of the same objective (meaning) by alternative means.

If one compares the manipulatory activity of a child (or of a young chimpanzee) and a prosimian, such as a loris, the most striking difference is precisely the extent to which manual activity of human and chimpanzee is constructed of components to meet the properties of the task. The wide range of combinations in the use of the component gestures that go into the making of the final prehension – relatively independent movement of fingers, of hand, of wrist, etc. – is striking. But as Bishop (1964) pointed out, prosimians use virtually the same grip for a variety of activities: taking hold of a branch, grooming, taking a piece of fruit, etc. My own informal observation on slow loris confirms this. The grip is adapted to the task by changing the orientation of the whole hand, by altering speed or force, etc. Napier (1962) has noted how the development of flexibility is facilitated morphologically by the evolutionary selection of phalangeal flexibility, and change in the hamate and trapezium with emergence of power and precision grips, but I part company with Napier in that it is *not* so much a change of manual morphology that separates baboon from ape from man, but the nature of the *programme* that controls the use of the hands.

Imitation as 'serious play' – incorporating what is observed into behaviour that is not mere mimicry but is directed intelligently to an end – must of course depend on 'matching to model', on constructing behaviour in the manner we have just examined, and must be concerned with the kind of deictic anchoring that permits one to distinguish and relate what is analogous in my behaviour and in that of another member of the species.

Effect of tools

We must consider now the question of tools and their use, and what effect this evolutionary step may have had on the management of immaturity. We might begin with its first emergence in chimpanzees, but before we do, it is worth considering initially a speculation by DeVore (1965) on the emergence of bipedalism and the freeing of hands. According to this speculation, and it can be nothing more, two contradictory selection pressures operated on the emerging protohominid. The first was for bipedal locomotion and easy standing, freeing the hands. The second was for a larger brain to provide the more flexible programming for the hands (as discussed above). Bipedalism, involving stronger impact on the pelvic girdle, led to selection of a smaller bony aperture of the birth canal to assure greater structural strength of the pelvis. If a bigger brained creature is to get through a smaller canal, there is required, of course, a smaller initial brain size and, therefore, greater initial immaturity (the human brain grows from approximately 335 to 1 300 cm^3 during development).[3] To assure the larger brain, the argument goes, there had also to be a recession in such apelike features as a heavy prognathous jaw as a base for effective dentition. *En route*, there is a critical point where the basic adaptation of the hominid must change.

So we may begin with the fact that tool using at its first appearance in apes comes before that point: it is an optional and not an obligatory adaptation. Chimpanzee survival does not depend on the use of sticks for fishing termites or on the use of crushed leaves as drinking or grooming sponges. As Jane Lancaster (1968) put it in a closely reasoned article on tool use, there is 'a major change from the kind of tool use that is incidental to the life of a chimpanzee to the kind that is absolutely essential for survival of the human individual' (p. 62). Yet, in spite of the absence of 'obligatory pressures', chimpanzees use tools optionally in an extraordinary variety of ways: for eating, drinking, self-cleaning, agonistic displays, constructing sleeping platforms, etc. Nor is it some accident of morphology: 'the hands of monkeys and apes are equally suited to picking up a stick and making poking or scratching movements with it but differences in the brain make these much more likely behaviour patterns for the chimpanzee' (p. 61).

I would like to make the rather unorthodox suggestion that in order for tool using to develop, it was essential to have a long period of optional, pressure-free opportunity for combinatorial activity. By its very nature, tool using (Or the incorporation of objects into skilled activity) required a chance to achieve the kind of wide variation upon which selection could operate.

Dolhinow and Bishop (1970) made the point most directly. Commenting first that 'many special skills and behaviours important in the life of the individual are developed and practised in playful activity long before they are used in adult life' (p. 142); they then note that play 'occurs only in an atmosphere of familiarity, emotional reassurance, and lack of tension or danger' (p. 142). Schiller (1952) reported, 'with no incentive the chimpanzee displayed a higher variety of handling objects than under the pressure of a lure which they attempted to obtain' (p. 186). He reported, actually, that attempting to direct play by reinforcing chimpanzees for play behaviour had the effect of inhibiting play.

Functions of play

Play appears to serve several centrally important functions. First, it is a means of minimizing the consequences of one's actions and of learning, therefore, in a less risky situation. This is particularly true of social play, where, by adopting a play face or a 'galumphing gait' (Millar, 1968) or some other form of metacommunication (Dolhinow and Bishop, 1970), the young animal signals his intent to play. Now, so to speak, he can test limits with relative impunity: 'There are many rules of what can and cannot be done in a: troop, and most of these are learned early in life, when the consequences of violating them are less severe than later on' (Dolhinow and Bishop, 1970, p. 148).

Second, play provides an excellent opportunity to try combinations of behaviour that would, under functional pressure, never be tried.

> The tendency to manipulate sticks, to lick the ends, to poke them into any available hole are responses that occur over and over again in captive chimpanzees. These responses are not necessarily organized into the efficient use of sticks to probe for objects, but they probably form the basis of complex motor patterns such as termiting.
>
> (Lancaster, 1968, p. 61)

Or in Van Lawick-Goodall's (1968) account:

> With the fruit, Figan devised a game of his own: lying on his back, he spins a *Strychnos* ball round and round, balancing it on his hands and kicking gently with his feet, like a circus bear ... Toys like this are not always at hand, but then the youngsters seem just as content to play with stones, leaves, or twigs. They may throw them, rub them over their bodies, pull leaves off stems, break and bend twigs, or poke them into holes in the ground. This form of play may be of tremendous importance in developing dexterity in manipulating objects. As the chimps grow older this skill becomes invaluable not only in routine activities such as nest-making and food-gathering, but also in the most specialized field of tool use.
>
> (pp. 36–37)

And even in captivity, this same tendency to incorporate objects into manipulative pattern goes on undiminished, as one may judge from this report by Caroline Loizos (1967) of a young female chimpanzee habituating to and then 'mastering in play' a tennis ball:

> I bounce a tennis ball in front of the cage several times so that she hears as well as sees it and place it inside on the floor. She backs away, watching ball fixedly – approaches with pouted lips, pats it – it rolls. She backs hurriedly to the wall. Hair erection ... J. pokes at it from a distance, arm maximally extended, watching intently; looks at me; pokes ball and immediately sniffs finger ... She

dabs at ball and misses; sniffs fingers; she backs away and circles ball from a distance of several feet, watching it intently. Sits and watches ball...(pause of several minutes)...walks around ball. J. walks past the ball again even closer but quite hurriedly. She lifts some of the woodwool in the cage to peer at the ball from a new angle, approaches ball by sliding forward on stomach with arms and legs tucked underneath her, so that protruded lips are very close to ball without actually touching it. Withdraws. Pokes a finger towards it and sniffs finger...returns to ball, again slides forward on stomach with protruded lips without actually connecting. Pokes with extended forefinger, connects and it moves; she scurries backwards; more dabs at it with forefinger and it moves again (but not far because of the woodwool in that area of the cage). J. dabs, ball rolls and she follows, but jumps back in a hurry as it hits the far wall. She rolls the ball on the spot with her finger resting on it, then rolls it forward, watching intently the whole time. She dabs again – arm movement now more exaggerated, flung upwards at end of movement. Tries to pick ball up between thumb and forefinger very gingerly...fails. Rolls it towards her, sniffs with lowered head. Picks it up and places it in front of her – *just* touches it with lips – pushes it into straw with right fore-finger – touches it with lower lip pushed out, pokes, flicking up hand at end of movement, but backs away as it rolls towards her. Bites at own thumb. Dabs at it with lips, pulls it towards her and backs away. Examines own lip, squinting down, where it touched ball. Picks at it with forefinger and covers ball as it rolls (walking on all fours, with head down to watch ball as it rolls along at a point approximately under her belly). Pushes with outside knuckles. Stamps on it, dabbing at it with foot. Sits on it, rolls it with foot; carries it gingerly with hand and puts it on shelf, climbing up to sit beside it. It drops down – she holds it in one hand and pats it increasingly hard with the other. Holds it in right hand, picks at stripe on ball with her left. Rolls it between two hands. Rolls it between hand and shelf. Holds and pats; bangs it on shelf. Holds and *bites*, examining ball after each bite. Ball drops from shelf and she pats at it on ground with right hand. Lies on her back, balances ball on her feet, holding it there with hands; sits up, holds ball under chin and rolls it two or three times round back of neck and under chin. It rolls away and she chases it immediately and brings it back to shelf. Lies on back and holds it on feet. Presses it against teeth with her feet and bites – all fear appears to be gone – lies and bites at ball held in feet, hands. Rolls it in feet, hands. Climbs to ceiling, ball drops and she chases it at once, J. makes playface, rolls and tumbles with ball, around, over, under ball, bangs it; rolls it over her own body.

(pp. 194–195)

Various writers (Dolhinow and Bishop, 1970; Loizos, 1967; Van Lawick-Goodall, 1968) are convinced that the mastery of complex tool skills among subhuman anthropoids depends not only on observation learning but also on whether or not they take place in the close setting of the infant–mother interaction. Reference was made in passing to one of the infants in the Gombe Stream Reserve, Merlin, who lost his mother at age three and was 'taken over' by older siblings. He mastered neither termiting nor nest building, skills that apparently require repeated observation.

Van Lawick-Goodall (1968) made it clear in her detailed reporting why such repeated opportunity to observe and play is necessary; mastery of a complex skill like termiting is a complex process of mastering *features* of the task – a non-mimicking approach – and then combining the mastered features. There is, for example, mastery of pushing a stick or grass into an opening, though initially this will be done without regard to appropriate rigidity of the probe or appropriate diameter, or appropriate length. It will be played with as a part skill once mastered – as Flint (208 years who had started at play termiting) pushing a grass stalk through the hairs of his leg. And sheer repetition will provide the familiar routinization that permits an act to be combined with other acts to meet the complex requirement of a stick of a particular diameter and rigidity, pushed in a particular way, withdrawn at a particular angle at a certain speed, etc. A comparable set of observations on human infants by Wood *et al.*[4] shows the importance of skill to three–five-year-olds in enabling them to benefit from demonstrations of how to put together an interlocking set of blocks to make a pyramid. Unless the child can master the subroutines, the demonstration of the whole task is about as helpful as a demonstration by an accomplished skier is to a beginner. As with the young chimps, so too with the young children: they take selectively from the demonstration those features of performance that are within the range of their capacity for constructing skilled acts. They are helped, but the process is slow.

One very crucial feature of tool skills in chimpanzees, as in humans is the trying out of variants of the new skill in different contexts. Once Köhler's (1926) ape Sultan had 'learned' to use a stick to draw in food, he tried using it very soon for poking other animals, for digging, and for dipping it through an opening in a cesspool. Once Rana had learned to climb up stacked boxes to get a suspended piece of fruit, she rapidly tried her new climbing routine on a ladder, a board, a keeper, and Köhler himself – most often forgetting the fruit in preference for the combinatory activity *per se*. Nor is this a response to the boredom of captivity, since the same variant exploration is to be found in the Gombe Stream animals studied by Van Lawick-Goodall (1968) – one of the most ingenious instances being the use of a twig as an olfactory probe by the juvenile female Fifi, an accomplished termiter:

> On three occasions (she) pushed a long grass stalk right into my trouser pocket, subsequently sniffing the end, when I prevented her feeling there with her hand for a banana. Each time there was in fact a banana there, and she followed me whimpering until I gave it to her.
>
> (p. 206)

It is probably this 'push to variation' (rather than fixation by positive reinforcement) that gives chimpanzee manipulation such widespread efficacy – such opportunism as dipping sticks into beehives for honey (Merfield and Miller, 1956), using sticks for clubbing lizards and rodents (Köhler, 1926), and using branches for striking at or throwing at big felines (Kortland and Koöij, 1963). The ecological significance of this wide potential repertory is attested to by observations of Kortland and his collaborators (Kortland, 1965; Kortland and Koöij, 1963; Kortland and van Zon, 1969). They have reported striking differences between forest-dwelling chimpanzees from the rain forest of the Congo and Guinea and those from the Guinea savanna. An animated, dummy leopard was placed in the path of the chimpanzees. Forest apes broke and brandished branches and swung them in horizontal orbit at the dummy. The only hit was by one animal, punching the dummy in the face from in front. Savanna apes warmed up with such sabre rattling, but then attacked the dummy *from the rear* with strong vertical blows with the heaviest available branch and scored violent hits – 'showing both tactical cooperation between the actual assailants and vocal support by the onlookers' (Kortland and van Zon, 1969, p. 12). These authors suggest that open country prevents arboreal escape and thus poses for the animals a problem in tool manipulation that calls for great flexibility in adapting tools to local constraints.

The play aspect of tool use (and, indeed, complex problem solving in general) is underlined by the animal's loss of interest in the goal of the act being performed and by its preoccupation with means – also a characteristic of human children (Bruner and Koslowski, 1972).

Consider the following episode:

> Hebb recounted how a chimpanzee he tested solved problems for banana slice incentives. On one particular day, she arranged the banana slice rewards in a row instead of eating them! Apparently, she had solved the problems for their own sake. 'I was out of bananas, but I offered her another problem…she solved the problem: opened the correct box and put a slice of banana into it. I took it out and then set the box again…I ended up with thirty slices of banana'.
>
> (Rumbaugh, 1970, p. 56)

A far cry from reinforcement in any conventional sense!

Köhler's (1926) account contains an interesting happening. He gave a handful of straw to one animal who tried to use it to draw in an out-of-reach piece of fruit. Finding the straw too flexible, the animal doubled it up, but it was too short, so he abandoned the effort. Modification is systematic, most often directed to features relevant to the task, and is combinatorial. It follows first constructions or first efforts at copying a model. But it appears first in play, not in problem solving.

Play in relation to tool use

I have described these play activities at great length because I believe them to be crucial to the evolution of tool using – steps that help free the organism from the immediate requirements of his task. Play, given its concomitant freedom from reinforcement and its setting in a relatively pressureless environment, can produce the flexibility that makes tool using possible. At least two laboratory studies, one by Birch (1945) and the other by Schiller (1952), indicate the necessity of initial play with materials in order for them to be converted to instrumental ends. They both used problems involving the raking in of food with sticks of varying length – before and after an opportunity to play with sticks. Few succeeded before play. Observed during play, Birch's animals were seen to explore increasingly over three days the capacity of the sticks to lengthen an arm. When put back into the test situation, all of these animals solved the problem within half a minute. Perhaps, as Loizos (1967) has suggested, it is the very exaggeration and lack of economy of play that encourage extension of the limits.

Looked at logically, play has two crucial formal patterns: one consists of a function and its arguments; the other, an argument and the functions into which it can fit. A ball or a stick are fitted into as many acts as possible; or an act, climbing, is performed on as many objects to which it can be applied appropriately. This pattern, I would speculate, is close to one of the universal structures of language, predication, which is organized in terms of topic and comment:

John has a hat
John is a man
John jumps the fence, or

Brush the hat
Wear the hat
Toss the hat.

It is interesting that the language play after 'lights out' of the three-year-old, reported by Ruth Weir (1962) in her remarkable book *Language in the crib*, takes precisely such a form. And I will not be the first to comment that the simultaneous appearance in man of language and tool using suggests that the two may derive from some common programming capacities of the enlarging hominid nervous system.

Another feature of play that is crucial to tool use is the feature referred to by Barsh (1972) as *dissociation* – 'the ability to anticipate the potential component parts of an object' for use in a new arrangement. It is a question that occupied Köhler (1926) in terms of the ability of his animals to 'dissolve visual wholes' of great visual firmness. A Russian investigator, Khroustov (1968), performed a most elegant experiment on tool using in a chimpanzee, showing to what degree these animals are capable of dissociation. Fruit was to be extracted from a narrow tube, and sticks of appropriate diameter were provided. The animal succeeded, and knowing the capability of the species, we are not surprised. The experimenter then provided a wood plaque too wide for the job. After inspecting it, the animal broke it along the grain to obtain a stick of appropriate size. Khroustov then painted a false set of grain lines on a plaque at right angles to the true grain. The animal, using them to guide a first splintering attempt and failing, looked more closely for the true grain and used it.

To summarize once again, the great ape possesses manipulative subroutines that are practised, perfected, and varied in play. These are then put together clumsily and selectively to meet the requirements of more extended tasks, very often in response to observing an adult in a stable and relaxed setting. The imitation observed is akin to imitation by a child of an adult speech model: the child's output is *not* a copy of the adult's; it has its own form even though it is designed to fill the same function. These initial acts are then modified in a systematic manner to fulfil further requirements of the task. The acts themselves have a self-rewarding character. They are varied systematically, almost as if in play to test the limits of a new skill. A baboon living in the same habitat as the chimpanzee is as eager to eat termites as is the latter; yet he shows none of these capacities even though he is seen to observe the chimpanzee exercising them often. He too is equipped with a good pair of hands. Note that there is an association between play and tool use, and that the natural selection of one, tools, led to the selection of the other as well, in the evolution of the hominids and man.

Adults as models

Neither among chimpanzees nor in the infinitely more evolved society of hunter–gatherers is there much direct intervention by adults in the learning of the young. They serve principally as models and as sources of the necessary affection (Bruner, 1965). Among the primates, there is very little intentional pedagogy of any kind. Hinde (1971) recently reviewed the literature and concluded as follows:

> On the whole, the mothers of nonhuman primates seem not to teach their infants. In a number of species, a mother has been seen to move a little away from her infant and then to wait while it crawled after her (e.g. Howler

monkeys; Carpenter, 1934; rhesus, Hinde *et al.*, 1964; gorilla, Schaller, 1963; chimpanzees, van Lawick-Goodall, 1968): this has the effect of encouraging the infant to walk, but can hardly be called teaching. However, it is clear that infants learn a great deal from their mothers, especially in the context of avoidance and food-getting behavior. Even avoidance of snakes differs between laboratory and wild-reared monkeys and may depend in part on parental example (Joslin *et al.*, 1964). It has been shown in the laboratory that monkeys can learn to avoid situations or responses that are seen to cause pain to other individuals (Child, 1938; Hansen and Mason, 1962; Hall, 1968), and to accept food that other individuals are seen to take (Distant and Cowey, 1963). In nature, the infant's proximity to its mother ensures that it becomes rapidly conditioned by her fear responses (e.g. Baldwin, 1969) and that its feeding behavior is influenced by her (e.g. Baldwin, 1969). In the patas monkey (Hall and DeVore, 1965), Japanese macaque (*Macaca fuscata*) (Kwamura, 1969), and chimpanzee (van Lawick-Goodall, 1968), the young eat fragments that their mothers drop, as well as being especially likely to feed at the same food sources. Although by the time they are one year old, Japanese macaques are acquainted with all the types of food used by the troop, it is difficult to make them take new types of food in the laboratory. Apparently learning from the mother is normally important (Kawamura, 1959). Schaller (1963) records an infant gorilla removing food from its mother's mouth and eating it, and one case of a mother breaking off a stem for its infant to eat. Imitation, principally of the mother, is important for the development of tool-using behavior in wild-living chimpanzees (Goodall, 1964; van Lawick-Goodall, 1968); and the development of actions by imitation has also been recorded in hand-reared individuals (Hayes and Hayes, 1952; Kellogg, 1968). In the latter case, the actions may be used for social communication (Gardner and Gardner, 1971).

In squirrel monkeys, food-catching skill is learned by younger juveniles from older ones, rather than from their mothers (Baldwin, 1969). However, it is by no means always the younger animals that learn food habits from older ones. Under natural conditions, young animals investigate new objects more than do older individuals, and this may lead to a transfer of feeding habits from younger to older animals. Thus, among the Japanese macaques, new foods tended to be accepted first by juveniles, and their use then diffused through the colony via their mothers and then the mothers' younger offspring and consorts (Itani, 1958). Although diffusion sometimes occurs in the opposite direction (Frisch, 1968), kinship ties are probably always important (Kawamura, 1959; Tsumori, 1967).

(p. 32)

There may, however, be something like 'tutor proneness' among the young – an increased eagerness to learn from adults. One study now in progress suggests how such tutor proneness may come about. Rumbaugh *et al.* (1972) are training chimpanzees and orang-utans under the following conditions. One group receives tutoring modelling on a variety of tasks; each task is presented on each new encounter in the form of a new embodiment of the problem. A second group gets the same problems, but each time in the same form, so that this group is essentially repeating. The third group is presented with the materials used by the others, but the human tutor model neither presents them as tasks nor models the solutions as in the first two instances. The tasks are mechanical puzzles, packing fitted containers within each other, searching for a hidden object, transporting an object to another part of the room, extracting candy from a container, etc. The reward is some combination of task completion and the tutor's approval. A preliminary finding of this work-in-progress is of particular interest. The apes in the more challenging first condition are the ones most likely to wait for the tutor to provide a clue before beginning on their own.

Does it then require a certain level of challenge and novelty to create tutor proneness in primates? Schaller (1964) remarked of the gorillas he observed in the Congo:

> Why was the Australopithecus, with the brain capacity of a large gorilla, the maker of stone tools, a being with a culture in the human sense, while the free-living gorilla in no way reveals the marvellous potential of its brain? I suspect that the gorilla's failure to develop further is related to the ease with which it can satisfy its needs in the forest. In its lush realm there is no selective advantage for improvement...The need for tools...is more likely in a harsh and marginal habitat where a premium is placed on an alert mind...
>
> (p. 232)

And the same view was voiced by Yerkes and Yerkes (1929) in their classic work on the great apes, as well as by Vernon Reynolds (1965) who, in a penetrating article on the comparative analysis of selection pressures operating on chimpanzees and on gorilla, concluded:

> Finally, we may briefly consider the contrast in temperaments between these two anthropoid species. Comparative behavior studies in the past often stressed this difference. Tevis (1921), for instance, wrote, 'In mental characteristics there is the widest difference between the two apes that we are considering. The chimpanzee is lively, and at least when young, teachable and tameable. The gorilla, on the other hand, is gloomy and ferocious, and quite untameable' (p. 122). It is possible to suggest an explanation for this contrast between the morose, sullen, placid gorilla, and the lively, exciteable chimpanzee. The difference seems to be most clearly related to the difference in social organization and foraging behavior. The herbivorous gorilla is surrounded by food: the more intensively it feeds, the slower it travels; its survival needs are easily met, and it is protected from predators by the presence of powerful males. Here there is no advantage to any form of hyper-activity except in threat displays and the charge of the big male, which is a hyper-aggressive behavior form. Chimpanzee survival, on the other hand, depends heavily on the fluidity of social groups and the ability to communicate the whereabouts of food by intense forms of activity (wild vocalizing and strong drumming). Moving rapidly about the forest, meeting up with new chimpanzees every day, vocalizing and drumming, and locating other chimpanzees by following their calls, are the basic facts of chimpanzee existence. Here an advantage may be seen in having a responsive, expressive, and adaptable temperament. Hyper-activity is the chimpanzee norm in the wild, and with it goes a volatile temperament.
>
> (p. 704)

But here we encounter a seeming contradiction. The evolutionary trend we have been examining seems to have placed a major emphasis on a combination of developments: a relatively pressure-free environment with its concomitant increase in play, exploration, and observation; and at the same time, a certain challenge in the requirements of adaptation to a habitat. (Play in young gorillas and orang-utans in the wild, by the way, is not nearly as elaborate as in the chimpanzee (cf. Reynolds, 1965; Rodman, 1972; Schaller, 1963; Yerkes and Yerkes, 1929), and in neither of these species is there much challenge from the habitat.)

I believe that Desmond Morris (1964) has a resolution for this apparent dilemma – that, on the one hand, a non-pressureful habitat seems crucial and, on the other, challenge is significant. He made the distinction between two modes of adaptation to habitat, *specialist* and *opportunist* – the squirrel versus the rat, certain exclusively forest-dwelling monkeys like the vervet or green versus the adaptable rhesus (cf. Hinde, 1971). Non-specialists depend on high flexibility rather than on morphology or behavioural specialization. Aristarchus said it well and provided Isaiah Berlin (1953) with a famous book title: 'The fox knows many things; the hedgehog knows one big thing'.

One can only speculate that the evolution of intellectual processes in the primate stock from which man descended was in the direction of opportunism and away from specialism. It could be argued, indeed, that the original stock, as far as intellect goes, was closer to chimpanzee than to either of the contemporary pongids, though Rumbaugh (1970) believed that in certain forms of intellectual performance there are striking parallels between man and orang-utan. The argument for opportunism seems in fact essential to account for the rapid fanning out of the evolved species to such a variety of habitats.

Instructional interaction between adults and young

What can be said of 'instruction' of the young in the protohominids and early man? Alas, nothing definite. But contemporary 'simple' societies, hunter–gatherers, provide certain clues. No matter how constraining the ecological conditions, there is among such people 'an expansion in adult–child instructional interaction, both quantitatively and qualitatively, of a major order. Although one cannot reconstruct the Pleistocene hunter–gatherer by reference to such isolated hunter–gatherers as the contemporary !Kung Bushmen, their practices do suggest something about the magnitude of the change. !Kung adults and children play and dance together, sit together, participate in minor hunting together, join in song and storytelling together. At frequent intervals, moreover, children are the objects of intense rituals presided over by adults – minor, as in the first haircutting, or major, as when a boy kills his first Kudu buck and undergoes the proud but painful process of scarification. Children also are playing constantly at the rituals, with the implements, tools, and weapons of the adult world. However, in tens of thousands of feet of !Kung film prepared by the Marshalls (see Bruner, 1966), one virtually never finds an instance of teaching taking place outside the situation where the behaviour to be learned is relevant. Nobody teaches away from the scene, as in a school setting. Indeed, there is nothing like a school.

Often the adult seems to play the role of inducting the young into novel situations that, without the presence of a protecting and familiar adult, would be frightening – as in extended trekking, in witchcraft ceremonials, and in many other spheres where the child comes along and participates to the limit that he is able. This induction to the margin of anxiety, I believe, starts very early. A study by Sroufe and Wunsch (1972) provides a hint of just how early that may be. The study sets out to explore what makes human infants laugh. From four months (when laughing first appears in reliable and recognizable form) into the second year of life, the sufficient stimulus for laughter becomes increasingly distal – at first being principally tactile and close visual (e.g. tickle plus looming), with incongruities following later, as when the mother adopts an unusual position such as crawling on all fours. Note, however, that at all ages, the capers most likely to produce laughter when performed by the mother are the ones most likely to produce tears when performed by a stranger. The mother seems able to bring the young, so to speak, to the edge of terror. King (1966) has suggested that this feature of mothering is universal; that among birds as well as mammals, the presence of the mother reduces fear of novel stimuli and provides the assurance necessary for exploratory behaviour. But it is only among humans that the adult *introduces* the novel, inducts the young into new, challenging, and frightening situations – sometimes in a highly ritualistic way, as with the *rites de passage*.

There is little question that the human young (and the young of the primates generally) are quite ready to be lured by the novel, given even the minimum adult reassurance. 'Neophilia' is what Desmond Morris (1967) calls it. Such readiness for novelty may even be attested to by a superiority, at least among the great apes and man, of the young over the old in detecting or extracting the rules and regularities in new situations. At least one laboratory study, Rumbaugh and McCormack (1967), has even found a *negative* correlation between age and the ability to master learning-set problems – tasks that have a common principle but a new embodiment on each presentation, like 'pick the odd one when two are alike and one is different'.[5] But note that it is in man only that adults arrange play and ritual for children that capitalize on this tendency.

It is obvious that the play and ritual in which young and adult humans are involved are saturated heavily with symbolism. Though the kind of mastery play I have been at some pains to describe in the preceding discussion is still a feature of human play, there is added to it now an extraordinary range of play forms that have as their vehicle the use of *symbols* and *conventions* – two terms that will concern us in due course. Not only are sticks, so to speak, used as arrows or spears or even as novel and unusual tools, they may be used now in a symbolic way that transcends utility – as horses, for example when put between the legs (Vygotsky, 1967) or giant trees when propped up in the sand. The prop or 'pivot' or toy (it is difficult to name the stick) is not used as a *utilitandun* (as, say, Khroustov's chimpanzee used a separated splinter to poke food out of a tube) but as a point of departure from the present perceptual situation. Though the stick must have some feature that is horselike (it must at least be 'go-between-the-leggable'), it must now also fit into an imaginary situation. It is for this reason that the great Russian psychologist Vygotsky used the term pivot: the stick is a pivot between the real and the imagined.

Once the symbolic transformation of play has occurred, two consequences follow. Play can serve as a vehicle for teaching the nature of a society's conventions, and it can also teach about the nature of conventions *per se*. David Lewis (1969) defined a convention as an agreement about procedure, the procedure itself being trivial, but the agreement not. We drive to the right, or we exhibit a red light to port and a green to starboard. And it is evident immediately that a linguistic-cultural community depends on an easy and fluent grasp of convention on the part of its members. Symbolic play, whatever function it may serve for the individual child in working through his own problems or fulfilling his wishes at the fantasy level, has an even more crucial role in teaching that child fluency with rules and conventions.

As for pretraining in the particular system of conventions of the society, let me give an instance from an exotic culture. The reader can provide instances closer to home. This one is from Dolhinow and Bishop's (1970) review:

> In New Guinea the Tangu engage in a ritual food exchange in which strict equivalence is maintained (Burridge, 1957). Equivalence is determined by mutual agreement between trading partners. The Tangu children play a game called taketak in which two lots of thirty spines of coconut palm fronds are stuck into the ground five yards apart. Individual spines within the lot are placed approximately six inches apart. The children have tops that are spun and let loose to try to touch the spines of the opponent's lot. The teams need not be equal, but the number of tops must be equal. The game proceeds as a series of bouts; within each bout, both teams must complete their turn. The game ends when, after any bout, both teams have an equivalent number of spines in and out, or, since this rarely occurs, when an end is mutually agreed upon. The object of the game is equivalence, just as in the food exchange ritual of the adults, and in both cases the outcome or equivalence is decided upon by mutual agreement. There is no winner or loser; the object is to tie.
>
> (pp. 183–184)

Using symbolic means: language

Having gone this far into symbolic play, I now turn to language in order to be more precise about what is involved when symbolic means are used for preparing the human young for culture. Higher primate skill, as I have described it, has about it certain languagelike properties. Skilled action, like language, has paraphrases and a kind of grammar. But there is also a communicative function of language; and it is this function, in all probability, that determines many of its design features (cf. Hockett, 1960). I have emphasized the similarity between action and the structure of language in order to propose a critical hypothesis: the initial use of language is probably in support of and closely linked to action. The initial structure of language and, indeed, the universal structure of its syntax are extensions of the structure of action. Syntax is not arbitrary; its cases mirror the requirements of signalling about action and representing action: agent, action, object, location, attribution, and direction are among its cases. Whatever the language, the agent–action–object structure is the form soon realized by the young speaker. Propositions about the evolution of language are justly suspect. I offer this hypothesis not on the basis of evolutionary evidence but on developmental grounds. For what the child himself shows us is that initial development of language follows and does not lead his development of skill in action and thought. It is only *after* a distinction has been mastered in action that it appears in initial language; and when it first does so, it is referenced by paraphrase of previously learned words or phrases (cf. Slobin, 1971). Piaget (1967) put it succinctly: 'language is not enough to explain thought, because the structures that characterize thought have their roots in action and in sensorimotor mechanisms that are deeper than linguistics' (p. 98).[6] And, to use Cromer's (1968) words: 'once certain cognitive abilities have developed, we find an active search ... for new forms. Suddenly, forms (and words!) which the child has been exposed to for years become a part of his own speech' (p. 219).

At the onset of speech, then, language is virtually an outgrowth of the mastery of skilled action and perceptual discrimination. These abilities sensitize and almost drive the child to linguistic development. De Laguna (1963, orig. publ. 1927) remarked that the most likely evolutionary explanation of language lies in the human need for help, crucial to the 'social–technical way of life' that is distinctly human (cf. Washburn and Howell, 1960). De Laguna went on:

> Once we deliberately ask the question: What does speech do? What objective function does it perform in human life – the answer is not far to seek. Speech is the great medium through which human cooperation is brought about. It is the means by which the diverse activities of men are coordinated and correlated with each other for the attainment of common and reciprocal ends.
>
> (p. 19)

Having said that much, we must next note that with further growth, the major trend is a steadfast march *away* from the use of language as an adjunct of action or as a marker for representing the immediate experience. If in the beginning it is true (Block, p. 107, cited in De Laguna, 1963, orig. publ. 1927, pp. 89–90) that 'a substantive does not denote simply an object, but all the actions with which it is in relation in the experience of the child', it is soon the case that language in the human comes increasingly to be free of the context of action. Whereas 'to understand what a baby is saying, you must see what the baby is doing', nothing of the sort is true for the adult. This brings us to the famous De Laguna dictum, the implications of which will concern us for the remainder of this chapter:[7]

> The evolution of language is characterized by a progressive freeing of speech from dependence on the perceived conditions under which it is uttered and heard, and from the behavior which accompanies it. The extreme limit of this freedom is reached in language which is written (or printed) and read. For example, it is quite indifferent to the reader of these words, under what physical conditions they have been penned or typed. This represents, we repeat, the extreme limit of the process by which language comes to be increasingly independent of the conditions of its use.
>
> (p. 107)

We need not pause long on a comparison of language as it is acquired and used by man and by the chimpanzee – notably by the chimpanzee Washoe (Gardner and Gardner, 1971; Ploog and Melnechuk, 1971). For one thing, Washoe's language acquisition is not spontaneous, and she can be seen from the film record to be both reluctant and bored as a language learner. There is neither the play nor the drive of the human child, the *Funktionslust* (Bühlier, 1934), that keeps the child exploring and playing with language. The young chimpanzee's grammar is tied perpetually to action. The nominatives and the attributives of early childhood speech, naming objects and attributing properties to them, are lacking and never seem to appear in Washoe. The evident delight of Matthew (Greenfield *et al.*, 1972) in the use of such nominatives as 'airplane', 'apple', 'piece', and 'cow' is quite as important as the fact that these holophrases were used in a context of action. Roger Brown (1970, 1971) has commented that virtually all of the two-sign and three-sign 'utterances' in Washoe's use of American sign language were either 'emphasizers' of action (*Hurry open*), 'specifiers' of action (*Listen dog*, at sound of barking), or indicated agents for action (*You eat, Roger Washoe tickle*). David McNeill (1973) put it concisely: Washoe's grammar can be characterized by the single proposition:

$s \ldots p^n$

or, 'statement that raises a predicated action to a higher level', a grammatical form not spontaneously present in human adult speech.[8] In a word, chimpanzee use of a taught form of human speech is strongly tied to action, beyond which it tends not to go, either spontaneously or by dint of teaching effort.

On the other hand, the development of language in humans not only moves in the direction of becoming itself free of context and accompanying action, it also frees the attention of the user from his immediate surroundings, directing attention to what is being said rather than to what is being done or seen. In the process, language becomes a powerful instrument in selectively directing attention to features of the environment represented by it.

With respect to the first of these, language processing goes on in its very nature at different levels. We process the phonological output of a speaker, interpret his syntax, hold the head words of imbedding phrases until the imbedded phrase is completed and the tail is located to match the head word, etc. At the same time, we direct attention to meanings and to references. The acts of language, argue Miller and Johnson-Laird (see footnote 3, p. 15), by their very performance free attention from control by immediate stimulation in the environment. One might even argue that the requirement of organizing what one experiences into sentence form may impose upon experience itself a certain cast – the classic arguments of Humbolt (1836) and Benjamin Lee Whorf (1956). Once language captures control of attention, the swiftness and subtlety of attention change come to match the swiftness and subtlety of linguistic manoeuvring. Language permits search specifications to be set in such a fashion as to fulfil any question that may be asked. The eye-movement records collected by Yarbus (1967) provide stunning illustration of the tactics of the language user: how, while guiding his eye movements by physical features of a picture of scene, he manages at the same time to pick up the features that answer questions he is entertaining – looking now to pick up the ages of people, now to judge their furniture, now to see what they are doing, etc.

To summarize, then, though language springs from and aids action, it quickly becomes self-contained and free of the context of action. It is a device, moreover, that frees its possessor from the immediacy of the environment not only by pre-emption of attention during language use but by its capacity to direct attention toward those aspects of the environment that are singled out by language.

I have gone into this much detail regarding early language because it is a necessary preliminary to a crucial point about the management of immaturity in human culture. I have commented already on the fact that in simple, hunter–gatherer societies, there is very little formal teaching outside the sphere of action. The child is not drawn aside and told how to do it: he is shown while the action is going on, with language as an auxiliary and as a marker of action – an aid in calling attention to what is going on that is relevant. Over and beyond that, the principal use of language was probably some mix of guiding group action and giving shape to a believe system through myths and incantations, as Susanne Langer (1969) has long proposed. I rather suspect that increasing technology imposed an increasing demand on language to represent and store knowledge in a fashion to be helpful outside the immediate context of original use. L. S. B. Leaky[9] suggested that once stone instruments came to be made to match a pattern rather than by spontaneous breaking, as in fabricating an Acheulan pebble tool with a single-face edge, *models* could be fashioned and kept. He has found excellent, obsidian-grained hand axes at Olduvai that appear never to have been used; he speculates that they were 'models for copy', with a religious significance as well.

But an inert model is a poor thing; it is, in effect, an end state, something to be attained with no intervening instruction concerning means. Language does better than that, and it is interesting to see the extent to which magic becomes mixed with practice and imitation in a primitive technology. A good example is afforded by the boat building and inter-island navigation of the pre-literate Puluwat Islanders in the Marshalls, recently described in rich detail by Gladwin (1970) in a book entitled *East is a big bird*. Theirs is a system in which East is marked by Altair at horizon elevation, distance by a commonsense speed-estimating method, with distance 'logged' by noting the supposed parallax of islands at different distances over the horizon. Final homing on an island is accomplished by noting the direction of end-of-day nesting flights of boobies and frigate birds. And the lot is peppered with sundry omens given by weeds and sea turtles and the feel of things. I happen to be a navigator myself. I am impressed not only that the system works but that it is genuinely a *system*; it ties together means and ends. The framework of the system can be *told*; however, without language it would be impossible, for the ingredients of the system involve reference to the absent or invisible, to the possible, to the conditional, and even (I suspect) to the knowingly false (the white lies all navigators must tell to keep the trustful sailors trusting). There must have been hunting systems and seasonal marking systems of this sort, representable outside the setting of action, in use by very early man – probably much earlier than heretofore suspected (cf. Marshack, 1972).

Increasingly, then, language in its decontextualized form becomes among human beings the medium for passing on knowledge. And, of course, the emergence of written language – a very recent innovation from an evolutionary point of view – gives this tendency still further amplification. Once this mode of transmitting knowledge has become established, the conditions for the invention of school – a place where teaching occurs – are present. School is a very recent development in evolutionary terms, even in historical terms. I explore now some of the consequences of these developments for our mode of dealing with, informing, and shaping the immature.

From 'knowing how' to 'knowing that'

As soon as schools, pedagogues, and the storing of decontextualized information received legitimacy – and it was probably the written word that accomplished this legitimization – the emphasis shifted from *knowing how* to *knowing that*. Even growth becomes redefined in accordance with the shift – the adult 'having' more knowledge, that is, 'knowing about' more things. We have even come to define the needs of infancy in these terms, as 'the need for experience' (rather than, as Bowlby, 1969, noted, in terms of the need for love and for predictability). Knowledge in some way becomes a central desideratum. And when, as in the United States, attention turns to the children of the underprivileged and the exploited, their difficulty is likely to be, and indeed in this case was, attributed to 'cultural deprivation'. Hence, an 'enriched environment' was prescribed much as if the issue were avitaminosis.[10] Dewey (1916) referred early to this diagnosis as the 'cold-storage' ideal of knowledge and, of course, attacked it vigorously.

But this is too simple, for in fact there is great power inherent in decontextualized knowledge – knowledge represented in a form that is relatively free from the uses to which it is to be put or to which it has been put in the past.[11] It is not too serious an oversimplification to say that it is precisely such a process of reorganizing knowledge into formal systems that frees it of functional fixedness. By using a system of notation that redefines functional requirements in formal terms, far greater flexibility can be achieved. Rather than thinking in terms of 'hammers', with all of their associated conventionalized imagery, one thinks instead in terms of force to be applied in excess of a certain level of resistance to be overcome. It is, in effect, the way of science to render the problem into this form in order to make the solving of *particular* problems mere instances of much simpler general problems and thereby to increase the range of applicability of knowledge. Why should the Puluwatan navigator struggle with such a set of complexities as I have described, when all it gets him is competence over a few hundred miles of ocean, and a shaky competence at that! He would be more accurate and more general, as well as more flexible, if he learned to take the elevation of a heavenly body, note the time, and reduce the sight to the easily solved spherical triangle of the western navigator. Such a system would serve him anywhere.

But there are two problems (at least!) in this ideal of efficient formal knowledge rather than implicit knowledge, to use Polanyi's (1958) phrase. The first grows out of the point already made about skill and its de-emphasis. That de-emphasis comes out of what I believe to be a misplaced confidence in the ease with which we go from *knowing that* to *knowing how*. It is not easy; it is a deep and perplexing problem. Let me call it the effectiveness problem. Just as deep is a second problem: it may well be that the message of decontextualization and formal structure is implicitly antifantasy and antiplay: call this the engagement problem. The two together – effectiveness and engagement – bring us to the heart of the matter.

With respect to effectiveness, it is probably a reasonable hypothesis that as technology advances, the effector and the energy components of industrial activity become increasingly remote from human empathy; neither the arm nor the hand any longer give the models for energy or for artificing. Energy and the tool kit become, for planning purposes, black boxes, and the major human functions are *control* and the *organization* of work. There is a spiral. It becomes possible to talk about the conduct of work almost without reference to skill or vocation – wheat production and steel production and gross national product and energy production and balance of payments. With work and competence presented in that mode, the young become more and more remote from the nature of the effort involved in running a society. Vocation, competence, skill, a sense of place in the system – these become more and more difficult for the young to fathom – or, for that matter, for the adult. It is difficult for the child to say what he will do or what he will 'be' as an adult. Effectiveness becomes elusive.

For while the new technological complexity produces an enormous increase in production processes and distribution processes, it produces no increase either in the number or in the clarity of comprehensible vocations. Production and distribution, in high technology, do not provide an operator with an opportunity to carry through from the initiation of a recognizable problem to its completion, or to see plainly how his task relates to the cycle from task initiation to task completion. Intrinsic structure and reward are removed. The result is what Norbert Wiener (1950) long ago called 'work unfit for human production'. The industrial revolution removed the worker from the home. Its technological elaboration made the worker's work away from home incomprehensible to the young and the uninitiated – the latter, often a worker himself. The greatest tribute to technique decontextualized from vocation, carried to an extreme where it becomes fascinating, is the *Whole earth catalogue*. Even the counterculture reaches a point where it is without vocations but offers only spontaneity as a contrast to over-rationalized 'vocationless' work.

School, separated from work which itself has grown difficult to understand, becomes its own world. As McLuhan (1964) insists, it becomes a medium and has its own message, regardless of what is taught. The message is its irrelevance to work, to adult life. For those who wish to pursue knowledge for its own sake, this is not upsetting. But for those who do not or cannot, school provides no guide – only knowledge, the relevance of which is clear neither to students nor to teachers. These are the conditions for alienation and confusion. I would urge that when adult models become incomprehensible, they lose the power either to guide or to inspire. I do not mean to settle the question here as to whether present adult models are in fact totally relevant to the problems of those entering society now. I will, however, return to it later.

Bronfenbrenner (1970) in his book on child rearing commented on the accelerating trend toward generational separation in technical cultures. The self-sealing peer culture, the denigration of adult ideal figures, the counter-culture committed to protest and romanticized ideals – these are by now familiar instruments of separation. But I believe them to be symptoms of the struggle to adjust to a social–technical order that changes at a rate faster than comprehension of it can be achieved and widely transmitted. This, you recall, is the problem with which we started: how can a system for preparing the immature for entry into the society deal with a future that is increasingly difficult to predict within a single lifetime? Many of the means for inducting the young into the social group, a heritage of the evolution of man's capacity for culture, appear to become ineffective under such conditions when such rapid change becomes the rule. Observation and imitative play, demonstration in context of skilled problem solving, induced tutor pror- ieness, an effective microcosm in the form of an extended family or a habitat group, and the concept of vocation – are all seemingly threatened. Yet, I wonder.

I do not propose to become gloomy. Surely human culture and our species are in deep trouble, not the least of which is loss of heart. But much of the trouble is real: we are degrading the biosphere, failing to cope with population, permitting technology to degrade individuality, and failing to plan. Many of the experimental and often radical efforts of the young represent, I believe, new variants of ancient, biologically rooted modes by which the young characteristically work through to maturity. And a great many of these efforts are in response to the new conditions we have been at such pains to describe – a rate of change faster than can be trans- mitted intergenerationally with concomitant likelihood of disastrous conse- quences. Let me conclude with a closer analysis of this point and, in so doing, come to what was referred to above as the problem of engagement.

Problem of engagement

A great many of the world's schools are conventional and dull places. They do not foster much productive play and little of what Jeremy Bentham (1840), in his *Theory of legislation*, called 'deep play' and condemned as irrational and in viola- tion of the utilitarian ideal. By deep play, Bentham meant play in which the stakes are so high that it is irrational for men to engage in it at all – a situation in which the marginal utility of what one stands to win is clearly less than the marginal disu- tility of what one stands to lose. Bentham proposed, good utilitarian that he was, that such play should be outlawed. But as the anthropologist Geertz (1972) com- mented in his close analysis of cockfighting in Bali, 'despite the logical force of Bentham's analysis men engage in such play, both passionately and often, and even in the face of law's revenge' (p. 15). Deep play is playing with fire. It is the kind of serious play that tidy and even permissive institutions for educating the young cannot live with happily, for their mandate from the society requires them to carry out their work with due regard for minimizing chagrin concerning outcomes achieved. And deep play is a poor vehicle for that.

What strikes me about the decade just past is the enormous increase in the depth of play in adolescence and, by reflection downward into lower age groups, among the young. Willingness to risk future preferment by dropping out of the system that is designed to qualify one for the future, in return for a season of communcal mutuality – surely the balance of utility to disutility is not Benthamite. Such wagers are highly dangerous for the lives of the individuals involved in them. (Note that Russian roulette is the worst bargain to be had in deep play.) When one finds deep play, the inference must be that there are deep and unresolved problems in the culture. There always are, but that does not mean that one should not look carefully at what these are and what they signify for the future. There is ample reason to believe that the present forms of deep play point to a thwarted, backed-up need for defining competence, both individually and socially, to oneself and to others. Recall that in most previous cultural eras, adults provided challenge and excitement and a certain sense of muted terror for the young by induction into rituals and skills that had momentous consequences. Engagement was built into the system. One knew the steps to growing up, both ritually and in terms of skill.

If adult life ceases to be comprehensible, or begins to be less a challenge than a drag, then engagement is lost – but only for a while. I have the impression of something new emerging. What takes the place of the deposed, incomprehensible, or worn-out competence figure, the classical adult image of skill? At first, of course, protest–withdrawal figures will – the pop figures of rock and the Timothy Leary prophets who offer an intravenous version of competence via subjectivity. I believe that gradually there is emerging a new form of role bearer – the *intermediate generation* – adolescents and young adults who take over the role of acting as models. They exist visibly in context. Their skills and vocation are proclaimed, miniaturized to appropriate size, and personalized. I should like to propose that such an intermediate generation is a response to the crisis of a change rate that goes faster than we can transmit from generation to generation.

Lest we go too rapidly, consider the pointlessness of an intergeneration in a society *with* continuity. Turnbull's (1961) account of a Pygmy group in Africa serves well:

> When a hunting party goes off there are always people left in the camp – usually some of the older men and women, some children, and perhaps one or two younger men and women. The children always have their own playground, called bopi, a few yards off from the main camp....
>
> There were always trees for the youngsters to climb, and this is one of the main sports even for those not yet old enough to walk properly. The great game is for half a dozen or more children to climb to the top of a young tree, bending it down until its top touches the ground. They then all leap off at once, and if anyone is too slow he goes flying back upward as the tree springs upright, to the jeers and laughter of his friends.
>
> Like children everywhere, Pygmy children love to imitate their adult idols. This is the beginning of their, schooling, for the adults will always encourage and help them. What else is there for them to learn except to grow into good adults? So a fond father will make a tiny bow for his son, and arrows of soft wood with blunt points. He may also give him a strip of a hunting net.

A mother will delight herself and her daughter by weaving a miniature carrying basket. At an early age, boys and girls are 'playing house'...

They will also play at hunting, the boys stretching out their little bits of net while the girls beat the ground with bunches of leaves and drive some poor. tired old frog in toward the boys... And one day they find that the games they have been playing are not games any longer, but the real thing, for they have become adults. Their hunting is now real hunting; their tree climbing is in earnest search of inaccessible honey; their acrobatics on the swings are repeated almost daily, in other forms, in the pursuit of elusive game, or in avoiding malicious forest buffalo. It happens so gradually that they hardly notice the change at first, for even when they are proud and famous hunters their life is still full of fun and laughter.

(pp. 128–129)

The transition is gradual, its excitement increased from time to time by rituals. But technological societies move away from such gradualism as they become increasingly developed. Indeed, the Protestant ethic made very early a sharp separation between what one does when young and what one does later, with the transition very sharply defined. In the western tradition there grew a puritan separation of the 'works of the adult' and 'the play of the babes'. But it was clear to both sides what the two were about. Now 'the play of the babes' has become separate from, dissociated from, the adult community and not understood by that community any better than the young comprehend or accept the ideals of the adult community.

A place is made automatically, perhaps for the first time in our cultural tradition, for an intermediate generation, with power to model new forms of behaviour. Their power comes precisely, I think, from the fact that they offer deep play, that irresistible charisma that so disturbed the tidy Jeremy Bentham. They are modelling new life styles to fit better what is perceived as the new and changing conditions, new changes that they claim to be able to see – perhaps rightly, perhaps not – more clearly than those who had adapted to something still earlier. The great question is whether the intermediate generation can reduce the uncertainty of growing up under conditions of unpredictable change, can serve as mentors as well as charismatic vendors of deep play, and as purveyors of effectiveness as well as of engagement.

I do not think that intermediate models are a transitory phenomenon. I believe that we would do well to recognize the new phenomenon and to incorporate it, even make it easier for the young adult and later juvenile to get more expert at it. Nobody can offer a blueprint on how an intermediate generation can help ready the less mature for life in an unforeseeably changing world. It is not altogether a comfortable problem either for the way of cultural revolutions and Red Guards (both composed of intermediates) can only inspire caution. But letting the young have more of a hand in the teaching of the younger, letting them have a better sense of the dilemmas of society as a whole, all of these may be part of the way in which a new community can be helped to emerge. What may be in order is a mode of inducting the young by the use of a more communal system of education in which each takes responsibility for teaching or aiding or abetting or provoking those less able less knowledgeable, and less provoked than he.

It was in the universities that these current matters first surfaced – a long way from the high savannas of East Africa where we began our quest for an understanding of immaturity and its uses. One becomes increasingly shaky the closer one comes to man in his contemporary technological society. I would only urge that in considering these deep issues of educability we keep our perspective broad and remember that the human race has a biological past from which we can read lessons for the culture of the present. We cannot adapt to everything, and in designing a way to the future we would do well to examine again what we are and what our limits are. Such a course does not mean opposition to change but, rather, using man's natural modes of adapting to render change both as intelligent and as stable as possible.

Notes

This chapter was prepared for the Study Group on Early Competence and presented later to a broader audience at the XXth International Congress of Psychology in Tokyo. In connection with its presentation at Tokyo, it was published for distribution there as a separate in the August 1972 issue of the *Am. Psychol.*

1 It should be noted carefully that in certain crucial ways, both mountain and lowland gorilla are exceptions to what is described here. For some interesting speculations about the lack of curiosity and imitativeness in the gorilla as related to his undemanding habitat and food supply as well as to his lack of need for cooperative efforts, see Yerkes and Yerkes (1929), Rumbaugh (1970), and particularly Reynolds (1965).

2 G. Miller and P. Johnson-Laird. *Presuppositions of language.* (privately circulated) 1961.

3 For an excellent account of the changes that occur during this enlargement, making possible greater flexibility of connection and possibly better memory storage, see Altman (1967). Some of the same changes during this period of expansion also occur as a result of challenging environments (Bennet *et al.*, 1964), and in the course of phylogeny (Altman, 1967).

4 D. Wood, J. S. Bruner and G. Ross. *Modelling and mastery in construction task.* In preparation.

5 Rumbaugh (1970) commented in a recent review of the learning capacities of great apes: 'It is frequently observed, however, that an animal that excels in learning when young remains excellent *if* frequently worked with as it grows to adulthood (at least eight years of age) and beyond. Might it be the case that early experience in some manner determines the avenues along which intelligent behavior will be manifest. If early experiences are with formal test and learning situations, will the animal's adaptability be maximally manifest as an adult in contexts of that order?' (p. 65).

6 This is not to say that once a language has been mastered to a certain level (unfortunately, not easily specifiable), it cannot then be used to signal properties of action and events that up to then had *not* been mastered by the child. It is in this sense that language can in fact be used as a medium for instruction (see Bruner *et al.*, 1966).

7 For excellent accounts of the process of decontextualization in language, see Werner and Kaplan (1963) and Luria and Yudovich (1959). Both of these volumes provide rich documentation and interesting commentary on the point.

8 McNeill also made the cogent point that perhaps (as with Premack, 1971) chimpanzees can be taught a human-like syntax, a not uninteresting point; but they seem not to acquire it as children do, by a process not so much of detailed learning or imitation as of spontaneous constructions of grammatical utterances most often exhibiting initial grammatical rules not present in the adult speech to which they are exposed.

9 L. S. B. Leaky, personal communication, April 1966.

10 For a discussion of these problems in childhood as reflecting the growth of skills for surviving under hopeless conditions, see Bruner (1970), Cole and Bruner (1971), and Denenberg (1970).

11 For a fuller discussion of the nature of thought processes employing formal and functional modes of organizing knowledge, the reader is referred to Bruner *et al.* (1956); Polanyi (1958); Popper (1954); Bartlett (1958); and Piaget's (1971) striking little volume on structuralism.

References

Altman, J. 1967. Postnatal growth and differentiation of the mammalian brain, with implications for a morphological theory of memory. In G. C. Quarton, T. Melnechuk and

F. O. Schmitt (Eds), *The neurosciences: a study program*, Vol. 1. Rockefeller University Press, New York.

Barsh, R. 1972. The evolution of tool use. Unpublished research paper. Center for Cognitive Studies, Harvard University.

Bartlett, F. C. 1958. *Thinking: an experimental and social study*. Basic Books, New York.

Beach, F. 1965. *Sex and behavior*. Wiley, New York, London and Sydney.

Bennett, E. L., Diamond, M. C., Krech, D. and Rosenzweig, M. R. 1964. Chemical and anatomical plasticity of the brain. *Science, N. Y.*, **146**, 610–619.

Bentham, J. 1840. *The theory of legislation*. Weeks, Jordan, Boston.

Berlin, I. 1953. *The hedgehog and the fox*. Simon and Schuster, New York.

Bernstein, N. 1967. *The coordination and regulation of movements*. Pergamon Press, Oxford.

Birch, H. G. 1945. The relation of previous experience to insightful problem-solving. *J. comp. physiol. Psychol.*, **38**, 367–383.

Bishop, A. 1964. Use of the hand in lower primates. In J. Buettner-Janusch (Ed.), *Evolutionary and genetic biology of primates*, Vol. 2. Academic Press, London and New York.

Block, S. C. 1974. Early competence in problem-solving. In K. J. Connolly and J. S. Bruner (Eds), *Growth of Competence*. Academic Press, New York and London.

Bloom, B. (Ed.). 1956. *Taxonomy of educational objectives*. McKay, New York.

Bowlby, J. 1969. *Attachment and loss*, Vol. 1. Basic Books, New York.

Bronfenbrenner, U. 1970. *Two worlds of childhood, U.S. and U.S.S.R.* Russell Sage Foundation, New York.

Brown, R. W. 1970. The first sentence of child chimpanzee. In *Psycholinguistics: selected papers by Roger Brown*. Free Press, New York.

Brown, R. W. 1971. Are apes capable of language? *Neurosci. Res. Prog. Bull.*, **9** (5).

Bruner, J. S. 1965. The growth of mind. *Amer. Psychol.*, **20**, 1007–1017.

Bruner, J. S. 1966. *Toward a theory of instruction*. Harvard University Press, Cambridge.

Bruner, J. S. 1970. *Poverty and childhood*. Merrill-Palmer Institute, Detroit.

Bruner, J. S. and Koslowski, B. 1972. Preadaptation in initial visually guided reaching. *Perception*, **1**, 3–14.

Bruner, J. S., Goodnow, J. J. and Austin, G. A. 1956. *A study of thinking*. Wiley, New York.

Bruner, J. S., Greenfield, P. M. and Olver, R. R. 1966. *Studies in cognitive growth*. Wiley, New York.

Bühler, K. 1934. *Sprachtheorie*. Jena.

Chance, M. R. A. 1967. Attention structure as the basis of primate rank orders. *Man*, **2**, 503–518.

Clark, W. E. Le Gros. 1963. *The antecedents of man: an introduction to the evolution of the primates*. Harper and Row, New York.

Cole, M. and Bruner, J. S. 1971. Cultural differences and inferences about psychological processes. *Amer. Psychol.*, **26**, 867–876.

Cromer, R. F. 1968. The development of temporal reference during the acquisition of language. Unpublished doctoral dissertation. Department of Social Relations, Harvard University.

Denenberg, V. H. (Ed.). 1970. *Education of the infant and the young child*. Academic Press, New York and London.

Devore, 1. 1965. *The primates*. Time-Life Books, New York.

Dewey, J. 1916. *Democracy and education*. Macmillan, New York.

Dolhinow, P. J. and Bishop, N. 1970. The development of motor skills and social relationships among primates through play. *Minnesota Symposium on Child Psychology*, Vol. 4.

Gallup, G. G., Jr 1970. Chimpanzees: self-recognition. *Science, N. Y.*, **167**, 86–87.

Gardner, B. J. and Gardner, R. A. 1971. Two-way communication with an infant chimpanzee. In A. M. Schrier and F. Stollnitz (Eds), *Behavior of nonhuman primates*, Vol. 4. Academic Press, New York and London.

Geertz, C. 1972. Deep play: notes on the Balinese cockfight. *Daedalus*, **101**, 1–38.

Gladwin, T. 1970. *East is a big bird*. Harvard University Press, Cambridge.

Goodall, J. 1965. Chimpanzees of the Gombe Stream Reserve. In I. DeVore (Ed.), *Primate behavior: field studies of monkeys and apes*. Holt, Rinehart and Winston, New York.

Gouldner, A. 1960. The norm of reciprocity: A preliminary statement. *Amer. Sociol. Rev.*, **25**, 161–178.

Greenfield, P., May, A. A. and Bruner, J. S. 1972. *Early words* (a film). Wiley, New York.

Hall, K. R. L. and DeVore, I. 1965. Baboon social behavior. In I. DeVore (Ed.), *Primate behavior: field studies of monkeys and apes*. Holt, Rinehart and Winston, New York.

Hamburg, D. 1968. Evolution of emotional responses: Evidence from recent research on nonhuman primates. *Science and Psychoanalysis*, **12**, 39–54.

Harlow, H. F. 1959. Love in infant monkeys. *Scientific American*, **200**, 68–74.

Harlow, H. F. and Harlow, M. K. 1962. The effect of rearing conditions on behavior. *Bull. Menninger Clinic*, **26**, 213–224.

Hayes, K. J. and Hayes, C. 1952. Imitation in a home-raised chimpanzee. *J. comp. physiol. Psychol.*, **45**, 450–459.

Herbert, M. J. and Harsh, C. M. 1944. Observational learning in cats. *J. comp. physiol. Psychol.*, **37**, 81–95.

Hinde, R. A. 1971. Development of social behavior. In A. M. Schrier and F. Stollnitz (Eds), *Behavior of nonhuman primates*. Academic Press, New York and London.

Hockett, C. D. 1960. The origins of speech. *Scientific American*, **203**, 88–96.

Humboldt, W., von. 1836. *Ueber die Verschiedenheit des menschlichen Sprachbaues*. Berlin (facsimile ed., Bonn, 1960).

Itani, J. 1958. On the acquisition and propagation of a new food habit in the natural group of the Japanese monkey at Takasakiyama. *Primates*, **1**, 84–98.

Jolly, A. 1966. *Lemur behavior: a Madagascar field study*. University of Chicago Press, Chicago.

Kawamura, S. 1959. The process of subculture propagation among Japanese macaques. *Primates*, **2**, 43–54.

Khroustov, G. F. 1968. Formation and highest frontier of the implemental activity of anthropoids. In *Seventh International Congress of Anthropological and Ethnological Sciences*, Moscow, 503–509.

King, D. L. 1966. A review and interpretation of some aspects of the infant–mother relationship in mammals and birds. *Psychol. Bull.*, **65**, 143–155.

Köhler, W. 1926. *The mentality of apes*. Harcourt, Brace, New York.

Kortland, A. 1965. How do chimpanzees use weapons when fighting leopards? *Yearbook of the American Philosophical Society*, 327–332.

Kortland, A. and Koöij, M. 1963. Protohominid behaviour in primates. In J. Napier and N. A. Bamicot (Eds), *The primates*. Symposia Zoological Society of London, **10**, 61–88.

Kortland, A. and van Zon, J. C. J. 1969. The present state of research on the dehumanization hypothesis of African ape evolution. *Proceedings of the International Congress of Primatology*, **3**, 10–13.

Laguna, G. A., de. 1963. *Speech: its function and development* (orig. publ. 1927). Indiana University Press, Bloomington, Illinois.

Lancaster, J. B. 1968. On the evolution of tool-using behavior. *Amer. Anthrop.*, **70**, 56–66.

Langer, S. 1969. *Philosophy in a new key* (rev. ed.; orig. publ. 1942). Harvard University Press, Cambridge.

Lashley, K. S. 1951. The problem of serial order in behavior. In L. A. Jeffress (Ed.), *Cerebral mechanisms in behavior: the Hixon symposium*. Wiley, New York.

Lee, R. B. and DeVore, I. (Eds). 1968. *Man the hunter*. Aldine, Chicago.

Levi-Strauss, C. 1963. *Structural anthropology*. Basic Books, New York.

Lewis, D. 1969. *Convention*. Harvard University Press, Cambridge.

Loizos, C. 1967. Play behavior in higher primates: a review. In D. Morris (Ed.), *Primate ethology*. Aldine, Chicago.

Luria, A. R. and Yudovich, F. Y. 1959. *Speech and the development of mental processes in the child*. Moscow, 1956. Staples Press, London.

McLuhan, M. 1964. *Understanding media*. McGraw-Hill, New York.

McNeill, D. 1972. Sentence Structure in Chimpanzee Communication. In K. J. Connolly and J. S. Bruner (Eds), *Growth of Competence*, Academic Press, New York and London.

Marshack, H. 1972. *The roots of civilization*. McGraw-Hill, New York.

Mayr, E. 1963. *Animal species and evolution*. Harvard University Press, Cambridge.

Merfield, F. G. and Miller, H. 1956. *Gorilla hunter*. Farrar, Strauss, New York.

Millar, S. 1968. *The psychology of play*. Penguin Books, Baltimore, Md.

Morris, D. 1964. The response of animals to a restricted environment. *Symposium of the Zoological. Society of London*, **13**, 99–118.

Morris, D. (Ed.). 1967. *Primate ethology.* Weidenfeld and Nicolson, London.

Napier, J. R. 1962. The evolution of the hand. *Scientific American, 207,* 56–62.

Piaget, J. 1967. *Six psychological studies* (Ed. by D. Elkind). Random House, New York.

Piaget, J. 1971. *Structuralism.* Routledge and Kegan Paul, London.

Ploog, D. and Melnechuk, T. 1971. Are apes capable of language? *Neurosci. Res. Prog. Bull., 9,* 600–700.

Polanyi, I. 1958. *Personal knowledge.* University of Chicago Press, Chicago.

Popper, K. 1954. *Nature, mind and modern science.* Hutchinson. London.

Premack, D. 1971. On the assessment of language competence in the chimpanzee. In A. M. Schrier and F. Stollnitz (Eds), *Behavior of nonhuman primates,* Vol. 4. Academic Press, New York and London.

Reynolds, V. 1965. Behavioral comparisons between the chimpanzee and the mountain gorilla in the wild. *American Anthropologist, 67,* 691–706.

Rodman, P. 1972. Observations of free-ranging orangutans in Borneo. Colloquium talk at the Center for Cognitive Studies, Harvard University.

Rumbaugh, D. M. 1970. Learning skills of anthropoids. In, *Primate behavior,* Vol. 1. Academic Press, New York.

Rumbaugh, D. M. and McCormack, C. 1967. The learning skills of primates: A Comparative study of apes and monkeys. In D. Stark, R. Schneider and H. J. Kuhn (Eds), *Progress in primatology,* Fischer, Stuttgart.

Rumbaugh, D. M., Riesen, A. H. and Wright, S. C. 1972. Creative responsiveness to objects: A report of a pilot study with young apes. Privately distributed paper from Yerkes Laboratory of Psychobiology, Atlanta, GA.

Schaller, G. 1963. *Mountain gorilla.* University of Chicago Press, Chicago, IL.

Schaller, G. 1964. *The year of the gorilla.* University of Chicago Press, Chicago, IL.

Schiller, P. H. 1952. Innate constituents of complex responses in primates. *Psychol. Rev., 59,* 177–191.

Singh, S. D. 1969. Urban monkeys. *Scientific American, 221,* 108–115.

Slobin, D. 1971. Cognitive prerequisites of language. In W. O. Dingwall (Ed.), *Developmental psycholinguistics: a survey of linguistic science.* University of Maryland Linguistics Program, College Park.

Sroufe, A. and Wunsch, J. P. The development of laughter in the first year of life. *Child. Dev., 43,* 1326–1344.

Tinbergen, N. 1953. *The herring gull's world: A study of the social behavior of birds.* Collins, London.

Trivers, R. 1971. The evolution of reciprocal altrusim. *Quart. Rev. Biol., 46,* 35–57.

Turnbull, C. 1961. *The forest people.* Simon and Schuster, New York.

Van Lawick-Goodall, J. 1968. The behavior of free living chimpanzees in the Gombe Stream Reserve. *Arim. Behav. Monogr., 1,* 165–301.

Vygotsky, L. S. 1967. Play and its role in the mental development of the child (1933). *Soviet Psychology, 5,* 6–18.

Washburn, S. L. and Howell, F. C. 1960, Human evolution and culture. In S. Tax (Ed.), *The evolution of man.* University of Chicago Press, Chicago, IL.

Weir, R. H. 1962. *Language in the crib.* Mouton, the Hague.

Werner, H. and Kaplan, B. 1963. *Symbol formation.* Wiley, New York.

Whorf, B. L. 1956. *Language, thought and reality: selected writings* (Ed. by J. B. Carroll). M.I.T. Press, Cambridge; Wiley, New York.

Wiener, N. 1950. *The human use of human beings; cybernetics and society.* Houghton Mifflin, Boston.

Yarbus, A. L. 1967. *Eye movements and vision.* Plenum Press, New York.

Yerkes, R. M. and Yerkes, A. W. 1929. *The great apes: a study of anthropoid life.* Yale University Press, New Haven.

CHAPTER 13

CHILD'S PLAY

New Scientist (1972) 62, 694, London: IPC Magazines Ltd

For many years psychologists viewed play as an unquantifiable behaviour. But it is now seen as an important guide to cultural and intellectual development.

Experimental psychology tends to be rather a sober discipline, tough-minded not only in its procedures, but in its choice of topics as well. They must be scientifically manageable. No surprise, then, that when it began extending its investigations into the realm of early human development it steered clear of so antic a phenomenon as play. For even as recently as a decade ago, Harold Schlosberg of Brown University, a highly respected critic, had published a carefully reasoned paper concluding sternly that, since play could not even be properly defined, it could scarcely be a manageable topic for experimental research. His paper was not without merit, for the phenomena of play cannot be impeccably framed into a single operational definition. How indeed can one encompass so motley a set of entries as childish punning, cowboys-and-Indians, and the construction of a tower of bricks into a single or even a sober dictionary entry?

Fortunately, the progress of research is subject to accidents of opportunity. Once data begin seriously to undermine presuppositions, the course can change very quickly. A decade ago, while Schlosberg's words still reverberated, work on primate ethology began to force a change in direction, raising new and basic questions about the nature and role of play in the evolution of the primate series. On closer inspection, play is not as diverse a phenomenon as had been thought, particularly when looked at in its natural setting. Nor is it that all antic in its structure, if analysed properly. But perhaps most important, its role during immaturity appears to be more and more central as one moves up, the living primate series from Old World monkeys through Great Apes, to Man – suggesting that in the evolution of primates, marked by an increase in the number of years of immaturity, the selection of a capacity for play during those years may have been crucial. So if play seemed to the methodologically vexed to be an unmanageable laboratory topic, primatologists were pondering its possible centrality in evolution!

A first field finding served to reduce the apparently dizzying variety of forms that play could take. On closer inspection, it turns out that play is universally accompanied in subhuman primates by a recognisable form of metasignalling, a 'play face', first carefully studied by the Dutch primatologist van Hooff (Figure 13.1). It signifies within the species the message, to use Gregory Bateson's phrase, 'this is play'. It is a powerful signal – redundant in its features, which include a particular kind of open-mouthed gesture, a slack but exaggerated gait,

Figure 13.1 Sketch showing a chimpanzee play face.

and a marked 'galumphing' in movement – and its function is plainly not to be understood simply as 'practice of instinctive activities crucial for survival'. When, for example, Stephen Miller and I set about analysing filmed field records of juvenile play behaviour made by Irven DeVore while studying Savanna baboons in the Amboseli Game Reserve in East Africa, we very quickly discovered that if one young animal did not see the 'metasignal' of another who was seeking to play-fight with him, a real fight broke out with no lack of skill. But once the signal was perceived by both parties the fight was transformed into the universally recognisable clownish ballet of monkeys feigning a fight. They obviously knew how to do it both ways. What was it for, then, play fighting? And why should the accompanying form of metasignalling have been selected, in evolution?

We begin to get a hint of the functional significance of play in higher primates from the pioneering observations of the group led by Jane van Lawick-Goodall studying free-ranging chimpanzees at the Gombe Stream Reserve in Tanzania. Recall first the considerably longer childhood in chimpanzees than in Old World monkeys – the young chimp in close contact with the mother for four or five years during which the mother has no other offspring, whilst in monkeys, the oestrus cycle assures that within a year new young are born, with the rapidly maturing animals of last year's crop relegated to a peer group of juveniles in which play declines rapidly.

Sitting with mother

David Hamburg of Stanford, a psychiatrist-primatologist working at Gombe Stream, has noted the extent to which young chimpanzees in the first five years spend time observing adult behaviour, incorporating observed patterns of adult behaviour into their play. Van Lawick-Goodall has a telling observation to report that relates this early observation-cum-play to adult skilled behaviour – an observation that deepens our understanding of the function of early play. Adult chimps develop (when the ecology permits) a very skilled technique of termiting, in which they put mouth-wetted, stripped sticks into the opening of a termite hill, wait a bit for the termites to adhere to the stick, then carefully remove their fishing 'instrument' with termites adhering to it which they then eat with relish. One of the young animals, Merlin, lost his mother in his third year. He had not learned to termite by four-and-a-half nearly as well as the others, though raised by older siblings. For the young animals appear to learn the 'art of termiting' by sitting by the mother, buffered from pressures, trying out in play and learning the individual constituent acts that make up termiting, and without the usual reinforcement of food from catching: learning to play with sticks, to strip leaves from twigs, and to pick the right length of twig for getting into different holes. These are the constituents that must be combined in the final act, and they are tried out in all manner of antic episodes.

Merlin, compared to his age mates, was inept and unequipped. He had not had the opportunity for such observation and play nor, probably, did he get the buffering from distraction and pressure normally provided by the presence of a mother. This would suggest, then, that play has the effect of providing practice not so much of survival-relevant instinctive behaviour but, rather, of making possible the playful practice of subroutines of behaviour later to be combined in more useful problem solving. What appears to be at stake in play is the opportunity for assembling and reassembling behaviour sequences for skilled action. That, at least, is one function of play.

It suggests a more general feature of play. It is able to reduce or neutralise the pressure of goal-directed action, the 'push' to successful completion of an act. There is a well known rule in the psychology of learning, the Yerkes-Dodson law, that states that the more complex a skill to be learned, the lower the *optimum* motivational level required for fastest learning. Play, then, may provide the means for reducing excessive drive. The distinguished Russian investigator Lev Vygotsky in a long-lost manuscript published a few years ago reports an investigation in which young children could easily be induced not to eat their favourite candy when laid before them when the candy was made part of a game of 'Poison'. And years before, Wolfgang Köhler had reported that when his chimps were learning to stack boxes to reach fruit suspended from the high tops of their cages, they often lost interest in eating the fruit when they were closing in on the solution. Indeed, Peter Reynolds in a widely acclaimed paper on play in primates given to the American Association for the Advancement of Science in Philadelphia in 1972 remarks that the essence of play is to dissociate goal-directed behaviour from its principal drive system and customary reinforcements. It is no surprise, then, to find results indicating that prior play with materials improves children's problem solving with those materials later.

Kathy Sylva of Harvard and I worked with children aged three to five who had the task of fishing a prize from a latched box out of reach. To do so, they had to extend two sticks by clamping them together. The children were given various 'training' procedures beforehand, including explaining the principle of clamping sticks together, or practice in fastening clamps on single sticks, or an opportunity to watch the experimenter carry out the task. One group was simply allowed to play with the materials. They did as well in solving the problem as the ones who had been given a demonstration of the principle of clamping sticks together and better than any of the other groups. In fact, what was striking about the play group was their tenacity in sticking with the task so that even when they were poor in their initial approach, they ended by solving the problem. What was particularly striking was their capacity to resist frustration and 'giving up'. They were playing.

The young lead the way

There are comparable results on primates below man where the pressure is taken off animals by other means – as by semi-domestication achieved by putting out food in a natural habitat, a technique pioneered by Japanese primatologists. It appears to have the effect of increasing innovation in the animals studied. Japanese macaques at Takasakiyama have taken to washing yams, to separating maize from the sand on which it is spread by dropping a handful of the mix into seawater and letting the sand sink. And once in the water, playing in this new medium to the edge of which they have been transplanted, the young learn to swim, first in play, and then begin swimming off, migrating to near islands. In all of these activities, it is the playful young who are centrally involved in the new enterprises, even if they may not always be the innovators of the new 'technologies'. But it is the young who are game for a change, and it is this gameness that predisposes the troop to change in ways – with the fully adult males often the most resistant or, at least the most out of touch, for the novelties are being tried out in the groups playing around the mother from which the big males are absent. Jean Claude Fady, the French primatologist, has shown that even ordinarily combative adult males will cooperate with each other in moving heavy rocks under which food is hidden – if the pressure is taken off by the technique of semi-domestication.

Ample early opportunity for play may have a more lasting effect still, as Corinne Hutt has shown. She designed a super-toy for children of three to five years old, consisting of a table with a lever, buzzer, bells and counters, different movements of the lever systematically sounding buzzers, and turning counters, etc. Children first explore its possibilities, then having contented themselves, often proceed to play. She was able to rate how inventive the children were in their play, dividing them into non-explorers, explorers, and inventive explorers, the last group carrying on all the way from initial exploration to full-blown play. Four years later, when the children were aged seven to ten, she tested them again on a creativity test designed by Mike Wallach and Nathan Kogan in the United States, as well as on some personality tests.

The more inventive and exploratory the children had been initially in playing with the super-toy, the higher their originality scores were four years later. The non-exploring boys in general had come to view themselves as unadventurous and inactive and their parents and teachers considered them as lacking curiosity. The non-exploratory and unplayful girls were later rather unforthcoming in social interaction as well and more tense than their originally more playful mates. Early unplayfulness may go with a lack of later originality.

Obviously, more studies of this kind are needed (and are in progress). But the psychiatrist Erik Erikson, reporting in his Godkin Lectures at Harvard in 1973 on a thirty-year follow-up of children earlier studied, has commented that the ones with the most interesting and fulfilling lives were the ones who had managed to keep a sense of playfulness at the centre of things.

Play has rules

Consider play now from a structural point of view as a form of activity. Rather than being 'random' it is usually found to be characterised by a recognisable rule structure.

New studies by the young American psycholinguist Catherine Garvey show how three- to five-year-old children, playing in pairs, manage implicitly even in their simplest games to create and recognise rules and expectancies, managing the while to distinguish sharply between the structure of make-believe or possibility and the real thing. Amusing though Catherine Garvey's protocols may be, they reveal a concise, almost grammatical quality in the interchanges and an extraordinary sensitivity on the part of the children to violations of implicit expectancies and codes.

It is hardly surprising then that different cultures encourage different forms of play as 'fitting'. Ours tend, in the main, to admire play and games of 'zero sum', one wins what the other loses. The anthropologist Kenelm Burridge contrasts our favourite form with a typical ritual food-exchange game of 'taketak' among the Tangu in New Guinea, a tribe that practices strict and equal sharing. The object of their game is to achieve equal shares among the players – not to win, not to lose, but to tie. It is reminiscent of a game reported years ago by James Sully. He tells of two sisters, five and seven, who played a game they called 'Sisters', a game with one rule: equal shares for each player, no matter what, in their case quite unlike life! We are only at the beginning of studying the functions of play in fitting children to their culture, but there are some classic studies.

If the rule structure of human play and games sensitises the child to the rules of culture, both generally and in preparation for a particular way of life, then surely play must have some special role in nurturing symbolic activity generally. For culture is symbolism in action. Does play then have some deep connection with the origins of language? One can never know. Yet, we have already noted the extraordinary combinatorial push behind play, its working out of variations. Play is certainly implicated in early language acquisition. Its structured interactions and 'rules' precede and are a part of the child's first mastery of language. Our own studies at Oxford on language acquisition suggest that in exchange games, in 'peek-bo', and in other structured interactions, young children learn to signal and to recognise signals and expectancies. They delight in primitive rule structures that come to govern their encounters. In these encounters they master the idea of 'privileges of occurrence' so central to grammar, as well as other constituents of language that must later be put together.

Indeed, there is a celebrated and highly technical volume by Ruth Weir on language play in a two-and-one-half year old child, Language in the Crib, in which she reports on the language of her son Anthony after he had been put to bed with lights out. He pushes combinatorial activity to the limit, phonologically, syntactically, and semantically, often to the point at which he remonstrates himself with an adult 'Oh no, no'.

Much more is being learned about play than we would have expected a decade ago. We have come a long way since Piaget's brilliant observations on the role of play in assimilating the child's experience to his personal schema of the world, as preparation for later accommodation to it. A new period of research on play is underway. Nick Blurton-Jones has shown that Niko Tinbergen's ethological methods can be applied to children at play as readily as to chimps in the forest. The new work begins to suggest why play is the principal business of childhood, the vehicle of improvisation and combination, the first carrier of rule systems through which a world of cultural restraint is substituted for the operation of impulse.

That such research as that reported raises deep questions about the role of play in our own society is, of course, self-evident. Although we do not yet know how important play is for growing up, we do know that it is serious business. How serious it is can perhaps be condensed by citing the conclusion of a study done on children's laughter by Alan Sroufe and his colleagues at Minnesota. They find that those things most likely to make a child laugh when done by his mother at a year are most likely to make him cry when done by a stranger.

CHAPTER 14

PATTERNS OF GROWTH

Inaugural Lecture at Oxford University, May 25, 1973

An Inaugural Lecture provides a rare chance not only for setting forth one's intellectual premises and crochets, but better still, for launching them into the future. For surely an Inaugural should be true to its Latin root: to begin, to install, with the sense of reading the future from the flight of birds or the entrails of beasts. So let me begin with some views about human development, its nature and function, including some thoughts about its proper study. After that, we can conjecture about future tasks. Or, in the voice of another American migrant to these shores,

> Calculating the future,
> Trying to unweave, unwind, unravel
> And piece together the past and the future,
> Between midnight and dawn . . . before the morning watch
> When time stops and time is never ending.

One does well to consider at the start a constraint on such an undertaking as this. The study of human behaviour, and even more so the study of its development, is not entirely a descriptive enterprise. It necessarily reflects the public demand that in the course of growth virtue be cultivated, evil rooted out, or inadvertent ill reduced to a bearable minimum. In this sense, the study of human development, for all that it may be a descriptive science, is a policy science as well, much as economics is. I take a policy science to be one in which the formulations of problems, the framing of hypotheses, and the kind of research carried out reflect the requirements of making decisions among feasible courses of action. And in the nurturing of the young, a society is required to make a continual series of decisions about such courses of action. Even at its most private and familial, child rearing still reflects a public requirement. A parent is bound by a deep if implicit contract to make the child into a certain kind of human being, to prepare him or her to take a place in a certain kind of society, to respect certain standards in order to be assured opportunity and reward. For its part, the study of human development mirrors these concerns: how to raise or even to define an intelligent human being, how to assure the growth of a proper moral judgement or an adequately evolved logical capability, how to increase independence or loyalty or tenderness, how to prevent alienation or anonymity. While these are questions that rarely affect our research directly, they none the less give it shape in subtle ways. And so it should be. Relevance is no embarrassment. I would just as soon participate in the culture. Yet this need not mean that our search for the sources of growth be any the less scientific for responding to the requirements of society. Like the economists, we will come under attack from time to time for speaking out on tender issues. So be it.

With that said, let me turn now to what for me is central to an understanding of the growth of human behaviour. Growth is organized around the acquisition of skill, skill in carrying out one's intentions. Skill implies knowledge that makes action flexible, foresightful, and open to new learning. To cultivate growth humanely is to provide conditions in which human beings can become alert and skilful in pursuit of their goals. All of this requires a communal setting, a social meshing of intentions and their pursuit. Human intentions are obviously not 'natural', though constrained by natural or biological factors. So too, skills may be culturally stylized, but constrained by biological requirements. Information must be got from short- to long-term memory in a few seconds or minutes. Our primate visual system operates with central detectors and peripheral locators, integrating information sequentially.

These are constraints, yet they are subject to cultural patterning, even to technological modification by prosthetic devices or 'instruments'. The pattern of looking and attending, for example, becomes stereotyped by social habit, and machines are already available for slowing down or speeding up what is too rapid or too slow for sequential integration. This mix, of course, is uniquely human and it makes the study of human development not only a natural and a social science, but also one of the sciences of the artificial.

Though I have chosen the enablement of human goal-seeking by the cultivation of skill as a *leitmotif*, you will see that I am mindful of the communal base of human skilled action. In most species, the 'communal' structure of adaptive action is built into the response mechanisms that have been selected in evolution, with a certain amount of room for idiosyncratic adaptation to off-beat niches. Such fixedness declines markedly as one ascends the primate order. In Man culture comes increasingly to provide rules for the communal enterprises of the species. It is probably a necessary condition for a species that constructs its own environments. So, culture and the learning of cultural rules thus become crucial to human development.

Human culture can then be said to regulate and 'socialize' the means–end activities of its members. Desirable ends are specified implicitly or explicitly, and the culture legitimizes certain means to their attainment while tabooing others. Man's goals and the paths to their attainment are then an uncertain mix of social convention and human biology. It follows from this that the raising of the young in our species will be drastically different from what one finds elsewhere in the primate order. For the young must come to cope with the world as nature indirectly, by the use of highly complex rules, ranging from the grammar of their language and the rules of their kinship to other less strictly formulated systems that govern the exchange of respect, goods, and services, etc. Perhaps it was the burden of having to transmit so much that has finally led our species, uniquely among species, deliberately to teach its young with the aim of achieving long-run effects. For in Man, the adult enters the life of the growing child in a manner and to a degree different from any other species. Pedagogy then is not an isolated feature, but a universal of the species – surely as widely distributed as the incest taboo.

Lest what I have said should create the impression that I believe there to be an irreconcilable discontinuity between how one studies human growth and how one studies growth in, say, other primates, let me note that while there are important discontinuities, these are themselves products of primate evolution and cannot be fully understood without reference to their evolving function. Alas, we have ignored until quite recently the *comparative* study of the development of behaviour. Culture, for all its uniqueness, is a resultant of biological forces in evolution, and its function in our own species is deepened by understanding its origins.

This gives us a start.

You will sense, I think, that my bias in the study of behaviour and its development is toward functionalism, toward an understanding of the means–end linkages in human behaviour and how they are perfected in the course of growth. Before turning more directly to this matter, let me say a filial word about the origin of my bias and, in doing so, tell about a long and very indirect connection with Oxford. As an undergraduate, I came under the influence, almost inadvertently, of Professor William McDougall, FRS, a former Wilde Reader in Mental Philosophy in this University, who had gone from Oxford to Harvard to take the Chair there in Psychology and then, some years later, had gone on to the newly transformed Duke University where I first encountered him as a most daunting lecturer in one of my courses. At that time I was involved in a headstrong, if lonely, confrontation with the University, involving compulsory chapel services that I had refused on principle to attend. It was a very adolescent and very unhappy incident. I was summarily suspended from the University. McDougall somehow persuaded the Dean to reinstate me and promised that I would work in his laboratory during the chapel hour. It was the start of my career as a psychologist. When the time came for me to go off for post-graduate study, I chose Harvard where I had gained a place as an assistant. McDougall had me to tea and warned me that Harvard, whence he had just fled, was a place where psychology was greatly oversimplified, mechanistic explanations flourishing, I recall him saying, like weeds. I also recall his remarking about Oxford at that time that it was notable not for oversimplification but, worse, for a total indifference to *any* form of psychological explanation. So, first to Harvard and then to Oxford went I, as if retracing McDougall's steps.

But if we migrated geographically in opposite directions, not so intellectually. For McDougall made a lasting and massive impression on me in one way: he convinced me early and irreversibly that one could not understand the organization of behaviour without taking into account its directionality, its purpose, its intention – its teleological structure, however heuristically one might formulate it. The conviction has guided me into studies of selectivity in perception, into work on strategies in thinking, and now to a functionalist theory of development in an age of structuralism. Being the first Watts Professor of Psychology in this University, I have no predecessor to salute. But I will take this occasion to salute McDougall, although he never quite thought of himself as an Oxford man.

Skill in the achievement of intention

Characteristically, an overt movement in an organism is triggered by a neural discharge to relevant effectors, but its coming is also widely signalled to many other parts of the nervous system by a corollary discharge or 'feedforward'. Close analysis of motor activity indicates that there is considerable information condensed into the corollary discharge or feedforward to assure adequate and widespread information in the nervous system about action about to occur or in process. Corollary discharge contains specifications concerning an act's intended course. Correction can therefore be effected on the basis of a discrepancy between the act as executed and the act as originally specified – what the neurophysiologist Bernstein (1967) has referred to as an *Istwert* and a *Sollwert*. The function of reafference, as this general phenomenon is called, has been widely studied. It is this reafference that enables us to discriminate between a point of light moving across the retina with the eye held still from the same point of light held stationary while the eye moves across it on an identical path. How else, von Holst and Mittelstaedt (1950) have asked, could we distinguish between shaking a branch ourselves and being shaken by it. Indeed, so important is this phenomenon that its elaboration has been proposed as central to the development of consciousness, the distribution of premonitory information being the *Anlage*, later much elaborated, of consciousness (Teuber, 1966).

It was, perhaps, Miller, Galanter, and Pribram (1960) who, among psychologists, saw the programmatic significance of such neural loops as elementary building blocks for more complex planful behaviour. For if acts at even this simplest level are tested against a criterion of expected outcome, then elementary acts can be combined into higher order acts, with the higher order outcome setting a criterion for subordinate actions. Such hierarchies could thus combine constituent acts whose outcomes were tied to attainments beyond themselves. We have, of course, become much more sophisticated about such matters in the last few decades – thanks not only to studies of neural activity and behaviour, but also to the formalism of computer programming. One could argue, and philosophers have, that it took only sustained reflection to recognize that a nervous system had to work in this way. Indeed, John Dewey's famous critique (1896) of the reflex arc over half a century ago is cited as a good illustration. But we psychologists are not as likely to be moved by good reflection as perhaps we should be. In any case, the result of all of this development has been to free us of the constricting mechanical models of behaviour that, in McDougall's words, had flourished like weeds.

I have elsewhere set forth the view (Bruner, 1973) that the acquisition of skilled action can be conceived as the construction of constituent skill hierarchies. Guidance and modification of action occurs by dint of a continuing task analysis that tests the fit of constituent acts to the over-all objective. We shall have much more to say later about task analysis. When we learn skilled actions, how to solve problems whether at the level of motor skills or intellectually, we appear to be learning not only *particular* solutions, but rather *classes* of solutions. We usually can solve problems thereafter that bear only a family resemblance to the original. In this sense, constituent acts are combined in carrying out skilled actions much as sentences, in language, are put together with a sense of what is needed to achieve an intended outcome (and it is interesting to note that Grice equates meaning with the transmission of intent). The constituents are analogous to parts of speech, the over-all act to a sentence. The uses of the human hand, including its extension into the wielding of tools and weapons have much this quality about them. They include some relatively large-scale subroutines, like differentiated but complementary power and precision grips, ready forms of cupping, etc., all of them transposable into many registers, forehand, and back, visible or not, with chopsticks or without. Indeed, even at the level of the hand, we are able to guide action by a notational system like music.

I have mentioned task analysis as guiding competent action: perceiving what is required in a given situation to achieve a particular objective. It is akin to what has recently been called 'communicative competence' in language, not so much knowing the rules by which utterances are constructed, the grammar of the language, but what it is appropriate to *say* in given situations to achieve what is intended. It is knowing how to assure a proper deployment of illocutionary force by an utterance, as Austin (1962) would have put it. Task analysis is usually viewed as a feature of problem solving or thinking. I think we would do better to think of it as a particular way of programming attention, to inquire how the selective processes of attention come to be directed to features of displays related to bringing off intended outcomes. I am of the view, on the basis of my own research with infants and children, that much of intellectual development must be seen as the ability to direct attention in a fashion to serve the skilled actions by which we reach goals – learning to *see what is needed*.

Let me note that there are two ways of viewing the development of competence in the child. One view of the difference between child and adult is that the two are both formed scientists or logicians, each with a different theory. The task of the student of development is to fathom the theory of the child – the child as scientist or logician. It is a powerful approach to the study of development, embodied in the ground-breaking work of Jean Piaget. It is an approach that has also inspired developmental linguistics. The acquisition of language can be described by a series of grammars characteristic of each level of development. And indeed, the child's problem solving, or at least his explanations, can be attributed to different forms of logic operating at different ages.

To quote the sibylline Niels Bohr: the opposites of small truths are false; the opposites of great truths may also be true. The opposite of the 'little scientist' view of the child, as Susan Carey-Block (1973) has recently called it, is that the young have the *same* theory and the *same* logic but have trouble registering the world and processing information about it. The troubles include limited attention span, limited memory capacity, inappropriate strategies for using information, etc. The diminished performance of the child may *appear* in the guise of a different theory about the world (at least in an adult's eyes) but if the child is given equal means for registering, processing, etc., he will reach conclusions much like those of an adult. So, for example, the child incapable of dealing simultaneously with variation in two attributes of a display – say the height and diameter of a container – will state that there is more water to drink when the contents of a standard beaker have been poured into a tall, narrower one, using a single dimension on which to judge. Yet, it helps to attempt to describe as formally as possible what the child's apparent theory is – so long as one avoids fruitless battles over whether or not the child 'conserves quantity across transformation in its dimensionality'.

As you already know, I am an exponent of the view that the growth of the child depends upon his mastery of skills appropriate to the tasks he must perform. And nowhere is this issue clearer than in the development of attention.

At the beginning, attention in the infant has an obligatory character – the infant is strongly held visually by movement, parallax, sharp contours, sharply defined figure-ground, and by various face-like configurations. During this early period, the opening months of life, it is very difficult for him to attend to more than one event at a time. If attending to one event at one place, he cannot even monitor a locus where another *might* occur. In time he comes to anticipate where things are going to occur, and even gives form to the anticipation by 'constructing' and following a supposed trajectory to account for change in position of the out-of-sight object. But there is an early shallowness in scanning the world. Perceptual similarity, even for the three-year-old, appears to be based on accepting those things as alike that happen on first inspection to share a common property. Later he will base judgements of likeness, not on point-for-point correspondence in two displays, but on the basis of a set of common features, however located. And he is past six before he reaches adult standard. During these early years, the child is building a model of what is redundant in his environment, is highly sensitized to novel stimuli. But early models of the environment are inflexible guides – as when the child is shown several times in a row a toy train moving from left to right, from point A to B, and then, on a new exposure the train moves further right to C. Rather than following, he returns his gaze to A, in expectancy of a train starting again from there.

What is most lacking early on is precisely the capacity for putting together parts and wholes, a formal requirement for dealing with means and ends. At age 3, for example, we find the child quite unable to use the constraint of scale in interpreting a rapidly exposed or blurred picture: this patch is an elephant, that mark on it is a house standing there, the red spot on top of that is a candied apple. Nor is there much evidence of the constraint of likelihood: 'it is underwater' may be followed by 'and there is a red bus'. And not until after five is the child able to pursue a voluntary order of visual search, specifying in advance the loci to be visited – like following instructions to inspect targets from one end to the other when they have been laid out along a line. And at that, the distractable six-year-old requires more than a hundred changes in eye position to visit forty-seven such targets, and with many errors. Indeed, where the purposeful inspection of displays is concerned, the child's performance is much like that of the frontal lesioned adult who does not modify his pattern of search in response to different questions about a scene. All this points to a marked deficiency in what has come to be called the skilled use of analysis-by-synthesis: looking at parts to help build hypotheses about the whole, checking these, and then returning to the parts to reinterpret them in the light of the whole. We have discovered that where an adult inspects large configurations of a scene and then returns to smaller ones and again to larger, the child goes steadily sampling in an indifferent, rather homogeneous way.

I have given, perhaps, an excessively detailed, if condensed, account of the development of attention. But it illustrates the troubles the child has in putting *any* theory of the environment to use. It may well be that he has a different theory of the world, but whatever that theory may be, it must be based upon and must lead to a search for information that is partial, fragmented, unco-ordinated, etc. There are great leaps forward in the child's development, leaps in theory and logic. But one cannot understand them or nurture them without having mind for the slow-growing control of attention, inference, retrieval from memory on which they are based.

But let us be clear about one thing. I am *not* urging a Lockeian view of the development of human powers – knowledge as a slow accretion of associations reflecting order in the world. Indeed, Kant has fared better than Locke – recalling, however, Bohr's injunction about truths and their opposite. There is much in the mind that is not written there so much by the experience of the individual as by the evolution of the species. Nothing so strikingly illustrates the point than the evolution of the two-component system of vision in primates, the one system being locative and spatially extended and derived from the phylogenetically ancient optic tectum, the other being detailed, feature sensitive, and central, depending heavily for its processing upon the evolving primate neocortex. And of what conceivable use could a fovea be to any but a species with a finely tuned hand to use and a vested interest in three-dimensional space? So we find that the pre-reaching infant bestirs himself in promising and appropriate ways in the presence of objects that are humanly manipulable in size, but not for others. By one year, if not sooner, he can recognize visually objects that before he had only touched. At the start of his reaching career, the infant is quite upset to encounter a virtual image with apparent externality but which cannot be touched, whilst an older, more experienced child is simply amused. Indeed, it would be. difficult to deny the preexperiential status of a 'sense of causation' in a threemonth-old who will suck on a dummy teat to clear the blur from a cinema display, but desist from sucking when it causes blur. The child must build models of the world and master skills for doing so, but he does not start from scratch. Theories are, to be sure, in the nervous system. But they operate, when skills are deficient, through a glass darkly.

I fear that the picture I have thus far sketched may have made of human growth something too purposeful, too joyless, too pedestrian. For, in fact, play is the major enterprise of childhood, and it becomes more prominent as one ascends the primate order (cf. Bruner, 1972). Play, surely, is behaviour without a means–end structure. But is it? On closer inspection, play seems to involve either an uncoupling of means and ends or their ritualization. The six-month-old infant, having learned to hold on to an object and get it easily to his mouth, then begins a process of variation – and does so with notable zest. He will successively hold it out for inspection, will shake it, will bang it, will drop it over the edge, and will fit the object into all the routines he has mastered. Conversely, once a new *routine* is mastered, as with power grip in one hand and precision grip in the other, he will. apply the skill to any and every object that has both mass and a loose end. A new object into old acts; a new act on old objects. Both absorb the child. Not only does play provide a tutorial in the consequences of one's acts, it also tempts into combinatorial exercises, the essence of problem solving.

Vygotsky (1967) urged that later play as well, particularly the development of symbolic play, must also be interpreted by reference to more ordinary striving. 'A child's play must always be interpreted as the imaginary, illusory realization of unrealizable desires.' At this higher level, play is displaced wish fulfilment often aided by what Vygotsky called a pivot – a prop that embodies a feature of the sought-for state, as a stick serves as a horse to ride. The pivot is the symbolic substitute. So play and aimed intention, while contrasting, seem of the same coin. The one holds the end constant, while varying the means; the other requires ends and means, but changes each to suit the other with a kind of measured zest.

Culture and growth

Culture, as Peter Medawar has remarked (1963), is Lamarckian in its transmission of acquired characteristics. It encompasses a pool of skills, values, and beliefs that give embodiment to what is carried in the gene pool. Language is the prime case, but one among many. Features of 'culture' and 'tradition' are to be found as far down the primate scale as the Old World monkeys, particularly when severe habitat pressures are lightened enough for the press of innate responses to be reduced. The Japanese macaque, baboons, and other species at a comparable level of evolution show, in semi-domestication, new and effective 'traditional' modes of coping with new situations (often emerging from the play of the young). The forms are transmitted among the young or within the group most in contact with them. In time, profound changes can occur in a troop, even affecting its ecology. Not only do semi-domesticated Japanese macaques learn to accept new sources of food, like the yam, but in time they learn to wash the dirt from the yam in the very sea that previous generations would not enter. They are now playing and beginning to swim in sea water, covering distances sufficient for inter-island migration. But the 'buffering' of semi-domestication appears to be essential. In one notable set of studies, for example, the co-operative moving of heavy stones disappears in a wilder setting under the impact of reasserted dominance behaviour. I cite such studies not to explain away the uniqueness of human culture. That would be absurd. Rather, it is to suggest that what may initially have been an optional adaptation, an extra that tapped unused resources in a species, finally becomes a target for evolutionary selection. In time, as with us, the capacity for culture becomes, so to speak, the obligatory mark of the species.

A most tempting way of conceiving culture is as a limited body of generative rules which, once learned, permits one to act, to anticipate, to predict in a wide variety of situations. Obviously, the rules are not rigorous, though there is a pervasiveness about their application that provides rich and seemingly endless material for study by sociologists and anthropologists. Lionel Trilling, two decades ago, commented that the sense of social actuality in such works as Riesman's *Lonely Crowd* was filling the void created when the novel ceased to be concerned with the investigation of manners. But we know very little as yet about the forms in which these pervasive rule structures present themselves for learning nor, alas, do we know much about rule learning. Our efforts to be physicalistically impeccable in a nineteenth century way kept us from the study of such a phenomenon as too mentalistic. But things are changing. Now, like ageing, converted village atheists, we seem prepared even to accept innate ideas as the base of our knowledge of such cultural universals as language. For my part, I can think of no more critically important area of inquiry for the psychologist of development than the phenomena of rule acquiring and rule using.

What is apparent about the learning of culture, as of language, is that it is what linguists would call *-emic* rather than *-etic*, that it involves the learning of structured relationships rather than isolated elements. Phonemics departs from phonetics by attempting to account for the structure of a higher level, words, by invoking the minimum set of features, change in which will change a word, for example /t/in, /b/in, /p/in...Phonetics is descriptive only. In an *-emic* system, the learner masters the particular by reference to the context in which it fits, and in turn develops hypotheses about the context from the particulars. The significance of an isolated act of greeting, say, depends on its context in some way analogous to the significance of a word depending on its grammatical context or a move in a game on the set of permissible moves possible in that context. Such patterning, of course, is characteristic of human culture, and it may well be that the nature of human attention is precisely of an order to make the learning of culture patterns altogether easier than it should be, if one took complexity as an index of potential difficulty.

Organized 'fields of knowledge', as we now call the results of scholarship, are simply an idealized form of culture in which the degree of connectivity of part to whole is amplified and idealized to the point where most of the particulars can he derived from a knowledge of the general organizing principles. These bodies of knowledge are codified in theories. A theory is a way of stating tersely what one already knows without the burden of detail. In this sense, it is a canny and economical way of keeping in mind a vast amount while thinking about a very little. Obviously, culture in the broadest sense and 'bodies of knowledge' in the narrowest require the use of a symbolic system – either 'ordinary' in the form of natural language, or more highly condensed and abstract as in formal theories. It is the construction and uses of these symbolic systems that led me earlier to characterize the study of intellectual development as one of the sciences of the artificial.

Let me explain what I mean, for it will lead me directly to a consideration of pedagogy, with which I shall end this inquiry. I must distinguish first what might be called 'spontaneous' knowing from 'cultivated' or 'artificial' knowing. Neither, obviously, exist in a pure form. The former, I believe, involves knowing in the context of action and interaction. It is knowing how to, with the knowledge inherent in the action. One learns such knowledge by engaging in activity in which the knowledge is implicit. One learns to catch fish, to handle an outrigger, to navigate from atoll to atoll – and, as we know from many close anthropological studies (e.g. Gladwin, 1970), one learns these things in doing them, usually starting young, doing whatever pieces of the action one can bring off, with an adult scaffolding the rest. Or with respect to social matters, the knowledge one has is intrinsic in the nature of one's interaction with the source: social knowledge cannot be separated from the person who imparted it in a particular interaction. We know from a recent study of Cole and Scribner how disruptive it is in a primitive society to introduce a form of schooling that separates knowledge from the action and the value of knowledge from the authority of the person who transmits it.

Cultivated knowledge, by contrast, is knowledge about. It is teachable away from the action – indeed, is teachable even in so detached a human institution as a school. In its most elaborated form, it is free of specification as to how the knowledge might be used. It is deeply dependent upon language and codification of a kind that is itself divorced from action – notably, written language which *must* be free of the context of action in order for it to be understood. Pedagogy has been the art or the science of arranging cultivated knowledge so that it may more easily be grasped and more easily used in thought. As such, it is a policy science *par excellence*, perhaps the major policy science through which the psychology of development expresses itself. To separate pedagogy, either from the disciplines of knowledge that must be translated by it, or from the study of human development, is to cripple pedagogy and impoverish us all. It would be as unwise as separating medicine from biology.

But I also believe that our understanding of how development proceeds argues for a radical reformulation of pedagogy that would include consideration of the many powerful but indirect, influences that affect the growth of mind. A culture is not only a repository of knowledge and skills and values. It is also a support system for giving hope and a sense of capability to. its members. The demoralization that ensues when a culture fails in this supportive role quickly telegraphs itself to the young, particularly to the offspring of the victims, whether the society is a developing one undergoing chaotic detribalization or a developed one with chronic unemployment. It seems particularly to be the case that the more highly elaborated forms of knowledge suffer in the transmission when the young feel that their situation is such that they will never need such knowledge. Both the American and the British experience show that equal opportunity to be educated does *not* overcome the effect produced by unequal access to power and well-being determined by class or race or religion. Children start school in the American system with matching IQs, and end up after a decade of schooling with the black child or the poor child ten or more points down.

It is evident enough, I think, that neither the study of development nor its application in pedagogy can, then, be divorced from the pervasive political, social, and economic forces that shape the society and thereby shape the conditions of growth. We psychologists, proud in our newfound competence, have till now been too separatist, too isolationist. There are times and occasions when we must withdraw into the laboratory to analyse the growth of attention as revealed by eye movements, or to study the emergence of case-grammatical rules in the child's first speech, to mention two of my own contemporary preoccupations. But I would hope that we have now achieved a sufficiently robust body of knowledge and methods to come back out again to ask afresh how it works for man living in society and how we may arrange the society so that competence can be achieved less stressfully, with more communal grace, and with less waste in rare human resources. Psychology is one of the sciences of culture, and it must be engaged in the culture. It is also a natural science and must be able in detachment to explore the mediating processes – behavioural, neural, biochemical. And finally, it is a science of the artificial, and as such must contribute to the man-made design of man's environment, to ensure that man can grow to the fullness of his powers.

Bibliography

Austin, J. L. *How to Do Things with Words*. Oxford: Clarendon Press, 1962.

Bernstein, *The Coordination and Regulation of Movement*. New York: Pergamon Press, 1967.

Bruner, J. S. 'Nature and uses of immaturity.' *American Psychologist*, 1972, **27** (8), 687–716.

—— 'Organization of early skilled action.' *Child Development*, 1973, **44**, 1–11.

Carey-Block, S. 'The child as little scientist or as inefficient information processor.' In K. J. Connolly and J. S. Bruner (eds), *The Growth of Competence*, London: Academic Press, 1973.

Dewey, J. 'The reflex arc concept in psychology.' *Psychological Review*, 1896, **3**, 357–70.

Gladwin, T. *East is a Big Bird*. Cambridge, MA: Harvard University Press, 1970.

von Holst, E. and Mittelstaedt, H. 'Das Reafferenzprinzip.' *Naturwissensehaften*, 1950, **37**, 464–76.

Medawar, P. 'Onwards from Spencer: evolution and evolutionism.' *Encounter*, 1963, **21** (3), 35–43.

Miller, G. A., Galanter, E., and Pribram, K. H. *Plans and the Structure of Behaviour*. New York: Henry Holt & Co., 1960.

Teuber, H. -L. 'Perception after brain injury.' In J. C. Eccles (ed.), *Brain and Conscious Experience*, New York: Springer-Verlag, 1966.

Vygotsky, L. 'Play and its role in the mental development of the child.' *Soviet Psychology*, 1967, **5** (3), 6–18. (From *Voprosy psikhologii*, 1966, **12** (6), 62–76.)

CHAPTER 15

POVERTY AND CHILDHOOD

Oxford Review of Education (1975) 1, 31–50

I should like to consider what we know about the education of the very young, about what may be formative influences during infancy and early childhood upon later intellectual competence and how these influences may be more compassionately deployed. Our focus will be upon the manner in which social and cultural background affects upbringing and thereby affects intellectual functioning. And within that wide compass, we shall limit ourselves further by concentrating principally upon the impact of poverty and dispossession.

There is little enough systematic knowledge about what in fact happens to children during infancy and early childhood and even less on what its latter effects on competence may be. Indeed, in the current debates, it is a moot point as to what is properly meant by intellectual competence, whether or in what degree competence comprises soul, mind, heart, or the general community. Nor can the topic be limited to education. For the charge has been made by Royal Commissions and advisers to presidents as well as by the anti-Establishment New Left that educational and socializing practice, before the school years as after, reflects and reinforces the inequities of a class system by limiting access to knowledge for the poor, while facilitating it for those better off. The charge is even more serious: that our practice of education, both in and out of school, assures uneven distribution not only of knowledge but also of competence to profit from knowledge. It does so by limiting and starving the capabilities of the children of the poor by leading them into failure until finally they are convinced that it is not worth their while to think about school-like things.

As Stodolsky and Lesser (1967) grimly put it, 'When intelligence data and early achievement data are combined we have a predictor's paradise, but an abysmal prognosis for most children who enter the school system from disadvantaged backgrounds'.

Why concentrate on the very young? The answer is, of course, in the form of a wager. For one thing, Bloom's (1964) careful and well-known work strongly suggests that a very major proportion of the variance in adult intellectual achievement, measured by a wide variety of procedures, is already accounted for by the time the child reaches the usual school-starting age of five. For another, there are enough studies to indicate, as we shall see, that certain possibly critical emotional, linguistic, and cognitive patterns associated with social background are already present by age three.

But principally, I am moved to concentrate on the very young by my own research (for example, Bruner, 1969; Bruner, Lyons, and Kaye, 1971). The staggering rate at which the preschool child acquires skills, expectancies, and notions about the world and about people; the degree to which culturally specialized attitudes shape the care of children during these years – these are impressive matters that lend concreteness to the official manifestos about the early years.

Our first task is to examine what is known about the effects of poverty on child development in our contemporary Western culture – whether this knowledge comes from attempted intervention, from naturalistic studies, or from the laboratory. I do not wish to make a special issue of poverty, of whether or not it represents a self-sustaining culture, as Oscar Lewis (1966) urges; nor do I want to make the claim that poverty is in every culture the same. Yet there are common elements that are crucial wherever it is encountered and in whatever culture embedded. We shall have more to say about these in context as we consider what it is that poverty and its attendant sense of powerlessness may do to the pattern of growth in children.

Our second task is to look briefly at modern theories of development with a view to assessing whether they aid in the understanding of the impact of culture on growth, generally, and of the impact of poverty, particularly.

Finally, and again too briefly, we must examine what the implications of this exercise are for public policy and for the conduct of early education. As Hess and Shipman (1968) put it, 'The current growth of programs in early education and the large-scale involvement of the schools and federal government in them is not a transitory concern. It represents a fundamental shift in the relative roles and potential influence of the two major socializing institutions of the society – the family and the school'.

Most of the work that compares children from different socio-economic backgrounds points to three interconnected influences associated with poverty.

> The first relates to the opportunity for, the encouragement of, and the management of goal seeking and of problem solving; it reflects differences in the degree to which one feels powerless or powerful, and in the realistic expectation of reward for effort. *What* the child strives for, *how* he goes about the task of means–end analysis, his expectations of success and failure, his approach to the *delay* of gratification, his *pacing* of goal setting – these are not only crucial, but they also affect how he uses language, deploys attention, processes information, and so on.
>
> The second influence is linguistic: by exposure to many situations and through the application of many demands, children come to use language in different ways, particularly as an instrument of thought, of social control and interaction, of planning, and so forth.
>
> The third influence comes from the pattern of reciprocity into which the child moves, whether middle class or poor and dispossessed. What parents expect, what teachers demand, what peers anticipate – all of these operate to shape outlook and approach in the young. We must consider each of these in turn.

Goal seeking and problem solving

A close reading of the evidence surely suggests that the major source of 'cognitive' difference between poor and better off, between those who feel powerless and those who feel less so, lies in the different way goals are defined and how means to their attainment are fashioned and brought into play.

Begin with a general proposition: that one feels competent about oneself before feeling competent about others or about the world at large. Moffett (1968) observes how language complexity increases when the child writes or speaks about events in which *he* participated in a goal-seeking process. Consider these unlikely initial subordinate constructions from third-graders uttered in describing a task in which they have had a central, directive role:

> *If I place a flame over the candle,*
>   *the candle goes out.*
> *When you throw alum on the candle,*
>   *the flame turns blue.*

Or take two speech samples from lower-class black children, one describing a TV episode in *The Man From U.N.C.L.E.*, the other a fight in which he, the speaker, was engaged:

> This kid – Napoleon got shot
> And he had to go on a mission
> And so this kid, he went with Solo.
> So they went.
> And this guy – they went through this window.
> And they caught him.
> And they beat up them other people.
> And they went
> and then he said that this
> old lady was his mother
> and then he – and at the end he say
> that he was the guy's friend.

And the fight:

> When I was in the fourth grade –
>   no it was the third grade
> This boy he stole my glove.
> He took my glove
> and said that his father found it downtown
>   on the ground.
> (And you fight him?)
> I told him that it was impossible for him
>   to find downtown 'cause all those people
>   was walking by and just his father
>   was the only one that found it?
> So he got all (mad).
> So then I fought him.
> I knocked him all out in the street.
> So he say he give
> and I kept on hitting him.
> Then he started crying
> and ran home to his father.
> And the father told him
> that he didn't find no glove.

As Labov (1969) remarks, the difference between the two is that the second has a consistent evaluative perspective or narrative line – from the speaker to the events that impinge upon him, and back to his reactions to these events.

A study by Strandberg and Griffith (1968) provides the third example. Four- and five-year-olds were given Kodak Instamatic cameras and told to take any pictures that interested them. Their subsequent utterances about these pictures were compared with what they said of comparable pictures that they had photographed when told to do so in order to learn.

In the first of the two excerpts, the child struggles – unsuccessfully – to find a context for an assigned picture. In the second, describing one he took on his own, it is built in.

The speaker is a five-year-old.

Assigned:

> That's a horse. You can ride it. I don't know any more about it. It's brown, black, and red. I don't know my story about the horse.

Own Choice:

> There's a picture of my tree that I climb in. There's – there's where it grows at and there's where I climb up – and sit up there – down there and that's where I look out at. First I get on this one and then I get on that other one. And then I put my foot under that big branch that are so strong. And then I pull my face up and when I, get a hold of a branch up at that place – and then I look around.

The bare, schoolish organisation of the first seems so detached next to the intentional, active, egocentric perspective of the second.

Shift now, without benefit of transition, to much younger children – infants of four to six weeks, studied at the Center for Cognitive Studies. In this study, conducted by Kalnins and Bruner (1970), infants control the focus of a lively motion picture by sucking at a preset rate on a special nipple. In one condition, sucking at or faster than the prescribed rate brings the moving picture into focus and keeps it there. In the other, sucking at this rate drives the picture out of focus and keeps it out. One group of infants starts with sucking for clarity and shifts to the suck-for-blur condition. The other begins with the suck-for-blur and shifts to the suck-for-clear condition – though the two conditions were never presented in the same session, or, indeed, on the same visit to the Center.

Note two crucial points about performance. The first is that the infants respond immediately and appropriately to the consequences produced by their sucking – the pauses averaging about four seconds in suck-for-clear and about eight seconds in suck-for-blur. As soon as the consequences of sucking alters, the infant's response pattern shifts abruptly and appropriately. As a further feature of reacting to consequences in both conditions, the infant averts his gaze from the picture when it is out of focus – while sucking in the case of suck-for-blur, and while pausing in the other case.

For those not acquainted with the data on infant learning, these findings may seem a trifle bizarre though otherwise quite to be expected. They are, in fact, rather unexpected in the immediacy of the learning reported, particularly in the light of the painfully slow process of *classical* conditioning found in infants of comparable age by Papoušek (1967), Lipsitt (1967) and others. Papoušek's infants turned their head one way or another *in response* to an environmental event, as did the babies in the Brown University experiments. Kalnins' babies were learning to respond not to a stimulus, *but to a change produced by their own act*, and to store the information thus gained as an instrumental sequence involving their own action. Indeed, it may well be that a special type of recurring 'critical period' is to be found in the few thousand milliseconds that follow upon a voluntarily initiated act. This is not the proper context in which to treat the matter in detail, yet it must be said emphatically that since the pioneer work of von Holst and Mittelstaedt (1950) the role of intention has become increasingly central in biology and psychology.

It was Held and Hein (1958) who first showed how crucial was the reafference output of 'intentional' movement for adaptation learning. In their now famous experiment with yoked kittens adapting to prismatically induced angular displacement in the visual field, one kitten actively walked about an environment, the other was passively transported in a gondola through an identical path. The former adapted to the prisms, the latter did not. While we are still far from understanding the neural mechanisms of intentionality – variously called reafference, feed-forward, motor-to-sensory mechanism corollary discharge, or 'Sollwert' – there are a sufficient number of leads to suggest that the pursuit will pay off.

In a word, probably the first type of acquired representation of the world the child achieves is in the form of an egocentrically oriented action schema: a joint representation of action intended along with the consequences of that action – a matter of which Piaget (1954) has devoted some of his most exquisite descriptions.

But if one thinks of acquired egocentric orientation only as a phase out of which the child must grow enroute to becoming operational and decentered, then a crucial point may be overlooked. In Vygotsky's (1962) terms, the stream of action and the stream of language begin to converge in the process of interacting with the world in just such an egocentric orientation.

My colleague, Dr Greenfield (1969) notes,

> Not only can people fail to realize goals, the environment can fail to provide a growth-promoting sequence for them. I should like to suggest that the goals set for the child by his caretakers and the relation of these to the child's available means is a critical factor in determining the rate and richness of cognitive growth in the early, formative years. If a mother believes her fate is controlled by external forces, that she does not control the means necessary to achieve her goals, what does this mean for her children?

The follow-up data from the Hess *et al.* (1969) group's study of the relation between maternal variables and the development of intelligence (to which we shall turn shortly) shows that the more a mother feels externally controlled when her child is four years old, the more likely the child is to have a low IQ and a poor academic record at age six or seven.

Striking documentation of these points is beginning to be available at the intimate level of family interaction (Shaw and Schoggen, 1969). One such study, now in progress, is Maxine Schoggen's (1969), an effort to elucidate differences in directed action that had been found in the children of the five-year study of Klaus and Gray (1968). She uses an 'environmental force unit' (EFU), which is defined as an act by any social agent in the child's environment directed toward getting the child to seek a goal. One crude finding already available – the data are only now in process of analysis – is that for lower-class families, some two-thirds of the children are below the total median rate for EFU's per minute, whereas only a quarter of the middle income children are. This suggests how great a difference there may be in sheer emphasis upon goal directedness in the two groups.

One must note also that in the two major studies of how middle class and poverty mothers instruct their children – Hess and Shipman (1965) and Bee *et al.* (1969) a quite comparable trend emerged. They found:

First, that middle-class mothers are more attentive to the continuous flow of goal directed action.
Second, they allow the child to set his own pace and make his own decisions more.
Third, they intrude less often and less directly in the process of problem solving itself.
Fourth, they structure the search task by questions that sharpen yet ease the search for means.
Fifth, they are more oriented toward the overall structure of the task than responsive to component acts in isolation.
Sixth, they react more to (or reinforce) the child's successful efforts than his errors (a practice far more likely to evoke further verbal interaction between tutor and child).

These surely suggest some of the crucial differences that emerge in the goal-seeking patterns of economically advantaged and disadvantaged children.

To this evidence must now be added still another type of research finding, resulting from longer-term longitudinal studies tracing human growth from infancy through adolescence.

Kagan and Moss (1962) state in their well-known monograph, 'It appears that the pattern most likely to lead to involvement in intellectual achievement in the boys is early maternal protection, followed by encouragement and acceleration of mastery behaviors'. And then, 'Following our best judgment in estimating the most desirable patterns to follow with young children, our educated guess remains that higher intelligence is fostered by warmth, support, and plentiful opportunity and reward for achievement and autonomy. Moreover, it is probably important to provide active, warm, achievement-oriented parental figures of both sexes after whom appropriate role patterns can be established' (pp. 221–222).

Add to this, finally, the conclusion reached by Robinson and Robinson (1968) in their review: 'Children with a high degree of achievement motivation tend to become brighter as they grow older; those with a more passive outlook tend to fall behind their developmental potential (Bayley and Schaefer, 1964; Sontag, Baker and Nelson, 1958).

The degree of achievement motivation is related to the socio-cultural background of the child; middle-class children are more strongly motivated toward achievement than are lower-class children (Douvan, 1956; Lott and Lott, 1963; Mussen *et al.*, 1961)'.

There is a further multiplier factor in the effects we have been discussing: the impact of urbanization on the care of children. We have, until now, argued that poverty, by its production of a sense of powerlessness, alters goal striving and problem solving in those it affects, whether the powerlessness occurs in a depressed London working class borough, among Kurdistani immigrants to Israel, in a black ghetto, among uneducated and abandoned Greenland Eskimo, mothers down-and-out in literate Copenhagen, or in the midst of Appalachia.

The evidence points to a magnification of this effect when poverty moves to the city. Perhaps the most comprehensive study to date is by Graves (1969), who has compared rural and urban Spanish Americans around Denver, as well as rural and urban Baganda around Kampala and Entebbe in Uganda.

Interviews with mothers in her study show that urban mothers come to believe more than rural mothers that their preschool children cannot understand, cannot be taught ideas or skills, cannot be depended on. City mothers rated their children lower in potentialities for independence, for self-reliance, and for ability to help with the family.

It is a cycle. When the poor mother moves to the city, she becomes trapped with her children – more irritable, more interested in keeping peace than in explaining and encouraging adventure. She often, then, produces the very behaviour she rates down. At the same time the urban environment itself restricts outlets for the child, it also reduces the mother's confidence in her children's capacity for coping with those that are left.

Warren Haggstrom (1964), in a masterful review of the literature on the effects of poverty, comes to the conclusion that 'the fact of being powerless, but with needs that must be met, leads the poor to be dependent on the organizations, persons, and institutions which can meet these needs. The situation of dependency and powerlessness, through internal personality characteristics as well as through social position, leads to apathy, hopelessness, conviction of the inability to act successfully, failure to develop skills, and so on' (p. 215).

Consider now some consequences of this pattern on the development of language usage in interactive speech, and likely as well in the internal use of speech in problem solving.

Language and poverty

It was perhaps the studies of Hess and Shipman (1965), inspired by Basil Bernstein (1961) that drew attention to *how* language was used in communicating with young children and what its significance was to the lower- and the middle-class child.

They asked mothers to instruct their own children to use an Etch-a-Sketch drawing pad, taking careful note of the mother's language and her mode of instruction. Their general conclusions have already been discussed.

Looking in detail at linguistic considerations, we turn to a more recent study that used Hess and Shipman's system of classification with further elaboration. It documents the work carried out by Helen Bee and her colleagues (1969) at the University of Washington with four–five-year-olds. The Washington group also asked the mother to help her child accomplish a task (copying a house of blocks); in addition they observed mother–child interaction in the well-supplied waiting room and interviewed the mother afterwards about her ideas on looking after children. An excerpt from their paper can serve as summary.

> The middle-class mother tended to allow her child to work at his own pace, offered many general structuring suggestions on how to search for the solution to a problem, and told the child what he was doing that was correct...The general structure offered by the mother may help the child acquire learning sets (strategies) which will generalize to future problem solving situations.
>
> In contrast, the lower-class mother did not behave in ways which would encourage the child to attend to the basic features of the problem. Her suggestions were highly specific, did not emphasize basic problem-solving strategies,

and seldom required reply from the child. Indeed, she often deprived the child of the opportunity to solve the problem on his own by her non-verbal intrusions into the problem-solving activity.

They comment on the fact that middle-class mothers ask so many more questions in an effort to help the child in his task, that their mode of operating linguistically could fairly be called 'interrogative' in contrast to the more indicative and imperative modes of lower class mothers.

Hess and Shipman (1965) had, of course, found quite comparable differences in mothers, though they distinguished three modes of communicating: cognitive-rational, imperative-normative, and personal-subjective.

In the first, the mother was task-oriented, informative, and analytic; in the second, she ordered and evaluated; and in the third, she pleaded for performance on grounds that it would please her. The highest concentration of the first mode was found among middle-class mothers.

Both studies point to early class differences in language use. One is the use of language to dissect a problem. In lower class discourse, mothers more often order, or plead, or complain, than set up a problem or give feedback. Such usage possibly accounts for the 'poor reinforcement value' of verbal reactions by the parents of less advantaged children (see, for example, Zigler *et al.*, 1968): language is not usually used for signalling outcome or hailing good tries. What is most lacking in the less-advantaged mother's use of language is analysis-and-synthesis: the dissection of relevant features in a task and their appropriate recombinings in terms of connection, cause-and-effect, and so on.

The evidence surely leads one to the conclusion that there is more demand for as well as more use of analytic language among middle class than among lower class speakers.

Turner and Pickvance (1970), for example, attempted to measure the difference by counting incidences of uncertainty in the verbal expressions of sixteen-year-olds from middle class and poverty backgrounds who were making up stories or interpreting uncertain events. 'Orientation toward the use of expressions of uncertainty is more strongly related to social class than to verbal ability... In every case in which social class has been shown to be related to the use of expressions of uncertainty, it was the middle-class child who used more of them'; the middle-class child had more recourse to Wh-questions, to the use of 'might be...' and 'could be...', to 'I think', and to refusals to commit himself. As the authors say, 'Bernstein's work suggests that the forms of socialization typically employed in middle-class families are likely to give the children reared in these families greater scope for self-regulation, for operating within a wide range of alternatives. These socialization procedures... are likely to give these children a greater awareness of uncertainty in certain areas of experience and are likely to encourage the children to be flexible in their thinking'.

Other evidence also suggests a difference in analytic discrimination. Klaus and Gray (1968), among impoverished black children in Murfreesboro, Tennessee, and Robinson and Creed (1968), with slum children in London's Borough of Newham, agree in finding less fine discriminations made by lower-class than by middle-class children – at least in rather impersonal, school-like tasks. Blank *et al.* (1969) shows that tutoring children from poverty backgrounds to extract features from displays – distance, direction, form, for example – increases their measured intelligence (long a belief of Maria Montessori). Indeed, it is not surprising that Earl Schaefer's (1969) careful intervention study with one–three-year-old children in poverty families emphasizes such discriminative training, with good results in raising standard intelligence scores.

Another index of the analytic use of language is the accumulation of vocabulary. As Cazden (1970) puts it, 'Consideration of vocabulary as an aspect of language cannot be separated from considerations of concepts as the whole of our personal knowledge. The content of our mental dictionary catalogs more than our knowledge of language; it catalogs our substantive knowledge of the world'. Brown, Cazden and Bellugi (1969) also point out that most instances of natural language instruction between parent and child relate to word meanings – true not only in their small Cambridge sample, but also for two lower-class black mothers in a Great Lakes city (Horner, 1968) and for mothers in Samoa (Slobin, 1968). It is of special interest then that Coleman (1966, pp. 292–295) noted that vocabulary subtests of an IQ test were more correlated with differences in quality of schools than were achievement tests in such more formal school subjects as arithmetic and reading.

This suggests that the push to analysis, differentiation, synthesis, and so on, is accompanied by a push to achieve economy of means of representation in words. Again, the more active the intellectual push of the environment, the more the differentiation of concepts and of words, their markers. Hence the richer, better stocked vocabulary of the middle-class child.

Perhaps the most telling example of increased analytic-synthetic activity in speech *per se* comes from Joan Tough's (1970) study of two groups of three-year-olds, matched for IQ and about equal in verbal output, one of middle-, the other of working-class background. Even at this age, middle-class children single out many more qualitative features of the environment to talk about, and indeed, also talk much more of such relations between them as cause-and-effect. So there is good reason to believe that there is an early start to the differentiating process whereby children from one social class move toward a programme of linguistic analysis-and-synthesis while the others move toward something else.

Klaus and Gray (1968) remark of this 'something else', 'the children with whom we worked tended to have little categorizing ability except in affective terms; they were highly concrete and immediate in their approaches to objects and situations' (p. 16). Berstein (1970) also comments on the fact that in carrying on a role-play type of conversation of the 'he said/she said' variety, the child from the slum area is often richer and less hesitant in his speech, as if the more direct and concrete affective tone of human interaction were the preferred mode. Perhaps the 'something else' is more thematic, personal and concrete.

Let me then suggest a tentative conclusion from the first part of this much too condensed survey of class differences in language use. Bruner, Goodnow and Austin (1956) drew a distinction between affective, functional, and formal categories. Affective categories involved the organization of events in terms of the immediate reactions they produced in the beholder, particular affect-laden reactions. Functional categories group objects and events in terms of fitness for the achievement of some particular goal or the carrying out of a particular task. Formal categories are those governed by a set of relatively universal criterial attributes in terms of which things can be placed without reference either to their use or to the 'gut reaction' they produce.

It would seem to be the case, though I am aware of how very insufficient the data still are, that 'middle-class upbringing' has the tendency to push the child toward a habitual use of formal categories and strategies appropriate to such categorizing – featural analysis of tasks, consideration of alternative possibilities, questioning and hypothesizing, and elaborating. It is a mode in which one uses language in a characteristic way: by constructing linguistically an analytic replica independent of the situation and its functional demands and manipulating the replica by the rules of language.

But note that it is *not* that children of different classes differ either in the *amount* of language that they 'have', nor in the variant *rules* that govern their language. Cazden (1970) and Labov (1969) have compiled enough evidence from the extant literature to cast serious doubt on both the 'less language' and the 'different language' theories of class difference. The critical issue seems to be language *use* in a variety of *situations* and the manner in which home and subculture affects such usage. Or as Hymes (in press) puts it, children not only learn to form and interpret sentences but 'also acquire knowledge of a set of ways in which sentences are used'.

A striking experiment by Heider, Cazden and Brown (1968), and an observation by Francis Palmer (1968), remind us again that the lower-class child, under appropriate conditions, *can* operate analytically quite well, though he might ordinarily or habitually not do so. Heider *et al.* asked lower-class and middle-class ten-year-old boys to describe a picture of an animal in a fashion that would later permit distinguishing it from many other similar pictures. Some of the attributes they used in their descriptions were criterial in the sense of uniquely defining the target or reducing materially the range of possibilities; others were irrelevant for guiding one to the correct target. Both groups mentioned about the same total number of attributes, and moreover, both mentioned about the same number of criterial attributes, 18 out of a total of 67 for middle-class boys, 16 out of 69 for lower-class. Where they differed was in the number of adult prompts and requests that were necessary to get the attributes out of them: an average of 6.11 for the lower-class children, and only 3.56 for the middle-class. And by the same token, Palmer (1968) finds that if seven or eight hours of prior, rapport-establishing contact is assured before testing, most differences between lower-class and middle-class children become minimal. This point was also established by Labov *et al.* (1968) when he concluded that Northern Negro English did not differ structurally or in underlying logic from Standard English.

What seems to be at issue again is the question of 'personalness' and the egocentric axis. If the situation is personal, egocentrically organized, then the lower-class child can be just as complex as the middle-class one. But the lower-class child seems far less able to achieve 'decentration', to analyse things in the world from a perspective other than his personal or local perspective. Perhaps this point will become more compelling when we examine a second feature of language that differentiates between social classes, to which we turn now.

This second feature involves communicating through language in a fashion independent of the situation. Grace de Laguna (1927, p. 107) says, 'The evolution of language is characterized by a progressive freeing of speech from dependence on the perceived conditions under which it is uttered, and heard, and from the behavior which accompanies it'. She argues that the superior power of a written language inheres in this freedom from the contexts of action and perception, that all of its 'semantic markers', to use a more familiar contemporary term (Katz and Fodor, 1964), are inherent in the utterance itself: they are 'intrasemantic' rather than 'extrasemantic'.

Greenfield (1968) remarks on how the speech of technologically oriented societies (in contrast to preliterate, more traditionally oriented ones) becomes more like a written language in its increasing context-independence. The theme of her paper, 'On speaking a Written Language', is apposite not only, I think, to the trend in spoken language from a preliterate to a literate society, but also from working-class to middle-class society in Western culture.

Basil Bernstein (1970) provides an interesting reason for the class difference.

> We can see that the class system has affected the distribution of knowledge. Historically and now, only a tiny proportion of the population has been socialized into knowledge at the level of the metalanguages of control and innovation, whereas the mass of population has been socialized into knowledge at the level of context tied operations... This suggests that we might be able to distinguish between two orders of meaning. One we would call universalistic, the other particularistic. Universalistic meanings are those in which principles and operations are made linguistically explicit, whereas particularistic orders of meaning are meanings in which principles and operations are relatively linguistically implicit. If orders of meaning are universalistic, then the meanings are less tied to a given context. The metalanguage of public forms of thought as these apply to objects and persons realize meanings of a universalistic type. Where meanings have this characteristic, then individuals have access to the grounds of their experience and can change the grounds... Where the meaning system is particularistic, much of the meaning is imbedded in the context of the social relationship. In this sense the meanings are tied to a context and may be restricted to those who share a similar contextual history. Where meanings are universalistic, they are in principle available to all, because the principles and operations have been made explicit and so public. I shall argue that forms of socialization orient the child toward speech codes which control access to relatively context-tied or relatively context-independent meanings.

In short, it is the parochializing effect of a culture of poverty that keeps language tied to context, tied to common experience, restricted to the habitual ways of one's own group.

The comparative context dependence of the language of disadvantaged children shows up early. In Joan Tough's work (1970) on three- to four-year-olds from middle- and lower-class backgrounds in an English industrial city, the children were matched on Stanford-Binet scores and, roughly, on verbal output. All of the children's items of representation were rated as to whether they required the presence of the concrete situation for effective communication. This concrete component constitutes 20.9 per cent of the representation of the favoured children and 34.5 per cent of the less favoured children. The most frequent form of the concrete component are pronouns whose only reference is to something pointed at in the environment. Such 'exophoric' reference is contrasted with 'anaphoric' reference, where pronouns refer to an antecedent previously supplied in words. The percentage of anaphoric references was 22.8 per cent for the favoured children and only 7.7 per cent for the less favoured. This finding replicated Bernstein's research with children five to seven years old (Hawkins, 1968). I do not know, save by everyday observation, whether the difference is greater still among adults, but my impression is that the difference in decontextualization is greater between an English barrister and a dock worker than it is between their children.

Two trends, then, seem to be operative in the *use* of language by middle-class children. One is the use of language as an instrument of analysis-and-synthesis in problem solving, wherein the analytic power of language aid, in abstraction or feature extraction, and the generative, transformational powers of language are used in reorganizing and synthesizing the features thus abstracted.

The second trend is toward decontextualization, toward learning to use language without dependence upon shared percepts or actions, with sole reliance on the linguistic self-sufficiency of the message. Decontextualization permits information to be conceived as independent of the speaker's vantage point, it permits communications with those who do not share one's daily experience or actions, and in fact does, as Bernstein (1970) insists, allow one to transcend restrictions of locale and affiliation.

Lower-class language, in contrast, is more affective and metaphoric than formal or analytic in its use, more given to narrative than to causal or generic form. It is more tied to place and affiliation, serving the interests of concrete familiarity rather than generality, more tied to finding than to seeking.

Both trends seem to reflect the kind of goal striving and problem solving characteristic of those who without protest have accepted occupancy of the bottom roles and statuses in the society that roughly constitute the position of poverty. It is not that the poor are 'victims' of the system – they are, but so is everybody else in some way. It is rather that a set of values, a way of goal seeking, a way of dealing with means and ends becomes associated with poverty.

Social reciprocity

Being socio-economically disadvantaged is no simple matter of deficit, of suffering a cultural avitaminosis that can be dosed by suitable inputs of compensation. It is a complex of circumstances at the centre of which is usually a family whose wage-earner is without a job or where there is no male wage earner. If there is a job, usually it is as demeaning in status as it is unremunerative. The setting is a neighborhood that has adapted itself often with much human bravura to 'being at the bottom', with little by way of long range perspective or hope, often alienated by a sense of ethnic separation from the main culture.

This is not the place to examine the economic, social, and political means whereby some societies segregate social classes by restricting access to knowledge and eroding in childhood the skills needed to gain and use knowledge. Obviously, the techniques of segregation by class are not deliberately planned, and they often resist deliberate efforts of abolition. More to the point is to ask how the behaviour patterns of the dispossessed are transmitted by the family to produce the forms of coping associated with poverty (or middle-class status).

We have already encountered a striking difference in the use of reward and punishment by the mother. One finding suggests that the transmission may be accomplished by so simple a factor as rewarding achievement in the middle-class while punishing or ridiculing failure among children of the poor (Bee *et al.*, 1969). Several studies point to a by-product in the form of a class difference in asking adults for help (e.g. Kohlberg, 1968) or in showing doubt in their presence (e.g. Hawkins, 1968). The poor do much less of both.

Modelling of 'class' patterns by adults – both in interaction with the child and in general – may be another source of family transmission. Hamburg (1968) draws some interesting inferences about such modelling from studies of higher primates. He writes 'The newer field studies suggest the adaptive significance of observational learning in a social context. Time and again, one observes the following sequence: (1) close observation of one animal by another; (2) imitation by the observing animal of the behavior of some observed animal; and (3) the later practice of the observed behavior, particularly in the play group of young animals'. A like point is made for preliterate people, as in the close study of Talensee education and play by Fortes (1938) and the detailed observation of children's play among the Bushmen by Lorna Marshall (1963). They too point to the conclusion that observation and imitative incorporation in play is widespread and seemingly central.

Early language acquisition seems almost to be the type case of modelling. In a recent and detailed review of the language acquisition of the three children being studied at Harvard by Brown, Cazden and Bellugi (1969), the importance of modelling is highlighted. But this work suggests that modelling is not a simple form of transmission.

The puzzling and challenging thing about learning language from a model is that the child is not so much copying specific language behaviour from observation-and-imitation, but rather is developing general rules about how to behave from which various specific acts can be appropriately derived or interpreted. It is not at all clear how much we should attribute in early learning to the reinforcing effects of reward and/or punishment and how much to such rule learning acquired by observing or interacting with a model. Discussing the role of approval and disapproval as possible influences in the acquisition of grammar, Brown and his colleagues (1969) say, 'In general, the parents fitted propositions to the child's utterances, however incomplete or distorted the utterances, and then approved or not according to the correspondence between proposition and reality. Thus *Her curl my hair* was approved because the mother was in fact curling Eve's hair. However, Sarah's gramatically impeccable, *There's the animal farmhouse* was disapproved because the building was a lighthouse.... It seems then to be truth value rather than syntactic well formedness that chiefly governs explicit verbal reinforcement by parents – which renders mildly paradoxical the fact that the usual product of such a training schedule is an adult whose speech is highly gramatical but not notably truthful' (p. 70–71).

If it turns out to be the case that the young child is learning not only linguistic rules but also 'rules about rules' and rules also about *ways* of thinking and *ways* of talking then indoctrination in class patterns must be, in the linguist's sense, generative and pervasive to a degree that is difficult to estimate. This would make even more meaningful the insistence of Smilansky (1968) that intervention programmes emphasize *rationale* and *explanation* in order to reach the deep conceptual level where the class-pattern rules operate. In sum, both through the compelling effects of approval and disapproval and by the modelling of 'rule-bound' behaviour, the family passes on class patterns of goal striving, problem solving, paying attention, and so forth.

Let me, in closing this section, make one thing clear. I am *not* arguing that middle-class culture is good for all or even good for the middle-class. Indeed, its denial of the problems of dispossession, poverty, and privilege make it contemptible in the eyes of even compassionate critics. Nor do I argue that the culture of the dispossessed is not rich and varied within its limits. (There are critics, like Baratz and Baratz (1970), who are too ready to cry 'racist' to what they sense to be derogation of Black culture, or Yemeni culture, or Cockney culture.) But, in effect, insofar as a subculture represents a reaction to defeat and insofar as it is caught by a sense of powerlessness, it suppresses the potential of those who grow up under its sway by discouraging problem solving. The source of powerlessness that such a subculture generates, no matter how moving its by-products, produces instability in the society and unfulfilled promise in human beings.

Culture and theories of development

Thus far we have concentrated upon how a culture of poverty reflects itself in child rearing. But there is no reason to believe that the effects of such child rearing are either inevitable or irreversible – there are ways of altering the impact of middle-class pressures or of poverty. Better to appreciate this likelihood of change, we must look briefly at the nature of human development and at theories designed to explicate it.

There is a paradox in contemporary formulations. We have, on the one hand, rejected the idea of culture-free intelligence, and probably the Coleman Report (1966) put the finishing blow to the idea of school-free tests of intelligence. In this view, intelligence depends on the incorporation of culture. At the same time, there is a current vogue for theories of intellectual development promoting education strategies that presumably are unaffected (or virtually unaffected) by class difference, cultural background, and other conditions of the life of the child short, perhaps, of pathology. The only differences, according to such theories, are in timetable, the steps being the same. It is a matter only of slower and faster, not of difference in kind. So on the one side we urge a context-sensitive view while on the other we propose that intelligence grows from the inside out with support from the environment being only in the form of aliments appropriate to the stage of development – a relatively context-free conception formulated most comprehensively by Piaget's Geneva School.

I suspect both kinds of theory are necessary – at least they have always existed. The strength of a context-free view is that it searches for universal structures of mind; its weakness is its intrinsic anticulturalism. Aebli (1970) notes the Geneva dilemma: if the child only takes in what he is 'ready to assimilate', why bother to teach before he is ready, and since he takes it in naturally once he *is* ready, why bother afterwards. The weakness of most context-sensitive views of development is that they give too much importance to individual and cultural differences and overlook the universals of growth. Their strength, of course, is in a sensitivity to the nature of the human plight and how this plight is fashioned by culture.

Two things, it seems to me, can keep us mindful of both universality and cultural diversity. The first is an appreciation of the universals of human culture, which revolve most often around reciprocal exchange through symbolic, affiliative, and economic systems. To alter man's participation in any of these systems of exchange is to force a change in how man carries out the enterprises of life. For what must be adjusted to is precisely these exchange systems – what we come to expect by way of respect, affiliation, and goods. Herein is where poverty is so crucial an issue – for poverty in economic life affects family structure, affects one's symbolic sense of worth, one's feeling of control.

But beyond the universals of culture, there are universals in man's primate heritage. The primate series illustrates to an extraordinary degree the emergence of curiosity, play, planfulness, anticipation, and, ultimately, the human species' characteristic ways of seeking, transforming, representing, and using information.

Our review thus far has surely shown us how hope, confidence, and a sense of the future can affect the unfolding and nurturing of these capacities. If the conditions imposed by a culture can alter hopes and shrink confidence it can surely alter the use of these species-typical patterns of behaviour.

Theories of development are guides for understanding the perfectibility of man as well as his vulnerability. They define man's place in nature and signal opportunities for improving or changing his lot by aiding growth. A theory of development that specifies nothing about intervention is blind to culture. One that specifies only intervention is blind to man's biological inheritance.

On intervention

With respect to virtually any criterion of equal opportunity and equal access to opportunity, the children of the poor, and particularly the urban poor, are plainly not getting as much schooling, or getting as much from their schooling as their middle-class age mates. By any conservative estimate of what happens before school, about a half million of the roughly four million children of each year of age in the United States are receiving sub-standard fare in day-care, nursery school, kindergarten, guidance, whatnot. This is not intended as a psychological assessment but as a description of resources, of officially agreed-upon facilities (cf. Sugarman, 1970). A few typical figures make the matter of facilities concrete.

> The kindergarten population in the United States in 1966 was 3,000,000 out of approximately 12,000,000 of the age group three through five. And the chances of a child in the lowest quarter of income being in kindergarten were immeasurably less than of a child in the top quarter.
>
> In 1967, there were 193,000 children in full-year Headstart, a definite improvement but a fraction of the estimated twenty per cent of the 8,000,000 three- and four-year-olds who needed it, or 1,600,000. One should note that more than 80 per cent of parents covered in the Westinghouse study (Cicirelli *et al.*, 1969) said that their children improved as a result of Headstart, a fact to be reckoned with in the light of the Rosenthal effect (1968) and Graves' (1969) findings on the ebbing confidence of poor urban mothers in their children.
>
> Finally, in 1968 there were some 2.2 million working mothers in America with children three to five many of whom were the sole breadwinner in the family. In that same year, there were approximately 310,000 places for children in registered day care centers and in approved 'private home' arrangements, one place per seven mothers. The present estimate, as of 1970, is that 9 per cent of children two to five or 14 per cent of children three to five with working mothers are catered for by day care.

I have been expressing the view that induction into this 'culture of failure' begins early. In cities like New York, half the children born in poverty are illegitimate. Growing up in an urban ghetto, in the family structure often produced by such a setting, in the neighbourhoods and schools that it spawns, surely diminishes the skills and confidence needed to use the benefits of modern industrial, democratic society on one's own behalf or on behalf of one's own group. Romanticism about poverty and its effects on growth is middle-class escapism.

Probably we cannot change this plight without changing the society that permitted such poverty to exist during a time of affluence. My first recommendation as a commonsense psychologist and as a concerned man is to transform radically the structure of our society. But that is not our topic. What can one do now, within the context of the changing society of today?

At a symposium on the 'Education of the Infant and Young Child' at the American Association for the Advancement of Science late in 1969 (Denenberg, 1970), I was asked to prepare a summary of reports on major programmes of intervention. Several common themes running through the reports struck me.

> The first was that there is an enormous influence exerted by the child's day-to-day caretaker, whatever the programme. Programmes had to consider the mother as a major factor. She had to be worked with, not compensated for.

Secondly, growth involves a small, step-wise acquisition of skill and competence on a day-to-day basis. Though theories of development emphasize principally the great leaps forward, it is in the management of day-to-day progress that discouragement or encouragement occur, where shaping has effect toward progress in one direction or another.

Thirdly, there is an enormous contribution to cognitive development from factors that, on the surface, are anything but traditionally cognitive. They are, instead, diffuse affective factors: confidence, the capacity to control one's environment, hope in the future, and the like. They too operate day-to-day, and they reflect the caretaker's mood.

Fourthly, it is now widely agreed that the idea of 'enrichment' puts the child in the position of a passive consumer. One study after another showed that for a child to benefit he must be helped to be on his own, to operate eventually on his own activation. It is this activation that must be cultivated and supported.

Fifthly, and very practically, there seem to be a wide range of alternative ways to succeed in an intervention programme – provided only they produce opportunities for mother and child to carry out activities that have some structure to them.

Beyond these specific conclusions, a general one stood out: the importance of initiative in the community as a means of activating parents and caretakers to do something for their children.

Haggstrom (1964) again makes telling points in discussing 'the power of the poor'.

In order to reduce poverty-related psychological and social problems in the United States, the major community will have to change its relationship to neighborhoods of poverty in such a fashion that families in the neighborhoods have a greater stake in the broader society and can more successfully participate in the decision making process...The poor must as a group be helped to secure opportunities for themselves. Only then will motivation be released that is now locked in the silent and usually successful battle of the neighborhoods of poverty to maintain themselves in an alien social world. This motivation...will enable them to enter the majority society and make it as nurturant of them as it is at present of the more prosperous.

'One way in which the poor can remedy the psychological consequences of their powerlessness and of the image of the poor as worthless is for them to undertake social action that redefines them...To be effective such social action should have the following characteristics:

1   The poor see themselves as the source of action.
2   The action affects in major ways the preconceptions, values, or interests of [those] defining the poor.
3   The action demands much in effort and skill...
4   The action ends in success; and
5   The successful self-originated important action [seen to increase the symbolic value of specific people who are poor]'.

Haggstrom's list is admittedly ambitious. Even so, it falls short of dealing with some intractable correlates of poverty, as race in the case of the American Black, as nationality with the Italian Swiss, and so on. Yet it surely provides a sense of the role of community action in providing a background for countering the very problems of goal seeking, problem solving, and language usage we have been discussing.

Granted the importance of community action and revolutionary aspirations in the struggle against poverty's effects, one can still discuss psychological help for the child of poverty so that he may grow more effectively, not into a middle-class suburban child (who has problems of his own), but into one capable of helping himself and his own community more effectively. It is with some considerations along these lines that I should like to end this chapter.

The expression, 'no room at the bottom' means something. With an increase in technological complexity, capital-intensive rather than labour-intensive techniques come to prevail. Instead of *more* labour to run the economy, more intensively *skilled* labour is used. While school rejects can be absorbed in a society built on stoop-labour, they can no longer find a place in one where even the street sweeper gives way to well designed, motorized brushing machines. Since the first steps toward dropping out take place at home, the home is where the first remedies must be applied – only the first, for it avails little to give help in the nursery only to defeat the child later in school.

The objective of 'curricula' for young children (as for older ones) is to produce the kind of generalist in skill, the 'skill intensive' worker who is capable of acting as a controlling factor in the regulating, running, or curbing of a technology such as we are developing in the West, or one who is capable of understanding it well enough to serve, to criticize, to be controller rather than victim.

I am assuming, to put it plainly, that man's cultural and biological evolution is toward general skill and intelligence and that the major difficulty we face is not in achieving such skill but in devising a society that can use it wisely. This means a society in which man feels at home and fulfilled enough to strive and to use his gifts.

I am taking for granted that we do *not* want to curb idiosyncrasy, surprise, and the inevitable raucousness that goes with freedom.

My colleagues at the Center for Cognitive Studies, Drs Greenfield and Tronick (1973), have devised a curriculum for a day-care centre at Bromley Heath in the Roxbury section of Boston. I have been enormously impressed with a set of implicit principles underlying their work – principles that I have extracted from one of their preliminary memoranda, but with which they may not agree. Nonetheless, let me briefly run through them, not with a view toward comprehensiveness, but toward illustration. There will be many echoes from earlier parts of this chapter.

1 The *active organism*. Human intelligence is active and seeking. It needs an environment to encourage such action.
2 *Effort after meaning*. The search for meaning and regularity begins at birth. There is a constant search for cues for significance that needs nurturing.
3 *Intentionality*. Action and the search for meaning are guided by intention and are self-directed. Help can be provided by sustaining such self-direction.
4 *Pace*. Each age and activity has a pace that requires respect and patience from those around the baby.
5 *Receptivity and state*. There is a state of alert awake receptivity when the child is hospitable to the environment. Use it for getting to the infant, rather than trying to break through unreceptive states.
6 *Cycles of competence*. Each newly emerging skill has a cycle of competence: initial crude effort, followed by consolidation and perfecting, followed by a

period of variation. The phases require recognition to be helped to their completion.

7   *Prerequisites.* Skills require prior skills for mastery, as, for example, in the 'fail-safe' method of sitting down from a standing position before risking walking. Opportunity to master prerequisites helps later skills.

8   *Appropriateness of play and objects.* Different activities have requirements that can be met by providing appropriate games, play, or objects. The child intent on exploring small irregularities with his fingers will work for hours on a board with irregular holes cut in it, each differently coloured.

9   *Principles of the enterprise.* Activity, as the child grows older, is more temporally organized under the control of intention. It is dependent upon mobilizing means to achieve an objective. Provision of means and encouragement for such enterprise and protection from distraction is of utmost importance to growth.

10 *Principle of representation.* Useful memory depends upon finding effective ways of representing information – be it in customary action, in a well-liked game, in a vivid picture, or in words. Marking something for later use or recognition is an important aspect of growth.

11 *Analysis and synthesis.* Problem solving often consists of reducing a task or situation to its component parts and then reorganizing them. Taking apart and putting together games, objects, stories, problems is practice for such activity.

12 *Time perspective.* The future is constructed by each human being by coming to expect, by planning and achieving planned objectives, by doing one thing so one may do the next, by learning how to hope and anticipate with realistic confidence. The process is long and begins early – probably with peek-a-boo.

13 *Principle of attachment.* Human young more than any other, perhaps, are dependent on a consistent caretaker who is there with warmth, certainty and effectiveness. It is in interaction with a caretaker that much of earliest learning occurs. A well-informed, decently satisfied, and hopeful caretaker is worth a pound of cure.

Summary and conclusion

Persistent poverty over generations creates a culture of survival. Goals are short range and restricted. The outsider and the outside are suspect. One stays inside and gets what one can. Beating the system takes the place of using the system.

Such a culture of poverty gets to the young early – how they learn to set goals, mobilize means, delay or fail to delay gratification. Very early too they learn in-group talk and thinking and just as their language use reflects less long-range goal analysis, it also tends toward a parochialism that makes it increasingly difficult to move or work outside the poverty neighbourhood and the group. Make no mistake about it: it is a rich culture, intensely personalized and full of immediate rather than remote concerns. The issue is certainly not cultural deprivation, to be handled, like avitaminosis with a massive dose of compensatory enrichment.

Rather the issue is to make it possible for the poor to gain a sense of their own power – through jobs, through community activation, through creating a sense of project in the future. Jobs, community action under community control, a decent revision of preschool and early school opportunities – all of these are crucial. But just as crucial is a sense of the change in the times – the insistence of the powerless that their plight is not a visitation of fate, but a remediable condition. If we cannot produce that kind of change, then our system that has worked fairly well (if exploitatively) since the industrial revolution will doubtless collapse, probably to be replaced by something premised far more on coercion for all rather than just for some. That is why the generation to be raised is so crucial a resource. It may be our last chance.

Note

This chapter was first published in J. S. Bruner *Relevance of Education*, W. W. Norton, New York, 1971, and George Allen and Unwin, London, 1972.

References

Aebli, H. Paper presented at the Center for Cognitive Studies, Harvard University, June 1970.

Baratz, S. S. and Baratz, J. C. (1970) Early childhood intervention: the social science base of institutional racism. *Harvard Educational Review*, 40, 1, pp. 29–50.

Bayley, Nancy and Schaefer, E. S. (1964) Correlations of maternal and child behaviors with the development of mental abilities: data from the Berkeley Growth Study. *Monographs of the Society for Research in Child Development*, 29, 6.

Bee, Helen L. *et al.* (1969) Social class differences in maternal teaching strategies and speech patterns. *Developmental Psychology*, 1, 6, pp. 726–734.

Bernstein, B. (1961) Social class and linguistics development: a theory of social learning. In A. H. Halsey, J. Floyd and C. A. Anderson (Eds). *Education, Economy, and Society*. (Glencoe, 111., Free Press).

Bernstein, B. (1970) Social class, language, and socialization. Unpublished paper.

Blank, Marion and Solomon, Frances (1968) A tutorial language program to develop abstract thinking in socially disadvantaged preschool children. *Child Development*, 39, pp. 379–389.

Blank, Marion and Solomon, Frances (1969) How shall the disadvantaged child be taught? *Child Development*, 40, 1, pp. 47–61.

Bloom, B. S. (1964) *Stability and Change in Human Characteristics*. (New York, John Wiley).

Brown, R., Cazden, C. B. and Bellugi, U. (1969) The child's grammar from I to III. In J. P. Hill (Ed.). 1967 *Minnesota Symposium on Child Psychology*. (Minneapolis, University of Minnesota Press).

Bruner, J. S. Origins of problem solving strategies in skill acquisition. Presented at the XIX International Congress of Psychology, London, July, 1969.

Bruner, J. S., Lyons, K. and Kaye, K. Studies in the growth of manual intelligence in infancy. Harvard University, Center for Cognitive Studies, research report in preparation.

Bruner, J. S., Goodnow, J. J. and Austin, G. A. (1956) *A Study of Thinking*. (New York, John Wiley).

Cazden, C. B. Language education: learning that, learning how, learning to. Presented at meeting of the Boston Colloquium for the Philosophy of Education, Boston University, April 13, 1970.

Cazden, C. B. (1970) The situation: a neglected source of social class differences in language use. *Journal of Social Issues*, 26, 3, pp. 35–60.

Cicirelli, V. *et al.* The impact of Head start; An evaluation of the effects of Head Start on children's cognitive and effective development. Westinghouse Learning Corporation and Ohio University, April 1969.

Coleman, J. S. *et al.* (1966) *Equality of Educational Opportunity*. (Washington, DC, U.S. Department of Health, Education, and Welfare, Office of Education).

Denenberg, V. H. (Ed.) (1970) *Education of the Infant and Young Child. Proceedings of the American Association for the Advancement of Science Symposium, Boston, December 1969*. (New York, Academic Press).

Douvan, Elizabeth (1956) Social status and success striving. *Journal of Abnormal and Social Psychology*, 52, pp. 291–223.

Fortes, M. (1938) Social and psychological aspects of education in Taleland. Supplement to *Africa*, 2, 4.

Graves, Nancy B. (1969) *City, Country, and Child Rearing in Three Cultures.* (Institute of Behavioral Sciences, University of Colorado).

Greenfield, Patricia. Oral or written language: the consequence for cognitive development in Africa and the United States. Presented at Symposium on Cross-Cultural Cognitive Studies, American Educational Research Association, Chicago, February 9, 1968.

Greenfield, Patricia. Goal as environmental variable in the development of intelligence. Presented at Conference on Contributions to Intelligence, University of Illinois, Urbana, IL, November 15, 1969.

Haggstrom, W. (1964) The power of the poor. In F. Riessman, J. Cohen and A. Pearl (Eds). *Menial Health of the Poor.* (New York, Free Press).

Hamburg, D. Evolution of emotional responses: evidence from recent research on non-human primates. *Science and Psychoanalysis*, **12**, pp. 39–54.

Hawkins, P. R. (1968) Social class, the nominal group, and reference. Sociological Research Unit, University of London, Institute of Education.

Heider, E. R., Cazden, C. B. and Brown, R. (1968) Social class differences in the effectiveness and style of children's coding ability. *Project Literary Reports*, no. 9. (Ithaca, NY, Cornell University).

Held, R. and Hein, A. V. (1958) Adaptation of disarranged hand-eye coordination contingent upon re-afferent stimulation. *Perceptual and Motor Skills*, **8**, pp. 87–90.

Hess, R. D. and Shipman, V. (1965) Early experience and socialization of cognitive modes in children. *Child Development*, **36**, pp. 869–886.

Hess, R. D. and Shipman, V. (1968) Maternal influences upon early learning: the cognitive environments of urban pre-school children. In R. D. Hess and R. M. Bear (Eds). *Early Education*. (Chicago, Aldine).

Hess, R. D. *et al.* (1969) *The Cognitive Environments of Urban Preschool Children.* (The Graduate School of Education, The University of Chicago).

von Holst, E. and Mittelstaedt, H. (1950) Das reafferenzprincip. *Naturwissenschaften*, **37**, pp. 464–476.

Horner, V. M. (1968) The verbal world of the lower-class three year old: a pilot study in linguistic ecology. Unpublished doctoral dissertation, University of Rochester.

Hymes, D. On communication competence. In R. Huxley and E. Ingram (Eds). *The Mechanism of Language Development*. (London, Ciba Foundation). In press.

Kagan, J. and Moss, H. A. (1962) *Birth to Maturity: A Study in Psychological Development.* (New York, John Wiley).

Kalnins, Ilze and Bruner, J. S. (1970) The use of sucking in instrumental learning. Presented as a doctoral thesis at the University of Toronto. Also in *Perception* (1973), **2**, pp. 307–314.

Katz, J. J. and Fodqr, J. A. (1964) The structure of a semantic theory. In J. A. Fodor and J. J. Katz (Eds). *The Structure of Language: Readings in the Philosophy of Language.* (Englewood Cliffs, NJ, Prentice-Hall).

Klaus, R. and Gray, S. (1968) The early training project for disadvantaged children: a report after five years. *Monographs of the Society for Research in Child Development*, **33**, 4.

Kohlberg, L. (1968) Early development: a cognitive-developmental view. *Child Development*, **39**, 4, pp. 1013–1062.

Labov, W. (1969) The logic of non-standard English. In James Alatis (Ed.). *Georgetown Monograph Series on Language and Linguistics*, **22**.

Labov, W. and Cohen, P., Robins, C. and Lewis, J. (1968) A study of the non standard English Negro and Puerto Rican speakers in New York City: Vol. 2, The use of language in the speech community. Final Report of Cooperative Research Project No. 3288, Columbia University.

de Laguna, G. A. (1927) *Speech: Its Function and Development.* (Bloomington, Indiana, Indiana University Press).

Lewis, O. (1961) *The Children of Sanchez.* (New York, Random House).

Lewis, O. (1966) The culture of poverty. *Scientific American*, **215**, 4, pp. 19–25.

Lipsitt, L. P. (1967) Learning in the human infant. In H. W. Stevenson, E. H. Hess and Harriet Rheingold (Eds). *Early Behavior: Comparative and Developmental Approach.* (New York, John Wiley).

Lott, A. J. and Lott, Bernice F. (1963) *Negro and White Youth.* (New York, Holt, Rinehart and Winston).

Marshall, L. and Marshall, Lorna (1963) The bushmen of Kalihari. *National Geographic*, **23**, 6, pp. 866–888.

Moffett, J. (1968) *Teaching the Universe of Discourse*. (Boston, Houghton Mifflin).

Mussen, P. H., Urbano, P. and Bouterline-Young, H. (1961) Esplorazione dei motivi per mezzo di un reattivo: II. Classi sociali e motivazione fra adolescenti di origine italiana (Exploration of motives through a projective technique). *Archivio di Psicologia, Neurologia e Psichiatria*, **22**, pp. 681–690.

Palmer, F. Unpublished research reported at a colloquium at Harvard University, November, 1968. Cited in J. S. Kagan (1969) Inadequate evidence and illogical conclusions. *Harvard Educational Review*, **39**, 2, pp. 274–277.

Papoušek, H. (1967) Experimental studies of appetitional behavior in human newborns and infants. In H. W. Stevenson, E. H. Hess and Harriet Rheingold (Eds). *Early Behavior: Comparative and Developmental Approach*. (New York, John Wiley).

Piaget, J. (1952) *The Origins of Intelligence in Children*. (New York, International Universities Press).

Piaget, J. (1954) *The Construction of Reality in the Child*. (New York, Basic Books).

Robinson, H. B. and Robinson, N. M. (1968) The problem of timing in preschool education. In R. D. Hess and R. M. Bear (Eds). *Early Education*. (Chicago, Aldine).

Robinson, W. P. and Creed, C. D. (1968) Perceptual and verbal discriminations of 'elaborated' and 'restricted' code users. *Language and Speech*, **2**, pp. 182–193.

Rosenthal, R. and Jacobsen, L. (1968) *Pygmalion in the Classroom*. (New York, Holt, Rinehart and Winston).

Schaefer, E. S. (1969) Need for early and continuing education. In Victor H. Denenberg (Ed.). *Proceedings of the AAAS Symposium on 'Education of the Infant and Young Child'*. (London, Academic Press).

Schoggen, Maxine. An ecological study of three-year-olds at home. George Peabody College for Teachers, November 7, 1969.

Shaw, Jean W. and Schoggen, Maxine. Children learning: Samples of everyday life of children at home. The Demonstration and Research Center for Early Education, George Peabody College for Teachers, 1969.

Slobin, D. I. Questions of language development in cross-cultural perspective. Presented at Symposium on 'Language learning in cross-cultural perspective', Michigan State University, September 1968.

Smilansky, Sarah (1968) The effect of certain learning conditions on the progress of disadvantaged children of kindergarten age. *Journal of School Psychology*, **4**, 3, pp. 68–81.

Sontag, L. W., Baker, C. T. and Nelson, V. L. (1958) Mental growth and personality development: a longitudinal study. In *Monographs of the Society for Research in Child Development*, **23**, 2.

Stodolsky, S. S. and Lesser, G. S. (1967) Learning patterns in the disadvantaged. *Harvard Educational Review*, **37**, 4, pp. 546–593.

Strandberg, T. E. and Griffith, J. (1968) A study of the effects of training in visual literacy on verbal language behavior. Eastern Illinois University.

Sugarman, J. M. The future of early childhood programs: an American perspective. Unpublished manuscript, 1970.

Tough, Joan. An interim report of a longitudinal study. Institute of Education, Language, and Environment, The University of Leeds, 1970.

Tronick, E. and Greenfield, Patricia (1973) *Infant Curriculum: The Bromley-Heath Guide to the Care of Infants in Groups*. (New York, Media Projects Inc.).

Turner, G. J. and Pickvance, R. E. (1970) Social class differences in the expression of uncertainty in five-year-old children. Sociological Research Unit, University of London, Institute of Education.

Vygotsky, L. S. (1962) *Thought and Language*. (New York, MIT Press and John Wiley).

Zigler, E. and Butterfield, E. (1968) Motivational aspects of changes in IQ test performance of culturally deprived nursery school children. *Child Development*, **39**, 1, pp. 1–14.

CHAPTER 16

THE ROLE OF TUTORING IN PROBLEM SOLVING

With David Wood and Gail Ross

D. Wood, J. S. Bruner, and G. Ross, *Journal of Child Psychology & Psychiatry and Allied Disciplines* (1976) 17, 89–100, Pergamon Press

This chapter is concerned with the nature of the tutorial process; the means whereby an adult or "expert" helps somebody who is less adult or less expert. Though its aim is general, it is expressed in terms of a particular task: a tutor seeks to teach children aged 3, 4, and 5 yrs to build a particular three-dimensional structure that requires a degree of skill that is initially beyond them. It is the usual type of tutoring situation in which one member "knows the answer" and the other does not, rather like a "practical" in which only the instructor "knows how". The changing interaction of tutor and children provide our data.

A great deal of early problem solving by the developing child is of this order. Although from the earliest months of life he is a "natural" problem solver in his own right (e.g. Bruner, 1973) it is often the case that his efforts are assisted and fostered by others who are more skilful than he is (Kaye, 1970). Whether he is learning the procedures that constitute the skills of attending, communicating, manipulating objects, locomoting, or, indeed, a more effective problem solving procedure itself, there are usually others in attendance who help him on his way. Tutorial interactions are, in short, a crucial feature of infancy and childhood. Our species, moreover, appears to be the only one in which any "intentional" tutoring goes on (Bruner, 1972; Hinde, 1971). For although it is true that many of the higher primate species learn by observation of their elders (Hamburg, 1968; van Lawick-Goodall, 1968), there is no evidence that those elders do anything to instruct their charges in the performance of the skill in question. What distinguishes man as a species is not only his capacity for learning, but for teaching as well. It is the main aim of this chapter to examine some of the major implications of this interactive, instructional relationship between the developing child and his elders for the study of skill acquisition and problem solving.

The acquisition of skill in the human child can be fruitfully conceived as a hierarchical programme in which component skills are combined into "higher skills" by appropriate orchestration to meet new, more complex task requirements (Bruner, 1973). This process is analogous to problem solving in which mastery of "lower order" or constituent problems in a *sine qita non* for success with a larger problem, each level influencing the other – as with reading where the deciphering of words makes possible the deciphering of sentences, and sentences then aid in the deciphering of particular words (F. Smith, 1971). Given persistent intention in the young learner, given a "lexicon" of constituent skills, the crucial task is often one of combining (usually in an appropriate serial order) the set of component acts necessary to achieve a particular end. The child, faced with new challenges, must match means to ends, and it is this matching (and the correction of mismatching) that is at the heart of problem solving (e.g. Miller *et al.*, 1960; Newell *et al.*, 1960; Saugstad and Raaheim, 1960).

Discussions of problem solving or skill acquisition are usually premised on the assumption that the learner is alone and unassisted. If the social context is taken into account, it is usually treated as an instance of modelling and imitation. But the intervention of a tutor may involve much more than this. More often than not, it involves a kind of "scaffolding" process that enables a child or novice to solve a problem, carry out a task or achieve a goal which would be beyond his unassisted efforts. This scaffolding consists essentially of the adult "controlling" those elements of the task that are initially beyond the learner's capacity, thus permitting him to concentrate upon and complete only those elements that are within his range of competence. The task thus proceeds to a successful conclusion. We assume, however, that the process can potentially achieve much more for the learner than an assisted completion of the task. It may result, eventually, in development of task competence by the learner at a pace that would far outstrip his unassisted efforts.

But, we would contend that the learner cannot benefit from such assistance unless one paramount condition is fulfilled. In the terminology of linguistics, 'comprehension of the solution must precede production'. That is to say, the learner must be able to recognize a solution to a particular class of problems before he is himself able to produce the steps leading to it without assistance. There is ample evidence from developmental psycholinguistics that for language acquisition such is almost universally the case (McNeill, 1970). Olson (1966, 1970) has similarly indicated that a child is capable of recognizing a diagonal design before he is able to construct one on a checker board, since the constituent acts of placement require more degrees of freedom (i.e. taking into account both horizontal and vertical axes) than he can handle simultaneously. Clinchy (1974), using the classic game of Twenty Questions, has likewise shown that her young subjects were able to discriminate between good strategy and bad, good questions and less good ones, if they were asked to choose between them, even though unaided they could not produce good strategies or even good questions.

It is quite obvious why comprehension must precede production and why in most instances it does. It must because without it there can be no effective feedback. One must recognize the relation between means and ends in order to benefit from "knowledge of results". There may be a marginal exception to this rule in the specialized area of learning without awareness, but it is probably a narrowly defined exception, since even bio-feedback procedures with human subjects are dependent upon the subject being able to realize when and by what means he has achieved an objective. Nevertheless, we should not overlook the role of serendipity, "the faculty of making happy and unexpected discoveries by accident". Plainly – and this will be very plain when we treat the observations of the children and their tutor – children do in fact gain a sense of possible outcomes as well as of means for achieving outcomes by a process of what on the surface looks like rather "blind" (though hardly random) trying-out behaviour. Such preliminary "blind" action may in fact be a necessary condition for the children to discover not only the nature of the final objective, but also some of the means for achieving it. Yet, such preliminary behaviour in search of the structure of the problem often requires the support of the tutor, and may indeed be directly attributable to the tutor's role as an activator – one of the features of scaffolding to which we return in the discussion of our results.

Our concern is to examine a "natural" tutorial in the hope of gaining knowledge about natural as well as automated teaching tasks. Our observations are not to be regarded as a test of an hypothesis about the tutoring process. Rather, they are attempts at systematic descriptions of how children respond to different forms of aid. We are, as it were, involved in problem-finding rather than in problem-solving (Mackworth, 1965).

The task

Thirty children, seen in individual sessions lasting from 20 min to 1 hr, formed the sample used in the study. They were equally divided into 3-, 4-, and 5-yr-olds, each age-group in turn being equally divided between girls and boys. All 30 children were accompanied by their parents who lived within a 5 mile radius of Cambridge, Mass., and had replied to advertisements for subject volunteers. They were predominantly middle-class or lower middle-class.

The task set for the children was designed with several objectives in mind. First and foremost, it had to be both entertaining and challenging to the child while also proving sufficiently complex to ensure that his behaviour over time could develop and change. It had to be "feature rich" in the sense of possessing a variety of relevant components. We tried to make its underlying structure repetitive so that experience at one point in task mastery could potentially be applied to later activity, and the child could benefit from after-the-fact knowledge or hindsight. But the task had not to be so difficult as to lie completely beyond the capability of any of the children. And finally, we did not want to make too great demands upon the child's manipulatory skills and sheer physical strength.

Note at the outset, then, that we have already constrained our results by the choice of a particular task, one that is "fun", one that is multifaceted and therefore "interesting", one that is within easy reach of a child's skills, and one that is continuous in its yield of knowledge. We shall revert to these matters in interpreting our results.

With these constraints in mind, we designed a rather complicated 9-inch high pyramid made of 21 square wooden blocks. The pyramid was 6 layers high, and measured 9 inches square at the base. What made it complicated was that the blocks had pegs and holes that had to be fitted into neighboring blocks in the correct orientation in order for the pyramid to stand firmly and without wobble. It was not an easy task, assembling the pyramid, but the children enjoyed and seemed to understand its challenge.

The tutoring procedure

The tutor's "program", which we now describe, was agreed upon in advance. By following a set of simple prescriptions the tutor endeavoured to gear her behaviour to the needs of the individual child while keeping reasonable comparability of procedure from child to child and age group to age group. Above all, her aim with every child was to allow him to do as much as possible for himself. She would always try to instruct verbally, for example, before intervening more directly, only doing the latter when the child failed to follow a verbal instruction. The child's success or failure at any point in time thus determined the tutor's next level of instruction.

When the child first came to the experimental room, he or she was seated at a small table, with the 21 blocks of various shapes and sizes spread out in a jumble. He was invited to play with the blocks. The child could have no idea what the blocks might look like when put together. He was left to his own devices for about 5 min so that he might become familiar with the blocks and the situation. The blocks were simply there, to play with if he wished.

The tutor would then usually take up two of the smallest blocks and show the child how these could be joined together to form a connected pair. If the child made up a correct pair on his own in free play, the tutor would use it as an example. She would then ask the child to "make some more like that one".

The tutor would then recognize and respond systematically to three types of response from her charge. Either the child ignored her and continued with his play; or he took up the blocks which she had just assembled and manipulated them; or he tried to make something with other blocks in a way more or less similar to the tutor's own method, by putting pegs into holes, for example. If the child had ignored her, the tutor would again present suitable and constrained material already assembled, perhaps simply joining and positioning two blocks to form a correct pair. If the child had tried to assemble pieces for himself but had over-looked a feature, then the tutor would verbally draw his attention to the fact that the construction was not completed. For example, if he had selected pieces himself and put them together wrongly, the tutor would ask him to compare his construction with hers and to make his similar. If, however, she herself had presented the material for construction to the child, she would herself correct any error that resulted.

Where possible, finally, she left the child to his own devices. It was only if he stopped constructing or got into difficulty that the tutor intervened. Her aim was to let the child pace the task for himself as far as possible.

There is one remaining issue that will not concern us formally in this study but which is of some importance. The tutor, the third author of this chapter but not of this paragraph, brought to the task a gentle, appreciative approach to the children. She did not so much praise them directly for their constructions or for their attention to the task, but rather created such an atmosphere of approval that the children seemed eager to complete their constructions – often, seemingly, to show her as well as to reach the goal *per se*. A testing procedure and a tutor create an atmosphere of encouragement or discouragement: in the present case it was the former, and the results certainly reflect it.

The matter does not stop there. The blocks are of good solid wood and the children, during the initial free period of 5 min enjoyed playing with them freely, often constructing in the service of highly imaginative themes. They did not always enjoy giving up imaginative play for the more constrained task of building a pyramid with due regard for geometric constraints. Imaginative work during free play was often followed by a rather uninspired performance of the presented task. The tutor was a spokesman, so to speak, for the geometry of the task. As such, she may have had a dampening, if helpful, function in terms of getting the children to do this task. But, doubtless, the behaviour we shall be describing in the following section reflects the nature of the task for which the tutor was an adherent. Yet, the same limitation may beset any tutor dedicated to a particular outcome.

System of scoring

At any point in time, the child could either be manipulating separate pieces which he was seeking to assemble, or assemblies of pieces previously made up. The assembly operations were further subdivided into two categories: assisted, in which the tutor either presented or specifically indicated the materials for assembly, and unassisted, where the child himself selected material. In both cases, the constructions created might or might not meet all task constraints. Where they did not – a mismatch – we noted whether the child rejected them, or simply laid them down as assembled. Similarly, when the child picked up and disassembled previous constructions, he might or might not go on to reassemble them. This too was noted.

We noted every intervention by the tutor. These were classified into one of three categories: (a) direct assistance, already defined above, (b) a verbal error prompt, which characteristically took the form, "Does this (a mismatched construction) look like this (a matched one)?", and (c) a straightforward verbal attempt to get the child to make more constructions, "Can you make any more like this?" In each case, we scored the child's subsequent behaviour into the aforementioned categories.

Interscorer reliability

Two scorers, working independently, achieved 94% agreement on a pool of 594 events scored directly from video-tape.

Observations on tutorials

Whenever a child picked up blocks and put them together or when he selected previous constructions and took them apart, the act was scored. Total number of acts were roughly similar for all ages. The fours performed a median 41, the threes 39, and the fives 32. The difference between fours and fives approaches, but does not achieve, significance ($U = 26$, $p < 0,1$). In terms of overall task activity, then, there were no significant differences between groups. However, the composition of these activities differed markedly from age group to age group.

It will come as no surprise that older children did better in the tasks. The older children produced a larger number of correct constructions in which they actually put self-made pieces of the puzzle together correctly themselves. The ratio of incorrect to correct solutions progressing from 9:0 to 2:8 to 1:2 for the three age groups. Or note that it takes 15 acts of pair construction to make a correct pyramid, and that more than 75% of these acts were unassisted among the 5-yr-olds, in contrast to 50% and 10% among the fours and threes respectively.

None of the 3 yr olds could put four blocks together correctly, while all the 4- and 5-yr-olds did so at least once. Older children frequently picked up matching pieces for construction with no prior "trial and error", a median of seven such quick constructions being made by each of them, in contrast to three per child at four years and less than one per child for the youngest group (5 yr vs. 4 yr, $U = 12$, $p < 0.02$; 4 yr vs. 3 yr, $U = 10$, $p < 0.002$). Increasing age, then, is marked not only by success but by the emergence of more complex, interlocking sequences of operations and by the development of more accurate, intuitive techniques of fitting blocks together.

Consider now the issue of recognition and production. The youngest children took apart almost as many constructions as they had together (a median of 13.0) while the older children were much less likely to "deconstruct" their assemblies (the 4-yr-olds taking apart a median 5.0, and the 5-yr-olds a median 4.0). But note that when a 3-yr-old took up and disassembled a correct construction he put it back together again two-thirds of the time on average (without any intervention by the tutor), the performance suggesting an appreciation of the fitness of the original. In contrast, having picked up an incorrect construction he would restore it only 14% of the time. In fact, not one 3-yr-old reassembled his incorrect constructions more frequently than his correct ones. More important still was the finding that the 3-yr-olds were just as sensitive as the 4-yr-olds to the difference between acceptable and unacceptable constructions. The two were equally likely to reassemble appropriate constructions and to leave scattered those that had been inappropriately constructed. Thus, although the youngest children were far inferior to the middle group when it came to constructing appropriate assemblies, they were as adept at recognizing an appropriate one when they encountered it. The oldest children had, of course, become more sophisticated still, reconstructing some 9 out of 10 correct constructions they had disassembled and only 2 in 10 of the incorrect ones that they had disassembled – but the difference is not very great between them and the younger groups.

This result surely suggests that, as noted, comprehension precedes production. The 3-yr-old recognizes what is appropriate before he can readily produce a sequence of operations to achieve it by his own actions. It is easier for him to recognize what "looks right" than to carry out a program of action to produce it.

The tutorial relationship

Obviously, the younger children need help more, For 3-yr-olds the proportion of totally unassisted constructions is 64.5 %, for the 4-yr-olds 79.3%, and for the 5-yr-olds 87.5%. The median instances per child of constructions carried out with pieces proffered by the tutor, as compared to self-selected pieces is 9.0 for the 3-yr-olds, 6.5 for the 4-yr-olds, and 3.0 for the 5-yr-olds. But it is not so much in amount as in the kind of dependence that one finds a difference in the tutorial interaction at the three ages.

For 3-yr-olds usually ignore the tutor's suggestions, paying little heed, particularly to her verbal overtures. This is illustrated by the sharp disparity between the median figure of eleven tutor rejections by the 3-yr-olds, in contrast to virtually none by the older children who were plainly ready to accept tutoring. This means that *vis-à-vis* the 3-yr-old the tutor has the initial task of enlisting the child as a tutoring partner. With the youngest ones, the tutor is principally concerned with luring them into the task either by demonstrating it or providing tempting material. Consequently, the tutor intervenes directly twice as often with the 3-yr-olds than with the 4 yr olds, and four times more often than with the eldest group (see Tables 16.1 and 16.2). The tutor, then, is both intervening more and being ignored more when working with 3 yr olds than with older children.

The predominant mode of interaction between tutor and the 4-yr-old tutee has become verbal, and the principal form of that verbal interaction is a combination of reminding the child of the task requirements and correcting his efforts as he seeks to carry on. So while we can say that the tutor acts principally as a lure to the youngest children, she acts more as a verbal prodder and corrector for the 4-yr-olds. The number of direct interventions drops by half from the 3- to the 4-yr-olds. Note, however, that the sum of demonstrations, corrections, and directions is about equal for the 3- and 4-yr-olds, though the balance has shifted (Tables 16.1 and 16.2).

When we come to the 5 yr olds, the median number of tutorial interventions per pupil drops again by half. Qualitatively speaking the best way of characterizing the tutor of the 5 yr olds is principally as a confirmer or checker of constructions, the children now having firmly in mind the nature of the task.

Table 16.1 Median instances of direct interventions, verbal corrections and general verbal directions (reminding subjects of task requirements)

	Age		
	3	*4*	*5*
Direct intervention (showing)	12.0	6.0	3.0
Verbal correction (telling)	3.0	5.0	3.5
Verbal direction and reminder (telling)	5.0	8.0	3.0
Total verbal intervention	8.0	13.0	7.5
Total help received[a]	20.0	19.0	10.5
Ratio: show/tell[b]	12.0/8.0 = 1.5	6.0/13.0 = 0.46	3.0/7.5 = 0.40

Notes
a The 5-yr-olds received significantly less help than both the 4-yr-olds ($U = 22$, $p < 0.05$) and the 3-yr-olds ($U = 22$, $p < 0.05$). The 3- and 4-yr-olds did not differ significantly.
b Both the 5-yr-olds ($U = 5$, $p < 0.002$) and the 4-yr-olds ($U = 6$, $p < 0.002$) received a significantly higher proportion of verbal assistance than the 3-yr-olds; 4- and 5-yr-olds did not differ in this respect.

Table 16.2 Relative successes of each age group with "showing" and "telling"

	Age		
	3	*4*	*5*
Showing succeeds	40%	63%	80%
Telling succeeds	18%	40%	57%

Table 16.3 Relative frequency of interventions by the tutor expressed as interventions per number of construction operations (both assisted and unassisted) performance by each child

	Age		
	3	*4*	*5*
Total construction operations	262	352	280
Total interventions	201	198	112
Operations per intervention	1.3	1.8	2.5

Note
The 5-yr-olds performed significantly more operations per intervention than the 4-yr-olds ($U = 16$, $p < 0.02$) who performed more than the 3-yr-olds ($U = 10$, $p < 0.002$).

In a word, the youngest children, although capable of recognizing the properties of a correct solution, had to be induced to try the task to learn through recognition of correct solutions. The tutor's role was to stimulate and to keep the goal before the child's eyes – not easy since the children had other notions of what could be done with the blocks. With the 4-yr-olds, already activated to construct, the tutor's task was more to help them recognize, usually by verbal marking, the nature of the discrepancy that existed between their attempted constructions and what was required by the task. It is this that shifts the balance from showing to telling as one goes from 3 to 4 yr. The 5-yr-old has recourse to the tutor only when he is experiencing difficulty or checking out a construction. The tutorial function, thus, withers away. Indeed, a tutor would be superfluous for a 6-yr-old.

It is in this sense that we may speak of a scaffolding function. Well executed scaffolding begins by luring the child into actions that produce recognizable-for-him solutions. Once that is achieved, the tutor can interpret discrepancies to the child. Finally, the tutor stands in a confirmatory role until the tutee is checked out to fly on his own. It is summed up in Table 16.3, where we see the number of acts the child can sustain between tutorial interventions rising steadily with age and experience.

Analysis of tutoring

Did the tutor manage to follow the pre-set rules? In 478 opportunities she conformed 86% of the time. She did so most frequently with the youngest children (92%) and less frequently with the 4-yr-olds (81%; $\chi^2 = 9.1$, $p < 001$). With the 5-yr-olds, her behavior fell mid-way (86%) though the difference between this group and the others was not statistically significant.

The majority of her "errors" with the 4-yr-olds was due to a tendency to offer more help than allowed by the rules (27 out of 36 cases). A closer inspection of the contexts in which she "transgressed" reveals an interesting consistency. When, for example, she offered a block rather than asking the child to find one, she would invariably transgress in this way when the particular child had recently failed several times to follow or understand a more difficult type of instruction. She appeared to be changing the rules to take account of larger segments of behaviour than written into the "rules".

The fact that she committed most violations with the middle group suggests an interesting observation regarding the tutorial process. As we have already seen, the tutor's role with the youngest children was largely one of task induction. The child seldom moved more than one "step" away from the tutor in terms of constructive activity. She might provide him with material for construction which he would probably then assemble, but having done so, the odds were that he would not attempt anything more. In short, though she might have difficulty getting the 3-yr-old started and keeping his attention on the task she was seldom left in doubt as to what the child had done in response to her instructions. With the 5-yr-olds too, her task was relatively straightforward. The child soon learned the task constraints and conducted his efforts in an appropriate serial order. But, the "try it and see" behaviour of the middle group was much harder to interpret. With the 4-yr-olds, then, the tutor is faced with a great deal of relatively unstructured behaviour from a child who initiates most of the task activity himself. These are the ones most difficult to accommodate within a fixed set of tutorial rules.

This result leads on to the conjecture as to whether formal programmes of "individualized" teaching may be most difficult to realize at the most critical point – the mid-phase of learning. Given the "disordered" structure of this mid-phase one cannot always know that a child is in fact simply ignoring a suggestion, whether he is systematically misunderstanding it or what. To the extent that the learner is at sea, so too is the tutor, who faces difficulties in interpreting responses appropriately. Problem-solving activity often has a deep structure that may not be apparent, until a long sequence in process is near completion. The tutor often cannot recognize hypotheses underlying long sequences and in the "middle phase" there are often too many complexities for either man or machine programmes to take into account.

Where the human tutor excels or errs, of course, is in being able to generate hypotheses about the learner's hypotheses and often to converge on the learner's interpretation. It is in this sense that the tutor's theory of the learner is so crucial to the transactional nature of tutoring. If a machine programme is to be effective, it too would have to be capable of generating hypotheses in a comparable way. In tutoring, moreover, effectiveness depends not only upon tutor and tutee modifying their behaviour over time to fit perceived requirements and/or suggestions of the other. The effective tutor must have at least two theoretical models to which he must attend. One is a theory of the task or problem and how it may be completed. The other is a theory of the performance characteristics of his tutee. Without both of these, he can neither generate feedback nor devise situations in which his feedback will be more appropriate for this tutee in this task at this point in task mastery. The actual pattern of effective instruction, then, will be both task and tutee dependent, the requirements of the tutorial being generated by the interaction of the tutor's two theories.

The "scaffolding" process

We may now return to the beginning of the discussion. Several functions of tutoring – "scaffolding functions" – were hinted at in the introduction. We can flow elaborate more generally upon their relation to a theory of instruction. What can be said about the function of the tutor as observed in this study?

1   *Recruitment.* The tutor's first and obvious task is to enlist the problem solver's interest in and adherence to the requirements of the task. In the present case, this often involved getting the children not only interested, but weaned from initial imaginative play with the blocks.

2   *Reduction in degrees of freedom.* This involves simplifying the task by reducing the number of constituent acts required to reach solution. It was N. Bernstein (1967) who first pointed to the importance of reducing the alternative movements during skill acquisition as an essential to regulating feedback so that it could be used for correction. In the present instances it involved reducing the size of the task to the level where the learner could recognize whether or not he had achieved a "fit" with task requirements. In effect, the "scaffolding" tutor fills in the rest and lets the learner perfect the component sub-routines that he can manage.

3   *Direction maintenance.* Learners lag and regress to other aims, given limits in their interests and capacities. The tutor has the role of keeping them in pursuit of a particular objective. Partly it involves keeping the child "in the field" and partly a deployment of zest and sympathy to keep him motivated. The children often made their constructions in order to show them to the tutor. In time, the activity itself became the goal – but even then, the older children often checked back.

One other aspect of direction maintenance is worth mention. Action, of course, tends to follow the line of previous success. There were instances, for example when subjects would work successfully (and apparently endlessly) on constructing pairs, rather than moving on from this success at a simpler level to trying out a more complex task – like the construction of a flat quadruple. Past success served to distract from the ultimate goal. The effective tutor also maintains direction by making it worthwhile for the learner to risk a next step.

4 *Marking critical features.* A tutor by a variety of means marks or accentuates certain features of the task that are relevant. His marking provides information about the discrepancy between what the child has produced and what he would recognize as a correct production. His task is to interpret discrepancies.

5 *Frustration control.* There should be some such maxim as "Problem solving should be less dangerous or stressful with a tutor than without". Whether this is accomplished by "face saving" for errors or by exploiting the learner's "wish to please" or by other means, is of only minor importance. The major risk is in creating too much dependency on the tutor.

6 *Demonstration.* Demonstrating or "modelling" solutions to a task, when closely observed, involves considerably more than simply performing in the presence of the tutee. It often involves an "idealization" of the act to be performed and it may involve completion or even explication of a solution already partially executed by the tutee himself. In this sense, the tutor is "imitating" in idealized form an attempted solution tried (or assumed to be tried) by the tutee in the expectation that the learner will then "imitate" it back in a more appropriate form.

In the introduction we said a few words about the subtlety of "modelling" an act that is to be "imitated". In fact, observed instances of "imitation" were all of a kind as to suggest that the only acts that children imitate are those they can already do fairly well. Typical was the following incident, involving a 4-yr-old.

> Tutor, noting that subject is constructing pairs quite easily, now takes two pairs and fits them together as a quadruple. Subject then takes the quadruple, disassembles it into two pairs, and hands these back to tutor. This in turn leads the tutor to a highly idealized version of constructing the quadruple: she now does it slowly and carefully, in contrast to a swift and casual construction of the constituent pairs. The child does not follow suit.

In fact, the study taught us little about imitation save that its occurrence depends upon the child's prior comprehension of the place of the act in the task. In all instances observed with these 30 children, there was not a single instance of what might be called "blind matching behaviour".

Summary

3-, 4-, and 5-yr-olds were tutored in the task of constructing a pyramid from complex, interlocking constituent blocks. The results indicate some of the properties of an interactive system of exchange in which the tutor operates with an implicit theory of the learner's acts in order to recruit his attention, reduces degrees of freedom in the task to manageable limits, maintains "direction" in the problem solving, marks critical feature, controls frustration, and demonstrates solutions when the learner can recognize them. The significance of the finding for instruction in general is considered.

Note

This research was conducted at the Center for Cognitive Studies at Harvard University under Grant MH-12623 of the U.S. National Institutes of Health.

References

Bernstein, N. (1967) *The Coordination and Regulation of Movement*. Pergamon Press, Oxford.

Bruner, J. S. (1972) Nature and uses of immaturity. *Am. Psychol.* **27**, 1–22.

Bruner, J. S. (1973) Organization of early skilled action. *Child Developm.* **44**, 92–96.

Clinchy, B. (1974) *Recognition and Production of Information – Processing Strategies in Children*. Unpublished doctoral thesis, Department of Psychology, Harvard University.

Hamburg, D. (1968) Evolution of emotional responses: evidence from recent research on non-human primates. *Sci. Psychoan.* **12**, 39–54.

Hinde, R. A. (1971) Development of social behaviour. In *Behavior of Non-Human Primates* (Edited by Schrier, A. M. and Stollnitz, F.), Vol. 3. Academic Press, New York.

Kaye, K. (1970) *Mother–Child Instructional Interaction*. Unpublished doctoral thesis, Department of Psychology, Harvard University.

Lawick-Goodall, J. van (1968) The behavior of free-living chimpanzees in the Gombe Stream Reserve. *Animal behaviour Monographs* 1 (3), 161–311.

Mackworth, N. H. (1965) Originality. *Am. Psychol.* **20** (1), 51–66.

McNeill, D. (1970) The development of language. In *Carmichael's Manual of Child Psychology* (Edited by Mussen, P. H.), Wiley, New York.

Miller, G. A., Galanter, E., and Pribram, K. H. (1960) *Plans and the Structure of Behavior*. Holt, New York.

Newell, A., Shaw, J. C., and Simon, H. A. (1960) Report on a general problem-solving program. In *Information processing*. UNESCO, Paris, pp. 256–264.

Olson, D. R. (1966) On conceptual strategies. In *Studies in Cognitive Growth* (Edited by Bruner, J. S., Olver, R. R., and Greenfield, P. M.), Wiley, New York, pp. 135–153.

Olson, D. R. (1970) *Cognitive Development: The Child's Acquisition of Diagonality*. Academic Press. New York.

Saugstad, P. and Raaheim, K. (1960) Problem-solving, past experience and availability of functions. *Br. J. Psychol.* **51**, 97–104.

Smith, F. (1971) *Understanding Reading*. Holt, Rinehart & Winston, New York.

INDEX